Accounting Commission
1971-1972

BERNARD T. STOTT, Chairman 1971-72
Comptroller
First National City Bank
New York, New York

DAVID C. BECK
Controller
Citizens Bank of Sheboygan
Sheboygan, Wisconsin

ROBERT C. CHRISTIE
Senior Vice President
& Comptroller
Pittsburgh National Bank
Pittsburgh, Pennsylvania

CHARLES C. ELLIS
Executive Vice President
& Comptroller
Irving Trust Company
New York, New York

JOHN J. GLEASON
Vice President
The Northern Trust Company
Chicago, Illinois

DAVID A. RADIUS
Vice President-
Management Systems
Old Kent Bank
and Trust Company
Grand Rapids, Michigan

JAMES C. TRAVIS
Senior Vice President
& Controller
National Bank of Tulsa
Tulsa, Oklahoma

WILLIAM H. WIELAND
Senior Vice President
& Comptroller
United California Bank
Los Angeles, California

EDWARD G. ZULTOWSKI
Comptroller
Garden State National Bank
Hackensack, New Jersey

1970-1971

THOMAS H. DOOLEY
Vice President & Comptroller
Manufacturers National Bank
Detroit, Michigan

ROBERT L. KEMPER
Executive Vice President
Wells Fargo Bank, NA
San Francisco, California

JAMES C. TRAVIS
Senior Vice President
& Controller
National Bank of Tulsa
Tulsa, Oklahoma

EUGENE F. ONCKEN
Vice President & Comptroller
First City National Bank
Houston, Texas

W. E. BREDESON, Smaller Bank Commission, BAI
President
Farmers and Merchants Bank
and Trust Company
Watertown, South Dakota

FOREWORD

The changing economy has brought into clearer perspective the merits of utilizing sound cost control programs for improving bank profits. Many bank operating functions are currently being identified as productive sources for profit improvement. A dollar saved through cost control goes directly to profits. Bank-wide programs called corporate planning, profit planning, and responsibility center accounting require a sound cost accounting system that produces essential facts for making correct decisions and implementing these management plans. These programs must be coordinated to produce the best bank-wide results. Furthermore, new banking ventures resulting from diversified programs add to the importance of sound cost accounting for pricing and control.

Since 1951 when NABAC published *Bank Costs* as its first formal effort in the field of cost accounting, it has continued to lead the industry in solving problems in this important administrative area.

In 1970 Bank Administration Institute published a timely manual *Successful Profit Planning for Banks,* which describes systematic profit planning, shows its role in management, and indicates what this effort requires.

Bank Costs for Planning and Control was written to further assist bankers in the important area of management, planning and control. It is concerned with the core of the planning process, namely, having all the cost facts before, during, and after the decision-making process. This requires the knowledge, support, participation, and cooperation of all levels of management, starting with the chief executive officer.

Many persons with diverse talents made this book possible. The number of banks that were intensively studied during the initial

Bank Costs for Planning and Control

Prepared for Bank Administration Institute
by
Haskins & Sells
Certified Public Accountants

Bank Administration Institute
Park Ridge, Illinois

Bank Administration Institute

Bank Administration Institute is a not-for-profit corporation whose broad goals are to help bank administrators achieve high levels of professional effectiveness and to help solve significant banking problems. These goals are pursued through programs of research and development, education, and technical assistance.

Founded in 1924, the Institute is today the largest technical banking association in the world. It is governed by a Board of Directors with the President acting as chairman. Responsibility for management of the Institute's activities within a framework of policy established by the Board rests with the Executive Director, who is assisted by a headquarters staff located in Park Ridge, Illinois.

Library of Congress Catalog Card Number: 70-173424

Copyright 1972 by Bank Administration Institute, Park Ridge, Illinois
All rights reserved. This book or any parts of it
may not be reproduced in any form without
written permission from the publisher

Printed in the United States of America

Price of book $15.00
Member discount price $7.50

phases of this project are too numerous to mention, but their assistance is greatly appreciated. I especially commend members of the Chicago, New York, and Houston offices of the firm of Haskins & Sells for their work in preparing this book. I commend Bernard L. Stott, Chairman of the Accounting Commission, and his subcommittee, Thomas H. Dooley, Chairman, Eugene F. Oncken, and James C. Travis for their leadership and guidance. Recognition also is given to the Technical Division of BAI, especially John D. Bryant, who coordinated the project, and Georgiana Yates, the Publications Division's technical writer, who edited and prepared the manuscript for publication.

Raymond C. Kolb
President

December 1971

PREFACE

This work has been compiled for Bank Administration Institute through the Cost Subcommittee of the Institute's Accounting Commission to meet the needs of the banking community in the 70's and beyond. During the 60's, increased interest rates and clerical costs, coupled with the lessened availability of funds, generated general interest on the part of banks of all sizes in profit improvement through better operations. It is natural that bankers should turn to a management tool that has been successful in industry. Cost accounting, as we know it today, had its origins in industry and, consequently, very few volumes have been oriented towards banking. Bank Administration Institute pioneered the subject of bank cost accounting in 1951 with the publication of *Bank Costs*—a 400-page manual designed to present a basic plan for bank cost determination. The manual was reprinted in 1962 and enlarged to include a section on trust costs.

Now BAI is publishing a new volume on cost accounting for bankers. The material in it is addressed to four audiences:

The Bank's Chief Executive Officer—for whom it offers an overview of cost accounting and its role in banking.

The Bank's Chief Accounting Officer—who will find in it easily accessible information on cost concepts, their application to banks, and specific down-to-earth approaches to frequently asked cost questions.

The Banking Student—for whom it will serve as a textbook.

The Business Community—for which it provides an authoritative reference on cost accounting as it relates to banking.

The book is divided into six parts:

- Part I, *Use of Cost by Bank Management,* is an overview of bank planning and control, describing how the two are related to costing. This part serves to provide a frame of reference within which costing can be considered.

- Part II, *Setting the Stage for Bank Costing,* presents a basic costing theory along with approaches to activity measurement. It introduces a structured approach to costing based on the characteristics of bank operations and management's need for cost performance.
- Part III, *Cost for Planning and Control of Resources,* relates the simpler aspects of bank costing to management's needs for planning and control of its resources. The use of costing for planning is treated in terms of ways to obtain the most from available resources. Its use for control is discussed in terms of accounting by responsibility centers and of project and program accounting.
- Part IV, *Allocation Techniques,* discusses cost allocation in detail, to provide the background for a later discussion of the more complex costing required to plan profitability and to measure profit for control purposes. The special problem of allocating the cost of funds is examined in detail.
- Part V, *Cost for Planning and Control of Profitability,* treats the use of costing to aid management in planning and controlling profitability. Profit centers are the focal point of this part of the book, which concludes with a review of cost for pricing, a special profitability problem.
- Part VI, *Special Cost Considerations,* the final section of the book, discusses standard costs, flexible budgets, and the allocation of data center costs.

Four appendixes have been provided. The first appendix sets forth the general organization and functional structure used throughout the book. The second discusses the general design of a basic processing and reporting system that smaller banks could consider. The third illustrates certain standards in some detail, and the final appendix provides the reader with a detailed solution of three illustrative costing problems using the principles discussed in this book.

HOW TO USE THE BOOK

This book has been designed for use as both a textbook and a reference work. It proceeds progressively from first principles to the complex applications of those principles. When it is used as a textbook, the chapters should be studied in sequence. When it is used for reference purposes, the reader who has a specific need in mind (e.g., a calculation to be made in a particular case) will derive the most benefit from the book if he proceeds in one of the following ways:

- If the purpose is *to select alternatives concerning resource use,* he should read Chapter 3 (*The Costing Process*), Chapter 4 (*Activity Measurement*), and Chapter 7 (*Planning Cost Performance—Resource Use*).

- If the purpose is *to analyze profitability,* he should read Chapter 3, then Chapter 4, Chapter 7, all of Part IV (*Allocation Techniques*), and Chapter 12 (*Planning Cost Performance—Resource Profitability*).

- If the purpose is *to control cost,* he should read Chapter 3, Chapter 4, and either Chapter 8 (*Controlling Cost Performance—Responsibility Center Accounting*) or Chapter 9 (*Controlling Cost Performance—Project and Program Accounting*).

- If the purpose is *to control profitability,* he should read Chapter 3, Chapter 4, Chapter 8, Part IV, and Chapter 13 (*Controlling Cost Performance—Profit Center Accounting*).

- If the purpose is *pricing,* he should read Chapter 3, Chapter 4, Part IV, and Chapter 14 (*Costs for Pricing*).

- If the purpose is *to allocate EDP costs,* he should read Chapter 3, Chapter 4, Part IV, Chapter 12, Chapter 15 (*Standard Costs*), and Chapter 16 (*Allocating Data Center Costs*).

- If he wishes to examine the general concept of costing as applied particularly to banks and to get the "feel" of an accounting system designed to facilitate bank costing, he should read Chapter 3, Chapter 4 (*Activity Measurement*), Chapter 5 (*The Characteristics of Bank Costs*), and Appendix B (*A Basic Processing and Reporting System*), which sets up a hypothetical bank to which many of the illustrations used in the book are related.

- Finally, if the reader wishes to review, in detail, the solution of typical bank costing problems using the approaches and principles discussed in the text, he can turn to Appendix D where three problems are presented with detailed solutions.

If the Purpose for Using the Book is:	These Chapters and Appendixes Apply:
Selection of a resource	(3) — (4) — (7)
Analysis of profitability	(3) — (4) — (7) — (10) — (11) — (12)
Control of cost	(3) — (4) — (8) or (9)
Control of profitability	(3) — (4) — (8) — (10) — (11) — (13)
Pricing	(3) — (4) — (10) — (11) — (14)
Allocation of EDP costs	(3) — (4) — (10) — (11) — (12) — (15) — (16)
General concept of bank costing	(3) — (4) — (5) — Appendix B
Review illustrative bank costing problems	Appendix D

CONTENTS

1

WHAT IS NEW ABOUT COSTS, PLANNING, AND CONTROL?

2

KEYS TO SUCCESSFUL COST MANAGEMENT

Figures

Part II: Setting the Stage for Bank Costing

3

THE COSTING PROCESS   21

Figures

4

ACTIVITY MEASUREMENT   49

Use of Activity Measurement to Determine Capacity
and Utilization 49

Use of Activity Measurement to Determine Transfer Units 51

Activity Measurement 53
    Defining the Activity Unit 53
    Methods for Counting Transactions 54
    Work Measurement 55

Summary 62

Figures

5

THE CHARACTERISTICS OF BANK COSTS 63

Figures

6

COST PERFORMANCE 71

Part III: Cost for Planning and Control of Resources

7

8

Figures

9

CONTROLLING COST PERFORMANCE—
PROJECT AND PROGRAM ACCOUNTING   107

Figures

Part IV: Allocation Techniques

10

COST ALLOCATION 133

Figures

11

ALLOCATING THE COST OF FUNDS 157

Figures

Part V: Cost for Planning and Control of Profitability

12

PLANNING COST PERFORMANCE— RESOURCE PROFITABILITY   181

Figures

13

CONTROLLING COST PERFORMANCE— PROFIT CENTER ACCOUNTING   217

Figures

14

COSTS FOR PRICING   231

Figures

Part VI: Special Cost Considerations

15

STANDARD COSTS   251

Figures

16

ALLOCATING DATA CENTER COSTS   263

Figures

Appendixes

A ORGANIZATION AND FUNCTION REFERENCE CHARTS   287

Figures

B A BASIC PROCESSING AND REPORTING SYSTEM   291

Figures

C STANDARD TIME VALUES
FOR WEIGHTING

Tables

D PRACTICAL EXAMPLES OF EFFECTIVE COSTING 323

Figures

Bank Costs for Planning and Control

Bank Costs for Planning and Control

Use of Cost for Planning

7. Planning Cost Performance—Resource Use

12. Planning Cost Performance—Resource Profitability

14. Cost for Pricing

15. Standard Costs

16. Allocating Data Center Cost

Costing

3. The Costing Process
4. Activity Measurement
5. Characteristics of Bank Costs
6. Cost Performance

10. Cost Allocation

11. Allocating the Cost of Funds

Use of Cost for Control

8. Controlling Cost Performance—Responsibility Center Accounting

9. Controlling Cost Performance—Project and Program Accounting

13. Controlling Cost Performance—Profit Center Accounting

Introduction—Bank Costs for Planning and Control

1. What's New About Costs, Planning, and Control

2. Keys to Successful Cost Management

Part I
Use of Cost by Bank Management

Part II
Setting the Stage for Bank Costing

Part III
Cost for Planning and Control of Resources

Part IV
Allocation Techniques

Part V
Cost for Planning and Control of Profitability

Part VI
Special Cost Considerations

—— Overview ——

—— Bank Costing ——

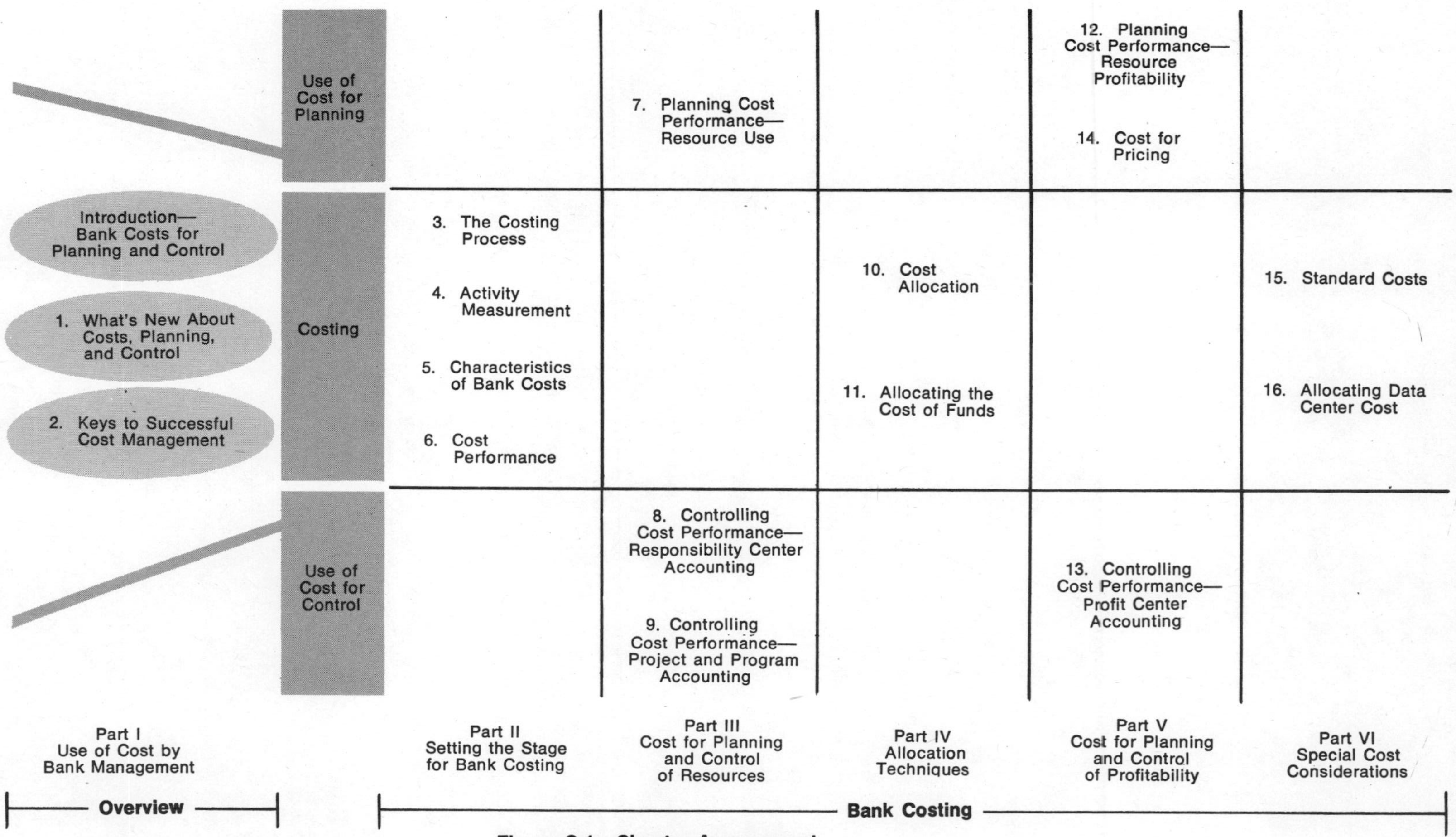

Figure O.1—Chapter Arrangement

INTRODUCTION

The dynamic, well-managed bank—one that is efficient and profitable—offers society an important public service. Conversely, the bank that is not well managed is likely to be unprofitable and a threat to the financial health of the community that it serves.

As a result, society has an interest in the efforts of bank managers who run their banks to benefit not only the owners and investors but also the public that depends heavily on bank services.

CONTEMPORARY CHALLENGES TO CHIEF EXECUTIVES OF BANKS

Today bankers are faced with demands that they not only carry out their historic public service obligation but that they refine and expand it as well. In the fields of equal employment and minority business development, for example, bankers are being asked to incorporate broad and ambitious objectives into their planning.

At the same time, a banker also must be prepared to compete more imaginatively and persistently than ever before with others in his industry. In the last 20 years, competition among bankers has taken on an aggressiveness comparable to that of other industries, and there is no sign that this new competitiveness will decline. Rather, it is sure to increase in intensity, primarily because customers' demands and investors' desires are sure to grow. This aggressive competition among banks has whetted the appetite of customers for more and better services. As a result, the banker must increase his efforts to serve. Similarly, the investing public shows a growing desire to get the greatest possible return on its invested dollar. The individual bank manager will have to accentuate profit performance or see the market value of his issues decline.

The bank chief executive, therefore, is confronted by a two-faceted challenge: he must increase profits and return more profit to investors (and therefore must compete more aggressively); and he must serve the public in new fields and new ways and with greater effectiveness.

PITFALLS AND OPPORTUNITIES

Perhaps one of the most significant matters that the bank executive must keep in mind is this: although he must delegate authority and assign responsibility to other managers in the bank, he cannot hope to diminish in any way his full and unavoidable responsibility for being involved in making bank operations effective. He personally must take part in every aspect of his bank's affairs, and he must understand that he will find no miraculous panaceas. He cannot go out and "buy" an organization chart that will solve all his problems, nor can he hire someone who will free him completely from the task of struggling with trying managerial problems. Too often leaders in other industries have sought ways to "get things running by themselves" only to find that "things" will only "run" properly when the chief executive himself participates personally with the entrepreneur's traditional energy and capacity for innovation.

Once the chief executive accepts this basic premise, the doors are open for him to benefit by the experience of others and to take advantage of important advances in the art and science of management.

It is the purpose of this book to focus on some of the more potentially rewarding managerial techniques available to the top executive in carrying out his total responsibility. For the banker this is the effective use of costs for planning and control, or what might be called "creative cost management."

1

WHAT IS NEW ABOUT COSTS, PLANNING, AND CONTROL?

Cost accounting has been practiced for at least 50 years. But it has never found complete favor with top management.

One reason for this lack of popularity is that many executives view it as a costly, detailed accounting system that goes far beyond reasonable bounds and into an area where complexity and sophisticated accounting techniques are out of proportion to the value of the information obtained.

A second reason is that many executives seem to lack a good understanding of what cost accounting can and cannot do for them.

A third reason is that many costing concepts that apply to manufacturing do not apply without adjustment and interpretation to banking.

A fundamental purpose of this book is to try to improve the executive's understanding of cost accounting (or costing) as it relates to banking. It is important to understand that cost accounting need not be an expensive and detailed extension of the present accounting system. In fact, a system may not be required—hence the use of the term "costing," which refers to an analytical approach, rather than cost accounting, which implies a system. Costing must be directed to the purpose it is to serve, and a short-term need for costing should not be met through a long-term commitment to a systematic, recurring preparation of cost information.

Further, some of the difficulty in understanding costing has been due to an overabundance of imprecise terms and ideas that can create more confusion than clarity. Costing is really no more complex than the actions it tries to depict.

PLANNING IN ITS PLACE

There are sophisticated new planning techniques for management to use, provided they are used *by* management—not *for* management. Costing constitutes just such a technique, one that can be used effectively for planning by a management that fully accepts its own responsibility to understand it and guide its use.

CONTROL CAN BE CREATIVE

The word "control" has sometimes led to confusion. Some have taken the view, or have created the impression, that control is the enforcement arm of management.

According to this interpretation, control involves a review of performance in order to punish those who do not meet expectations. It is a view that associates control with cost reduction, layoffs, and other, sometimes necessary, defensive measures.

This is, of course, an oversimplification of attitudes because control must be integrated into the total management process in such a way that it is progressive rather than repressive, creative and liberating rather than monotonous and confining. Control should be a constructive learning experience. Those who are subject to it should be able to look back and see evidence of progress because control was properly exercised.

Through this book it is hoped that bankers will be convinced that costing can be used by them to help them plan and control banking operations both to profit and to serve their community.

2

KEYS TO SUCCESSFUL
COST MANAGEMENT

What are the keys to successful overall management that, in turn, become the keys to effective cost management? There are six keys the banker must use:

1. He must devise an integrated, interrelating system for planning and control—called a *planning and control structure*—that fits harmoniously into his total management process.

2. He must activate the planning portion of his structure by specifying the *objectives* the bank is to pursue.

3. He must determine, in the light of these stated objectives, the general *areas of effort* that are to be managed, identifying them without regard to whatever scheme of organization might be used to manage them.

4. Having specified the areas to be managed, he must then design the *organizational structure* that can best carry out the management of these areas.

5. He must *analyze alternative courses of action* and *decide on a plan* to be carried out by his organization.

6. He must activate the control portion of his planning and control structure to *communicate clearly to his organization the plans to be carried out* and, as soon as the implementation of plans commences, *measure results against plans, evaluate differences, and make decisions.* These decisions then serve to reactivate the planning side of the structure for purposes of replanning, which starts the cycle all over again.

Any abstract attempt to identify keys to a process of action cannot apply completely to all situations. For example, it is implied here that the chief executive will accomplish all the tasks listed above, but in reality this would not be feasible except in the smallest institutions. Although it is stated that "he" must determine the objectives, this is for purposes of simplicity. The role of a board of directors and of other officials must be taken into consideration, and the chief executive must call upon others to assist him. Nevertheless, the point must still be stressed that the chief executive is the only one from whom coordinative direction can come.

Despite the inevitable abstractness of attempting to define steps in this way, it is still constructive to examine each of them in some detail, since they form the foundation upon which the theme of this book is developed.

DEVISING A PLANNING AND CONTROL STRUCTURE

As for the chief executive's first step (devising a planning and control structure), the most important point is that *he* must devise it (or in one way or another specify the criteria for its construction) and that *he* must work with it. (Figure 2.1 will be helpful in visualizing the planning and control structure in relationship to overall organization, resources, and day-to-day operations.)

Planning and control should be regarded as an operating function, and not as a "staff" function. There should be no arbitrary lines of demarcation separating those who plan, those who operate, and those who control. Moreover, there should be no implication that those who plan and control have any lesser stature than those who operate. A finance and control division, for example, must be considered to have as much "line" responsibility as a trust division, and the heads of each should coordinate their efforts in a cooperative and constructive way. Whenever an effort is made to establish lines of demarcation between staff and line functions or to place one on a level lower than the other, trouble inevitably results.

In devising his planning and control structure, the chief executive might choose to place the detailed operation of it in the hands of an executive vice president, or a committee of top executives, or he might operate it from his own office. Fundamentally, it makes no difference how he operates so long as he does not violate the concept that all responsible officials must participate in the planning and control process.

Some distinctions should be made here between planning and control. Planning might conceivably be effective with a minimum of

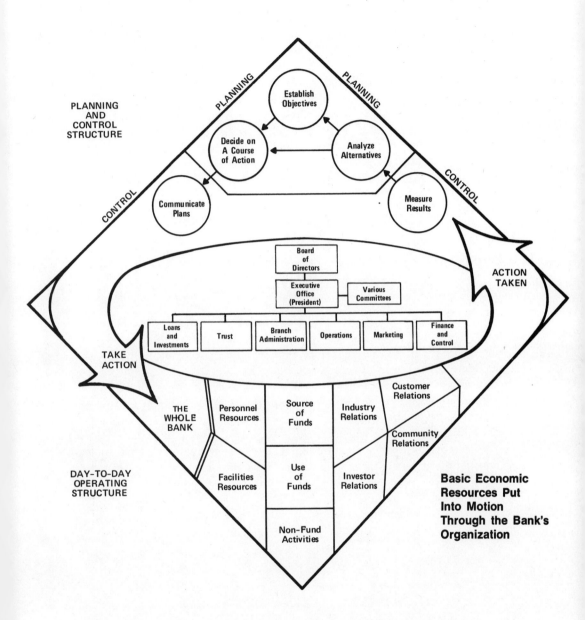

Figure 2.1—A Planning and Control Structure and Its Relationship to Organization, Resources and Day-to-Day Operations

participation by key personnel throughout an organization; however, control cannot be effective if everyone in an organization does not participate in the process of having their work reviewed, measured, assessed, evaluated, and redirected. If control becomes distant from day-to-day work, the groundwork has been laid for ensuing difficulties. Sooner or later men and women at all levels will find ways to frustrate any management that subjects them to what might be thought of as "absentee" control. This does not mean that there is no role for the objective appraisal of results, but it must be a cooperative supplement to a control process by which all responsible officials seek to assess performance so they can move collectively to greater levels of success.

SPECIFYING BANK-WIDE OBJECTIVES

The second key to successful management is specifying bank-wide objectives.

As in all efforts to compartmentalize activity neatly, it may seem that the need for objective-setting is so obvious that it hardly needs to be mentioned. Yet the job of setting objectives is complex and troublesome in any large organization and particularly so in a bank. A bank must keep public service objectives in mind along with profit-making objectives to an extent that probably applies to few other profit-making institutions in our economy. But these objectives often may be contradictory. For example, a bank might have an opportunity to increase its profits by an investment outside its geographic area. The bank's management may forego this opportunity in order to better serve the community in which it is located.

Moreover, time and human affairs have a bearing on the types of objectives that any enterprise must set. For example, a hundred years ago a banker might have said that his objectives were both to profit and to serve the community. But he did not necessarily regard the building of a strong corps of permanent employees as an objective worth standing beside the other two. Today, however, many bankers would undoubtedly feel that this objective has an importance comparable to that of the others.

IDENTIFYING AREAS OF EFFORT

Regardless of what objectives are spelled out, the chief executive is now ready to move on to the third step, namely, determining the areas of effort that are to be managed. In doing so, he specifies them without regard to any preconceived notion of the type of organization by which they might be managed.

It makes no fundamental difference how the executive sorts, groups, and subdivides the areas to be managed, so long as he does so in an effective way. The following ten areas to be managed can serve as an example:

1. *The Whole Bank*
   Certain matters that apply to the bank as a whole cannot be compartmentalized. For example, the "image" the bank proposes to project—whether staid, conservative, and austere or, conversely, dynamic, progressive, and friendly—cannot possibly be confined to any one area.

2. *Source of Funds*
   This area is concerned with the sources from which the bank draws investable funds into its hands—e.g., time deposits, demand deposits, international branches, etc.

3. *Use of Funds*
   This includes all loan and investment activities—e.g., commercial loans, instalment loans, credit cards, investment activities, etc.

4. *Nonfund Activities*
   The chief executive would group the following services: trust, EDP, travel, insurance, and mutual fund sales.

5. *Physical Resources*
   The chief executive would examine physical facilities on a bankwide basis, cutting across organizational and branch lines, and geographic locations.

6. *Human Resources*
   This entails managing the human resources of the bank on a total, coordinated basis. In some organizations, human resources are neglected or viewed as the responsibility of a specialized personnel organizational unit. If management takes the narrower view, it is possible that it will fail to manage human resources to maximum advantage and to grasp personnel problems clearly. On such matters as rate of turnover, for example, an enterprise should know what its turnover rate signifies.

7. *Customer Relations*
   In viewing customer relations on a bank-wide basis, the chief executive makes it clear that the management of customer relations should not be delegated to any one organizational unit. Even a maintenance department, for example, plays a direct role: snow and ice on the steps does not help customer relations.

8. *Investor Relations*

   In any free-enterprise organization, relations with investors are so important that they must be managed on a firm-wide basis (particularly when investors are customers or employees).

9. *Industry Relations*

   Intra-industry relations play a significant role in banking. Although competition with others in the industry may be intense, cooperation with industry members in other locations is made essential by the very nature of banking. Making sure that these cooperative relationships are sound and properly maintained cannot be left to any one segment of the bank. Moreover, there are few industries in which it is so important for individual members to work together. With the continuing impact of regulatory controls, it is mandatory for bankers to cooperate effectively if they are to be properly understood by the public, as well as by legislators and administrators.

10. *Community Relations*

    The bank's relationship to the community it serves is of paramount importance. The bank's participation in and support of community activities and its attention to the scope of banking and related services that the community should receive to retain its vigor and dynamic character is necessary for the welfare of its citizens.

THE SCHEME OF ORGANIZATION

When the chief executive has clearly identified the areas he must manage, he is ready to set up the organization scheme he feels will help him to manage these areas and accomplish his objectives. This is the fourth key to successful cost management. Too often, however, management leaders will not wait to design their organizations until the necessary preparatory work has been completed.

Bank management must approach organizational design with all possible deliberation. Whether a new organization is being created or an old one is being reshaped, nothing can be accomplished without an organization. Although there are a few cases in which one can almost do without an organization (such as a dam site that operates by remote control and requires only periodic inspection by one man), they are so rare that they merely serve to dramatize the need for organizational units to work towards specific objectives together with other units.

In structuring his organization, the chief executive should bear in mind that fundamentally he is arranging resources to carry out bank functions. What are these resources? They can be categorized as follows: funds, people, and facilities—either those now at his disposal or those he acquires or creates. Fundamentally, his task is to deploy and manage these resources—regardless of what kind of organization structure he utilizes—in carrying out bank activities on a day-to-day basis within the framework of broad areas to be managed. In the final analysis, no matter what objectives and functions the bank may have. it is the effective use of resources that is crucial. It will be pointed out that the analysis of costs for the entire bank can only be made in terms of these resources (funds, people, and facilities) because it is the acquisition or creation and use of these resources that gives rise to cost. Even though costs can be expressed in terms of such focal points as functions, profit centers, and activities, it is actually resources that are being costed.

ANALYZING ALTERNATIVES AND DECIDING ON A PLAN

The chief executive's fifth key is the analysis of alternative courses of action and the preparation of plans. Against the backdrop of bank objectives he must analyze the courses of action required to meet those objectives. This involves determining what resources are to be used and what the result of their use is likely to be.

Deciding upon those alternatives to be put into action is a fundamental managerial art. The fact that bank objectives may necessarily seem contradictory only serves to make the process more difficult. Costing plays an important part in determining the courses of action to be taken, and the chief executive's understanding of costs will likewise play an important role in the quality of his decisions.

The decisions made concerning the directions to be taken, the resources needed, and the results to be obtained constitute the plan. The chief executive now must decide how to communicate the plan to his organization; it is here that the control process begins.

THE CONTROL PROCESS

The sixth key is communicating plans and controlling results. Communicating plans may seem to be a fairly simple procedure if the necessary preparatory steps have been taken; however, if this procedure is not handled properly, the chief executive could lose the advantages he has gained so far. If he fails now to enlist the cooperation of his organization so that it will participate in detailed plan development, much of his preparatory work could be wasted. Or, if he plans only in terms of tight organizational components, his achievements may fall short of bank-wide objectives. If he merely passes plans down and expects them to be carried out without a sequential process of review and approval, he may be risking lackluster performance.

The chief executive must keep in mind that plans should be communicated in a way that clearly points out the actions to be taken by the organization and where the responsibility for such action lies. In structuring plans he must also recognize the need for comparing results of actions taken and provide a means for corrective action if necessary.

Once plans have been issued and subordinate plans have been developed and reviewed, action can take place. Planning must interrelate with action; planning cannot take the place of action. Moreover, action, measurement, and evaluation must begin simultaneously. Management must design this process so that the results of planned action can be measured and evaluated on a timely basis. Deficiencies can then be noted and corrective action taken before crises develop. This analytical process has to be carried out in such a way that it enlists cooperation and perhaps even excites enthusiasm throughout the organization. In this way control can be a creative process that stimulates productivity, offers incentives, and rewards enterprise.

When costs are given a new visibility, their impact on action can be assessed by management readily and with assurance. Those who know costs and understand costing can most accurately associate costs with action and with benefits to be derived.

THE BENEFITS OF COST MANAGEMENT

The six keys to successful management in general and successful cost management in particular have been described. Without them, it is most unlikely that cost management can be successful; with them, it can play a useful role. It is incumbent upon a bank to utilize creative cost management to advance its objectives by applying the costing process through a variety of costing techniques. This will enable management to analyze alternatives when planning and in communicating plans and measuring results for control purposes (Figure 2.2).

In devising this costing process, care has been taken to avoid presenting it in what many managers regard as the esoteric, somewhat mystifying terms of traditional cost accounting. Many bankers have

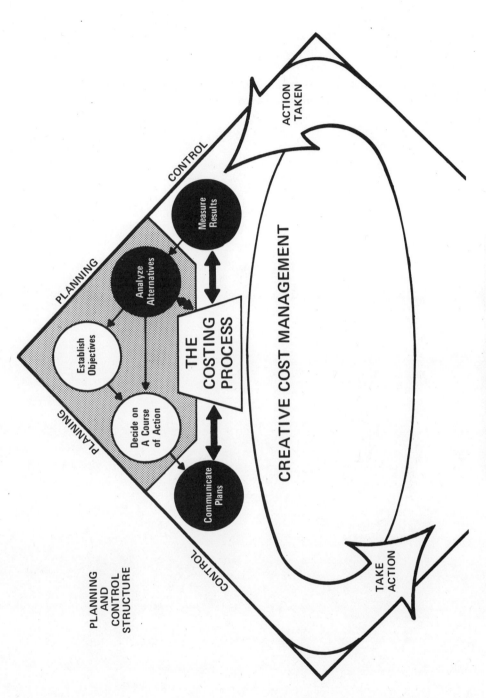

PLANNING
AND
CONTROL
STRUCTURE

PLANNING

CONTROL

Establish Objectives

Analyze Alternatives

Decide on A Course of Action

Measure Results

Communicate Plans

THE COSTING PROCESS

CREATIVE COST MANAGEMENT

ACTION TAKEN

TAKE ACTION

Figure 2.2—Relationship of Bank Costing to the Planning and Control Structure

understandably been afraid to grapple with the technical aspects of costing, and it is hoped that this book will be instrumental in overcoming fears once the subject is discussed in terms that show the underlying simplicity of a sometimes very complex subject. It is expected that bank managers will see that cost management is a technique that they can use fully and creatively without delegating it to others.

Part II

SETTING THE STAGE
FOR BANK COSTING

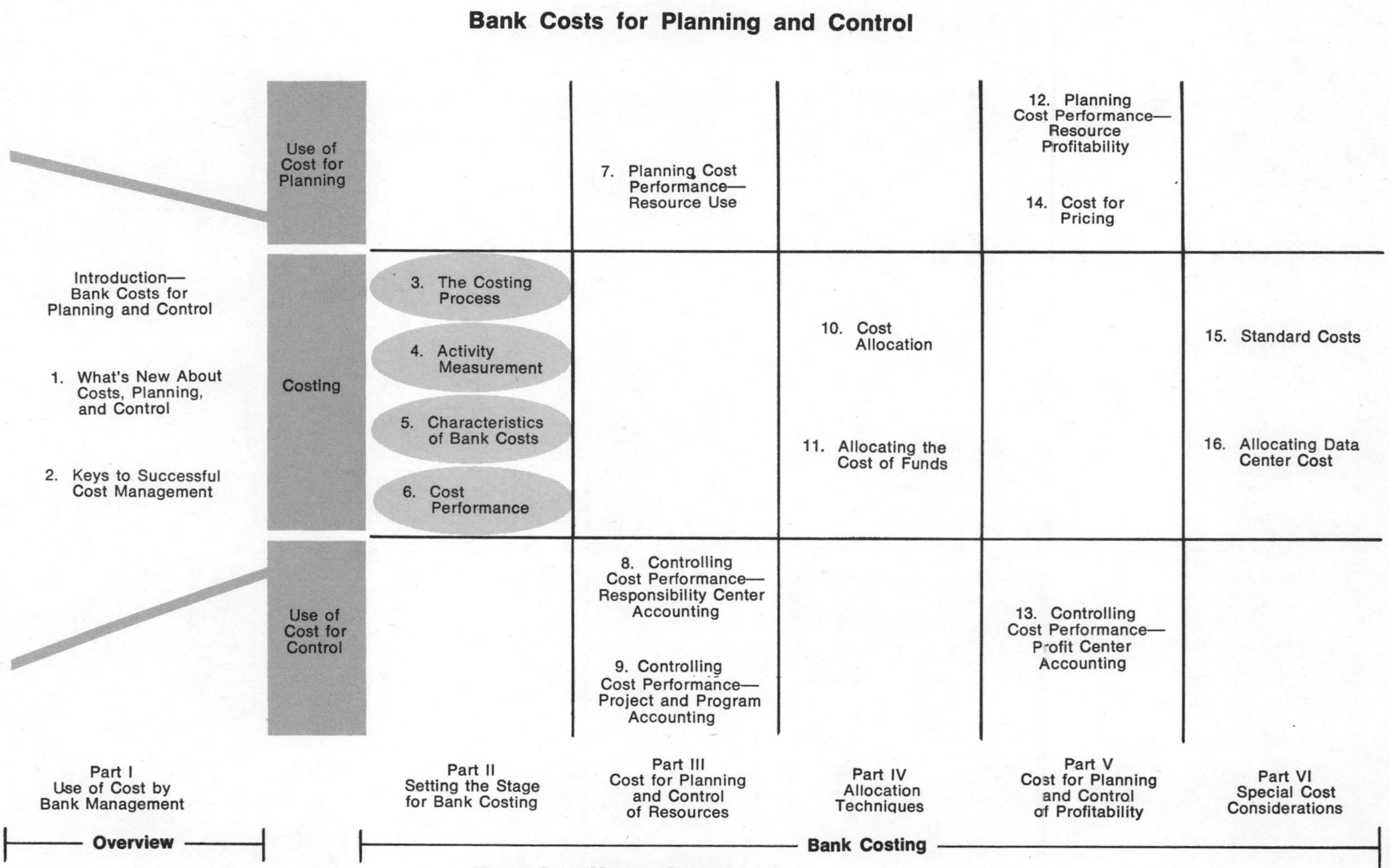

Bank Costs for Planning and Control

	Use of Cost for Planning	Costing	Use of Cost for Control		

Introduction—
Bank Costs for
Planning and Control

1. What's New About
   Costs, Planning,
   and Control

2. Keys to Successful
   Cost Management

Part I
Use of Cost by
Bank Management

7. Planning Cost
   Performance—
   Resource Use

3. The Costing
   Process

4. Activity
   Measurement

5. Characteristics
   of Bank Costs

6. Cost
   Performance

8. Controlling
   Cost Performance—
   Responsibility Center
   Accounting

9. Controlling
   Cost Performance—
   Project and Program
   Accounting

Part II
Setting the Stage
for Bank Costing

Part III
Cost for Planning
and Control
of Resources

10. Cost
    Allocation

11. Allocating the
    Cost of Funds

Part IV
Allocation
Techniques

12. Planning
    Cost Performance—
    Resource
    Profitability

14. Cost for
    Pricing

13. Controlling
    Cost Performance—
    Profit Center
    Accounting

Part V
Cost for Planning
and Control
of Profitability

15. Standard Costs

16. Allocating Data
    Center Cost

Part VI
Special Cost
Considerations

— Overview — ─── Bank Costing ───

Figure O.1—Chapter Arrangement

Part II

SETTING THE STAGE
FOR BANK COSTING

This section presents a generalized view of costing to enable the reader to visualize the entire costing process. It concludes with a discussion of cost characteristics in banks and the concept of cost performance upon which the remainder of the book is built.

Costing is presented in Chapter 3 with an introductory discussion of fundamental terms. These terms, which will be used throughout the book, are:

- Cost.
- Costing object.
- Allocation.
- Cost center.

The concluding part of Chapter 3 discusses five major steps required to produce useful cost information:

- Defining the purpose of the calculation.
- Defining the costing object.
- Specifying the cost data.
- Specifying the allocation process.
- Calculating the cost.

These steps have been developed around a concept of costing that is applicable to banking, manufacturing, government, or any other enterprise. They are required in any calculation of cost information and, in the course of considering alternatives, making decisions, communicating plans, and measuring results, these five steps are used frequently. Moreover, the reader has a frame of reference as more detailed concepts of costing are considered.

Determination of revenue is not discussed in this section to any extent, because determining revenue and relating it to cost does not generally present unusual problems. But when it does, it is discussed in sufficient detail to provide the reader with required techniques.

Discussion of the costing process is followed by a brief discussion of activity measurement (Chapter 4), an important aspect of both the costing process and controlling the use of bank resources.

Costing has had its greatest use and development in the manufacturing field. Consequently, there is a natural tendency to apply manufacturing cost concepts to banks. For the proper application of the costing process to the banking field, it is necessary to understand the characteristics of costs in banks. Cost characteristics strongly influence the validity of certain cost techniques. They are presented in Chapter 5 so that a subsequent discussion of costing techniques can be made more meaningful.

This section concludes with a discussion of cost performance, a useful concept for relating costing to management's responsibility for planning and control.

3

THE COSTING PROCESS

Any discussion of costing inevitably raises questions concerning the meanings assigned to various terms. Economists have their interpretations of cost and cost-related terms, accountants have theirs, and engineers, in turn, have theirs. These interpretations have been developed to meet the special requirements of each profession. The problem has been made more complex by the necessity to improvise to meet the special needs of an industry or an individual company. Consequently, there has been some misunderstanding about terms and concepts, which can lead to the misapplication of costing techniques.

In order to reduce the possibility of misunderstanding or misapplication, this chapter will provide meanings for the more significant terms used in this book, and will explain how they are applied in the costing process. When other cost-related terms are used later in the book, they will be explained at the point where they are first used.

Using the more significant terms (stated in parentheses), costing can be described as

The accumulation of costs *(Cost)* in some relevant and convenient form *(Cost Center)*, and
The transferring *(Allocation)* of the cost thus accumulated to that which is being costed *(Costing Object)*.

COST DEFINITIONS

Cost

"For business purposes, cost is a general term for a measured amount of value purposefully released or to be released in the acquisition or creation of economic resources, either tangible or intangible." [1]

This definition was developed by the Committee on Cost Concepts and Standards of the American Accounting Association.

There are two points concerning the definition of cost that should be noted:

- First, cost is generally expressed in monetary terms— ("measured amount of value") —and is measured by the dollar amount of cash expended or dollar value of other property transferred.
- Second, cost is assumed to have a purpose ("purposefully released"). "Purpose" in turn has two aspects:
  1. The release of value must have as its purpose the acquisition or creation of an economic resource. (For purposes of this book, these economic resources will be funds, people, and facilities. For a further discussion of the term "resources" see the following section.
  2. The cost measurement itself must serve a purpose.

For additional clarity there are two terms commonly used in accounting that should be defined here to explain their relationship to the term "cost." They are "expenditure" and "expense."

Expenditure. Expenditure has been defined as "the incurring of a liability, the payment of cash, or the transfer of property for the purpose of acquiring an asset or service or settling a loss." [2] All expenditures, as a practical matter, can be assumed to be costs.

Expense. An expense is a cost related to a time period for the purpose of reporting operating results. When salaries are paid to tellers on a monthly basis, the amounts are expenses of the bank that are part of its monthly operating costs.

To use another example, when money is paid for a machine that is expected to function for five years, the sum paid is the cost of the machine. One-fifth of that cost is applied against operations each year as depreciation, which is an expense, since it is a cost related to a time period.

[1] American Accounting Association: Tentative Statement of Cost Concepts Underlying Reports for Management Purposes, *Accounting Review*, Vol. 31, 1956, p. 183.
[2] Eric L. Kohler, *A Dictionary for Accountants*, 4th Ed. Englewood Cliffs, N.J.: Prentice-Hall, Inc., 1970, p. 182.

In accordance with accounting convention, expenses are classified by their nature under "natural expense categories." They include salaries, supplies, depreciation, rent, etc. Expenses also may be regrouped, still in natural expense categories, by organizational units.

Costing Object

The specifically identified economic resource or function, organizational unit, activity, service, etc., for which cost is being determined.

Economic resources are funds, people, and facilities (referred to in this book as resources). In using resources to accomplish its objectives, management combines them in a variety of ways. (In fact, many resources represent capabilities only in combination with others.) Sometimes resources are arranged by management along organizational lines (sections, departments, and divisions). Sometimes they are viewed in terms of their combined capabilities to provide services and carry out activities or functions, either within organizational units or cutting across them. Whether management views its resources from an organizational point of view or from a functional standpoint, the economic benefits it seeks are produced by the resources it utilizes.

When management enters the costing process, it may want to determine the cost of a given organizational unit or function, but it can only do so in terms of resources used since there is no other way to measure cost. The organizational unit or function becomes the costing object, the cost of which is measured and expressed in terms of resources.

In some cases, management may wish to cost a particular resource itself (such as an individual employee, a certain amount of funds borrowed or invested in the enterprise, or a specific piece of equipment purchased), in which case that resource becomes the costing object.

Since this text defines resources as being only funds, people, and facilities, it will not use the term "resource" to apply to a capability, a unit, or a function. However, one might easily regard a given organizational unit or function as a bank resource (or even the bank as a whole as a resource of some larger unit to which it may belong). For purposes of simplicity the term resource has been defined in the more narrow sense as stated above.

In any particular costing situation the costing object is the object of the ultimate purpose for undertaking the costing process. For example, if the bank desires to determine the cost of, say, the commercial loan function, the resources that, taken together, provide the capability of that function represent the costing object.

Allocation

The process of transferring cost data to a costing object according to benefits received or other logical measures of use.[3]

There are a number of other terms commonly used to convey the same idea. They include, for example: "transfer charge," "transfer cost," "transfer price," "distribution," "redistribution," "assignment," "association," and "classification." The distinction between them is not always clear because the words have slightly different meanings to different users, but they do convey the general idea of a transference of cost to a costing object. The word "allocation" will be used because it expresses this thought best, even though it may have different shades of meaning to some cost accountants.

Cost Center

An intermediate cost accumulation that facilitates the transference of cost to a costing object.

In finance and accounting, the term "cost center" also is used to mean an accumulation of cost by an organizational or other cost-significant unit which, in the terminology used here, would likely correspond to a costing object. For purposes of this book, however, the term will be restricted to situations in which costs are being accumulated in order to transfer cost to a costing object.

If cost centers do not exist, they may have to be created in order to carry out costing. The bank's general accounting system frequently will have accumulated costs by expense accounts, asset accounts, departments, etc., that, for costing, can often be cost centers. For example, if the general accounting system has classified all salaries of safe-deposit department personnel in one general ledger account, this account would serve as a cost center for transferring cost to the safe-deposit department, if that is the costing object. The account in which these salaries have been accumulated provides a ready-made cost center.

There are many situations, however, in which cost data must be specially accumulated in order to meet the costing situation at hand. For example, if safe-deposit salaries were not accumulated in one general ledger account, as they were in the situation referred to above, it may require creation of a special cost center containing those salaries. If a general ledger account contained all salaries for the bank,

---

[3] A similar definition of allocation is this: "Assigning one or more items of cost or revenue to one or more segments of an organization according to benefits received, responsibilities, or other logical measures of use." Charles T. Horngren, *Cost Accounting, A Managerial Emphasis*, 2nd Ed. Englewood Cliffs, N.J.: Prentice-Hall, Inc., 1967, p. 844.

the account would be reviewed, safe deposit salaries extracted and placed in a new cost center.

An example of cost center use in determining projected costs may serve to further clarify the cost center concept. In order to determine the projected cost of making an instalment loan, historical costs are obtained from the general accounting records (assuming that they are ready-made cost centers). Trend data is applied to these cost center accumulations and new, projected cost centers are created to contain the projected costs. These new cost centers are then used to transfer the costs to the costing object.

THE COSTING PROCESS

The costing process involves allocating cost data to a costing object for a purpose. The underlying concept is that of transferring cost data from its sources, through cost centers that act as "carriers," to the costing object.

The cost information to be developed through the costing process for planning and control purposes has two distinct uses: analysis of alternatives and communicating plans and measuring results.

Cost for Analyzing Alternatives

Analyzing alternatives is an integral part of developing plans and determining action to be taken to control operations. Put another way, analyzing alternatives is both initial planning and re-planning, and for both, the costing process is the same.

The search for alternative courses of action to meet management objectives is a difficult process. Frequently there are no precedents, and cost measurements may be, at best, difficult to make. The search is a highly creative process that requires a high level of managerial skill.

Costing for analysis requires cost determination for a number of alternative courses of action. The alternatives may be a simple "yes" or "no" concerning a suggested course of action, or they may involve a rather complex series of feasibility studies in which a number of alternatives are costed in order to select the best course of action.

When analyzing alternatives, the costing approach may vary markedly, depending on the specific purpose for which the cost is being determined. For example, one purpose for costing may be to evaluate a pricing structure. Another might be the consideration of dropping a bank service. In the former case, the costs to be used may include both those costs caused by the unit of service being priced and a share of all general overhead costs in order to provide sufficient revenue to cover all costs and provide a profit. In the latter case, the only costs that need to be considered are those that will be eliminated. Generally, costing for analysis requires more complex procedures than costing for communicating plans and measuring results due to the variety of circumstances encountered in analyzing alternatives.

Cost for Communicating Plans and Measuring Results

Once the alternative course of action has been selected, costing then plays the role of communicating the desired action to the bank organizations involved and measuring the results of action taken. Essentially, the nature of the costs for communicating plans (or budgets) and the costs for measuring results are structured in a uniform way, because it is necessary to express cost comparisons (actual to plan) in the same terms.

Of course, it is possible (and often desirable) to measure results of a chosen alternative course of action using the same costing approach as that used when analyzing the alternative. This can be useful in validating the assumptions contained in the original calculations. What it may not do, however, is to reflect the action taken by organizational units (or action required by organizational units), because analysis does not necessarily have to use costs expressed in terms of organizational units. For communicating plans and measuring results, however, it is essential to do so.

Costing Steps

Costing is an art that attempts to quantify in monetary terms some very complex interrelationships between bank resources, functions, units, activities, etc. It seeks to do this in a way that will result in understandable cost information that is useful to management in making decisions. Costing is referred to as an art because of the constant requirement for gaining new insights into cost relationships and for discovering new ways of quantifying them and presenting the results.

However, it is useful to consider the costing process as a series of definable steps, each having its own recognizable components. In order to do this, costing will be presented here as five costing steps for the purpose of making a complex process more understandable. The steps are as follows:

1. Define the purpose of the costing.
2. Define the costing object.
3.. Specify the cost data.
4. Specify the allocation process.
5. Calculate the cost.

Both the exercise of judgment and continual alertness to the many subtleties of any particular costing problem are of paramount importance in carrying out these steps. One cannot expect to go about performing them mechanically; as each step is accomplished, new light may be shed upon the previous steps and reiteration may be necessary.

In this chapter, each of the five steps in the costing process will be described in detail without making a distinction between their use for analyzing alternatives or for communicating plans and measuring results.

Step One: Define the Purpose

To develop a clearly stated definition of the purpose for making a cost calculation is the first and most important step in costing. The stated purpose influences each of the other steps, but it is frequently overlooked.

The statement of purpose should define the ultimate purpose for making the calculation (or, to put it another way, the nature of the decision to be made using the costs determined) and the criteria that are to be used in making the final decision. Although in an actual costing situation purpose is not always spelled out with the precision recommended here (a precision that will be used in later chapters when the five costing steps are used to illustrate costing problems), the same kind of information, nonetheless, should be available in some communicable form.

A clear definition of the ultimate purpose should indicate the context in which cost is to be used and provide a general guide to the coster in developing cost data. In general, the ultimate purpose will be to provide cost information to enable management to (1) analyze alternatives, or (2) communicate plans and measure results. These general purposes are elaborated upon in the following examples:

"Consider the alternative lending uses of excess funds."

"Determine the best alternative use of the 20% of the data center's computer capacity that is available."

"Prepare proof and transit department plans and measure results."

In many situations, the ultimate purpose can be further explained as being, for example, whether or not to add a service, to drop a service, expand an activity, contract an activity, develop or buy computer software, etc. Or the purpose may make it necessary to determine how to communicate plans and measure results in ways that will evoke the required reaction by management.

The criteria by which the decision is to be made also should be included in the purpose, in order to guide the coster in selecting relevant cost data (Step Three). Criteria include cost, profit, profit contribution, return on investment, cash flow, breakeven, etc.

To illustrate the importance of carefully defining the purpose, Figure 3.1 shows seven different purposes that might require calculating the cost of a credit card operation. The left-hand column of the figure also shows different groups of cost data, the use of which depends upon the purpose.

If consideration is being given to expanding or contracting a credit card operation (Figure 3.1), the cost impact of these actions must be determined. Costs that would be added or eliminated for the bank as a whole would have to be determined in making the cost calculation. These costs would then be compared to the benefits of expanding or contracting the operation (revenue, for example) in order to make a decision. Similar considerations would be required in deciding whether or not to add or drop a credit card operation.

As for the profitability of the credit card operation, the bank may wish to know whether it generates enough revenue to cover the costs it causes directly. If it does, the directly related costs would be used. If there is any question about the bank's ability also to cover those costs that are associated with other bank services used, these additional costs would have to be allocated.

If pricing is being evaluated, the bank may want to determine whether current or anticipated prices cover all costs of the credit card operation as well as a share of the bank's general overhead expenses.

If management wants plans and measurements of results to be expressed in terms of responsibility centers, only the costs that can be controlled by responsibility center managers should be used. These costs may differ from directly related costs if some of the latter are not under the control of the responsibility center managers.

Step Two: Define the Costing Object

It might seem that the costing object in any particular costing situation would be obvious, but failing to define it carefully can make it difficult to select the proper data and to carry out the allocation process.

Clear identification of the costing object is necessary to determine what costs are applicable and how they are to be accumulated by cost center. A simple example would be the selection of a proof machine, which should be identified by model, space and power requirements, performance specification, etc.

A more complicated example would be that of the credit card operation previously mentioned. If the bank wants to determine the

Costing Object: Credit Card Operation

Cost Group Affected \ Costing Purpose	Expand	Contract	Add	Drop	Determine Profitability	Evaluate Prices	Control by Responsibility Center
Costs added	X		X				
Costs eliminated		X		X			
Directly related costs					X	X	
Allocated portion of cost of data processing or other bank services used					X	X	
Allocated portion of general overhead expenses						X	
Controllable expenses							X

Figure 3.1—The Effect of Purpose on the Selection of Cost Data Required

profitability of that operation, all relevant resources used in it and by it would have to be determined. The resources used could be defined in terms of: funds used (this involves cost of funds); space (this involves occupancy cost); and the resources of those benefit-providing units that provide supporting services (data processing, for example).

To summarize, defining the costing object requires:

- A clear, concise statement identifying the resource, function, activity, or organizational unit that is to be costed.
- Specific identification of the resources and benefit-providing functions, activities, or organizational units that go to make up the costing object. This identification can be summarized as follows:
  - .. Funds (stated in terms of deposits and other sources, investable funds, or invested funds).
  - .. People (stated in terms of number, skills, etc.).
  - .. Facilities (stated in terms of premises, equipment, supplies used, etc.).
  - .. Resources of benefit-providing units (departments, functions, etc.).

Figure 3.2 illustrates the resource composition of a costing object.

Step Three: Specify the Cost Data

Once the purpose and the costing object of the cost calculation have been clearly defined, the next costing step is to specify the data necessary for the cost calculation. This involves:

1. Identifying the cost data associated with the resources that comprise the costing object.
2. Identifying the sources of each type of cost data.
3. Screening out data not relevant to the purpose of the calculation.
4. Determining the degree of precision required in the data.

Identify the Cost Data. To identify the cost data, thought must be given to the kinds of data that are related to the resources that make up the costing object. The data usually will take two forms—costs and activity measurements. The need for costs is evident. The activity measurements are required to determine resource capacity and utilization. Data concerning capacity and utilization is necessary to judge the relevancy of costs and also the degree of cost precision.

To illustrate identification of cost data, assume that telephones are one of the resources that make up a costing object (e.g., a credit card operation). It is necessary, therefore, to define the elements of

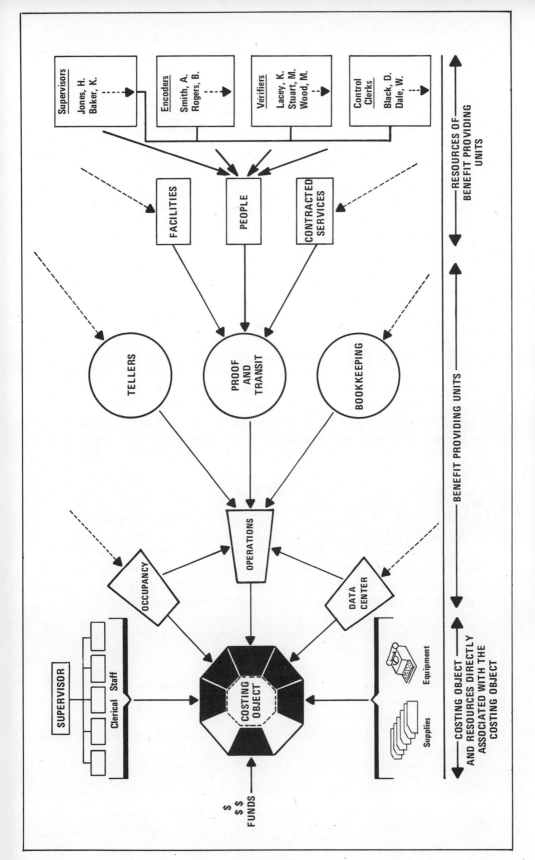

Figure 3.2—Illustration of Costing Object Resource Composition

cost that represent the telephones: installation cost, monthly rental of units, the cost of switching equipment, and the cost of switchboard operators. The type of activity data required might include the number of telephones used or needed. The more complicated the nature of the costing object, the more difficult it will be to identify cost and activity data.

Identify Sources of Cost Data. Cost data is available from many sources: general accounting records, previous cost projections, special studies, industry statistics, census summaries, work measurement statistics, etc.

Screen Out Nonrelevant Data. The data must be relevant to the cost purpose. Consideration of relevancy frequently depends on the capacity of the resource or combination of resources to handle changes in volume or use. For example, bookkeeping department supervisor salaries would not be likely to change if an additional bookkeeping machine were acquired. Therefore, if the purpose is to decide whether or not to buy another machine, the supervisor salaries are not relevant. Purchase of the machine might, however, necessitate hiring an additional bookkeeper, in which case the bookkeeper's salary would be relevant. Or, if the number of credit card accounts is increased, the number of telephones required to answer inquiries might be higher. Telephone costs would be relevant. Figure 3.3 shows examples of data that are relevant to a particular purpose and costing object.

Determine the Degree of Precision Required. Determining the requisite degree of precision centers around the effect that the range of probable error in the data may have on the decision. If the outcome is sensitive to a probable error, greater precision is required.

For example, if interest paid on time deposits is 60% of the cost of funds, a small change in the interest rate is material with respect to a decision involving the interest rate to be charged to a borrowing customer. On the other hand, a 100% error in an operating expense that amounts to one percent of the cost of funds would not significantly affect the decision. Therefore, in this situation greater precision is required in the projection of interest than is required in projecting that particular operating expense.

Data concerning capacity and utilization is often necessary to judge the degree of cost precision required. In the example discussed above concerning telephones used in the credit card operation an increase in inquiries of 15% might indicate that ten to twelve additional telephones are needed. It would not be necessary to determine the precise number needed (10, 11, or 12) if the range of the esti-

Purpose of Calculation	Costing Object	Cost Data Element	Relevancy
• To decide whether to close a branch or keep it open	• Existing branch	• Rental cost for space occupied by the branch	• Relevant—the rental cost could be avoided if the branch were closed or it would be incurred if kept open
• To decide whether to close a branch or keep it open	• Existing branch	• Salaries of president's staff	• Not relevant—the salary cost for the president's staff would continue whether the branch closes or remains open
• To decide whether or not to open a new branch	• Proposed branch	• Home office proof and transit cost	• Relevant—the increase in check volume to be handled at the home office will affect the utilization of the proof and transit department and may require additional people, equipment, etc.

Figure 3.3—Examples of Relevancy of Cost Data

mated number of telephones does not represent a significant cost difference.

Step Four: Specify the Allocation Process

Allocation is the most complicated aspect of costing, and it is probably this complexity that leads many businessmen and accountants to equate costing entirely with allocation. It is, however, only one step in the costing process.

In discussing the costing process thus far, three costing steps have been reviewed: the definition of purpose, the definition of the costing object, and the specification of appropriate cost data.

Step Four describes the process to be used in transferring the data specified in Step Three to the costing object.

Specifying the allocation process involves:

1. Determining the allocation basis.
2. Determining the transfer unit.
3. Determining the allocation method.

The concepts underlying these three parts of the process are described here, and the details involved in carrying them out are discussed in Chapters 10 and 11.

Allocation Basis. An allocation basis is always required in any transfer of cost. It is an expression of benefit received by the costing object, either directly or through intermediate cost centers. Examples of allocation bases are area occupied, transactions handled for a particular function, particular services received from employees, time spent by managers, loans processed, etc.

To determine the allocation basis required in a particular costing situation, it is necessary to begin with the definition of the costing object established in Step Two. This definition (Figure 3.2) identifies the relationships of the various resources and benefit-providing units that make up the costing object. Each of these relationships is further examined in order to determine an allocation basis (i.e., the benefit provided and received in each relationship). Figure 3.4 shows how allocation bases link the resources and benefit-providing units to the costing object.

Transfer Unit. Allocation basis provides the expression of the benefits provided that is needed to begin the allocation process. The next step is to express the allocation basis in some unit of measure that can be used to apportion the applicable costs in a cost center for transfer to a costing object. For convenience, this unit measure of the

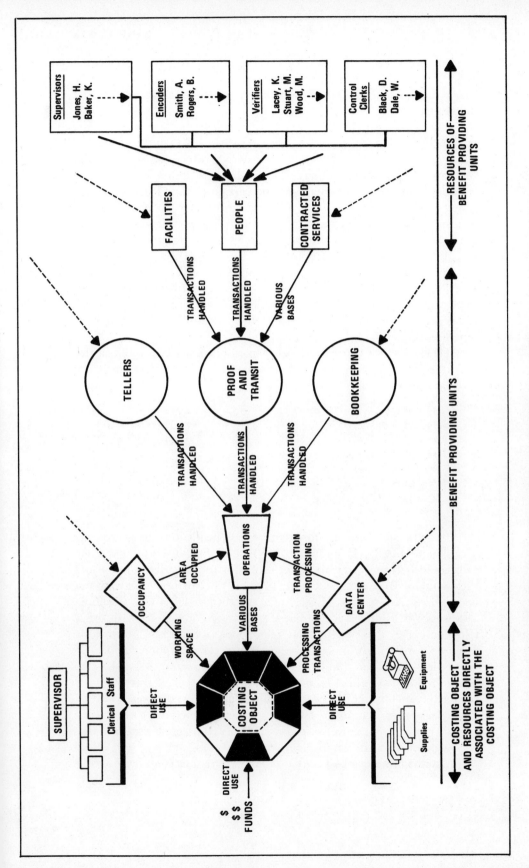

Figure 3.4—Allocation Bases Linking Resources and Benefits Received to the Costing Object

allocation basis will be referred to as a "transfer unit" since it is used for cost transfer.

There are situations, however, where it is not necessary to use transfer units to apportion the costs of a cost center and, instead, the whole cost of a cost center can be transferred directly to another cost center or to the costing object. This will occur frequently when accounting system data is being used and certain general ledger accounts contain only those costs applicable to the costing purpose and the costing object. Accounting systems that incorporate responsibility center or profit center accounting will tend to have a good deal of the cost data already accumulated in cost center form suitable for direct transfer. Theoretically the cost center in this case is a transfer unit of one. Since these situations require only a simple transfer of the cost center cost, the remainder of this section will be devoted to the more complex requirement, the use of a transfer unit to apportion cost center costs.

To clarify the distinction between allocation basis and transfer unit, typical allocation bases and frequently used transfer units are listed as follows:

Allocation Basis	Transfer Unit
Area occupied	Square foot
Transactions handled	Transaction
Services received from employees	Man-hour
Time spent by managers	Man-hour
Loans processed	Loan

The transfer unit to be used also depends on the degree of precision required. For example, the cost of long-distance telephone calls could be transferred to a cost center or to a costing object using each actual call as a transfer unit, but this kind of precision may not be required. As an alternative, under certain circumstances, the long-distance costs could be accumulated in a cost center along with other telephone costs and, using each telephone as a transfer unit, costs could be transferred using an average cost for each telephone used.

When calculating the cost (Step Five), the amount of cost to be transferred is determined by multiplying the number of transfer units received (which is another way of expressing the benefits received) by the benefiting cost center (or costing object) times the cost of each transfer unit. The relationship between cost center, allocation basis, and transfer unit is shown in Figure 3.5.

Figure 3.5 shows a cost center (which serves to accumulate costs in

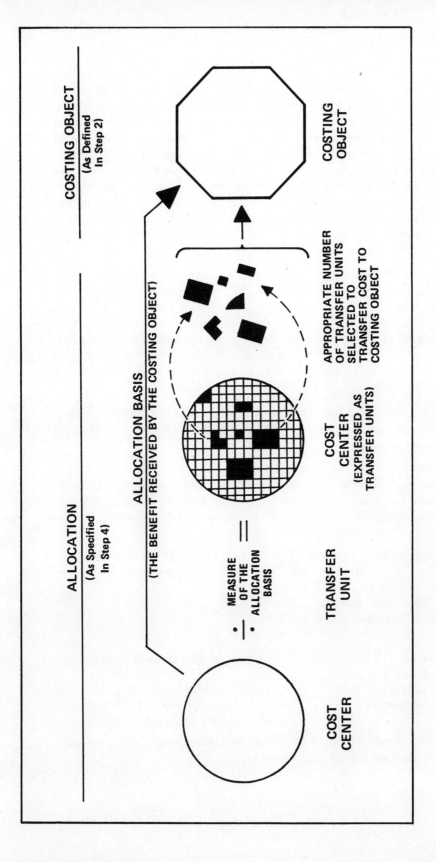

Figure 3.5—Relationships Between Cost Center, Allocation Basis and Transfer Unit

a convenient form for transfer to a costing object—or to another cost center), the cost of which must be apportioned to a costing object. The cost center could be created for a particular costing situation or it could be an existing general ledger account. The cost center is divided by the unit of measure of the allocation basis (transfer unit), which results in the cost center being expressed as a particular number of transfer units. The number of transfer units (man-hours, transactions, employees, etc.) received by the costing object is then used to apportion the cost center cost to the costing object. The assignment of cost to the transfer unit and the actual transfer is accomplished in Step Five of the costing process.

Method. In defining the resources and benefits received that go to make up the costing object (Figure 3.2) it becomes evident that costs can flow between resources and benefit-providing units and the costing object in several ways. The allocation method has as its objective a simulation of the cost flow for costing purposes. In summary, cost flow can be thought of in the following classifications (although cost flows are generally more complex due to the real-life complexity of the benefit-provided/received relationship):

Direct flow: Example: The data center serves the demand deposit function, and the cost flows from the data center to the demand deposit function.

Compound flow: Example: The data center, the administrative function, and the demand deposit function require space. Occupancy cost flows to the demand deposit function directly and also through the data center and the administrative function to the demand deposit function.

Complex flow: Example: The data center serves the administrative function, and the administrative function has responsibility for the data center. The costs flow both ways.

These cost flows are represented by methods used to simulate them for cost allocation purposes:

Flow	Allocation Method
Direct flow	Direct allocation
Compound flow	Step allocation
Complex flow	Reciprocal allocation

Chapter 10 explains these allocation methods in more detail; a simplified illustration is provided here as follows:

It will be assumed that the purpose of the costing is to compare the profitability of the safe-deposit function with that of another function. The definition of the safe-deposit function (the costing object) reveals that it is composed of the following: vault attendants (people), space occupied (facilities), and a share of the administrative function (services provided to it). It is assumed further that the costs related to these resources and the function are contained in the following general ledger accounts:

- Safe-deposit salaries expense.
- Vault depreciation.
- Building depreciation.
- Utility expense.
- Janitorial expense.
- Administrative expense (various expense accounts).

Figure 3.6 illustrates an allocation method for this situation.

Note that safe-deposit salaries have already been accumulated in a general ledger account in the accounting system suitable for direct transfer to the costing object. The use of transfer units is unnecessary. Only portions of the occupancy and administrative cost center are to be transferred to the cost object. This requires the use of transfer units. Since a portion of administrative costs are applicable to occupancy and to the safe-deposit function, transfers will be made to each. In turn, occupancy costs (including a portion of administrative costs) are transferred to the costing object. The transfer of safe-deposit salaries and a portion of administrative costs and safe-deposit expenses direct to the costing object illustrates the "direct" method of cost allocation. The transfer of a portion of administrative costs to the occupancy cost center and then of a portion of occupancy costs to the costing object illustrates the "step" method of cost allocation.

Step Five: Calculate the Cost

When the purpose and the costing object have been defined and both the required data and the allocation process have been specified, the stage has been set for the actual cost calculation.

- The cost data required and the sources have been specified. In the calculation step costs are assembled and accumulated by cost centers.
- The allocation bases, the transfer units (where required), and the allocation method have been specified. In the calculation step:
    .. If only a portion of the cost center is to be transferred, measurements are made of the number of transfer units con-

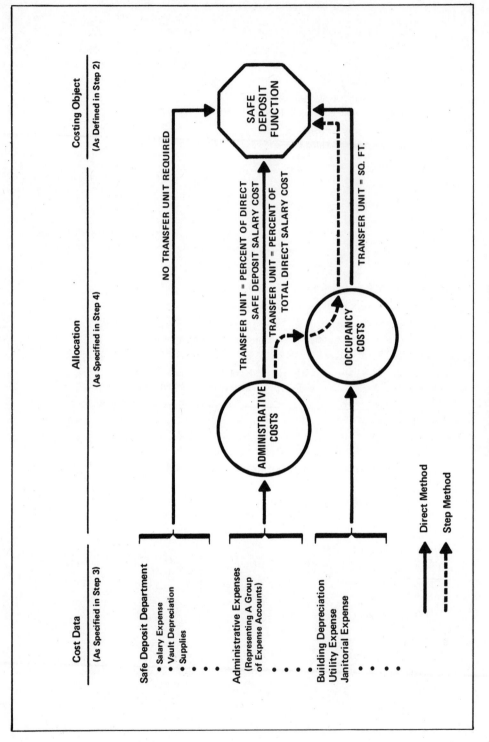

Figure 3.6—Illustration of Allocation Methods

tained in the cost center and the number in the receiving cost center (or costing object).

.. The unit transfer cost is determined by either specifically identifying a cost associated in a center with a transfer unit (salary cost with an individual employee for example) or by dividing the cost accumulated in the cost center by the number of transfer units applicable to the cost center. In the latter case, the unit cost result is an "average unit transfer cost."

.. The costs are then transferred to the costing object (through a multiplicity of cost centers, if necessary) by multiplying the applicable number of transfer units in the costing object by the unit transfer cost (or the average unit transfer cost). Where transfer units are unnecessary, the whole cost center is transferred directly to the costing object (or another cost center if the transfer is only intermediate in nature).

The costing process is completed by summarizing the costs transferred to the costing object. These steps are illustrated in Figure 3.7.

Several examples are used in Figures 3.8-3.11 to illustrate both the allocation process and the cost calculation.

Figure 3.8 illustrates a simple flow of cost. The example assumes that the purpose is to determine the cost of a particular bookkeeping machine in order to compare the cost to that of a similar model, assuming that such costs as incoming freight are prepaid in both cases. In this case, the cost as shown by the vendor's invoice is transferred directly to the costing object (the machine). Since apportionment of cost is not required, transfer units are unnecessary.

A similar example would be the transfer of salary to a safe-deposit function when the salary cost is already accumulated through the general accounting system in an account entitled, "safe deposit, attendant salaries" (Figure 3.9). The general ledger account serves as the cost center, which is transferred directly to the costing object. No apportionment is required.

Figure 3.10 illustrates a slightly more complicated situation in which the attendants' salaries, instead of being segregated in the safe-deposit attendant salary account, have been accumulated by the general accounting system in one salary account for the entire bank. In this situation, the salary costs in the "salaries" account that apply to the safe-deposit attendants are taken from that account and transferred to the costing object, using each individual employee identified as working in the safe-deposit function as a transfer unit.

The next level of cost flow complexity can be illustrated by

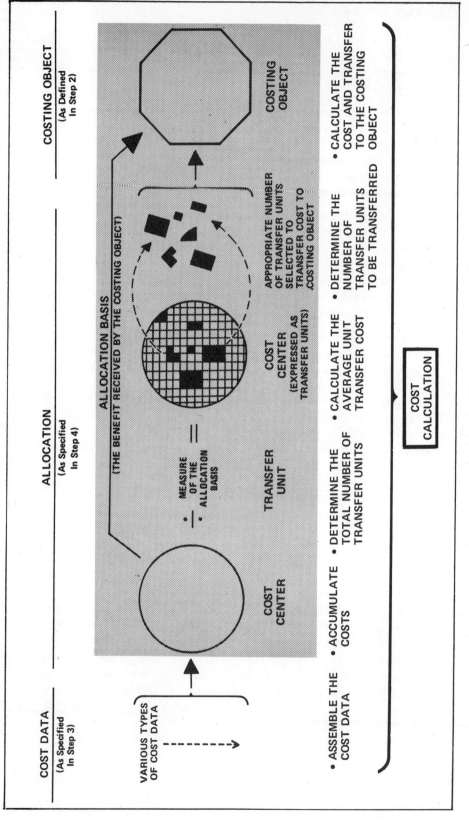

Figure 3.7—Step Five—Cost Calculation and Relationship to Previous Costing Steps

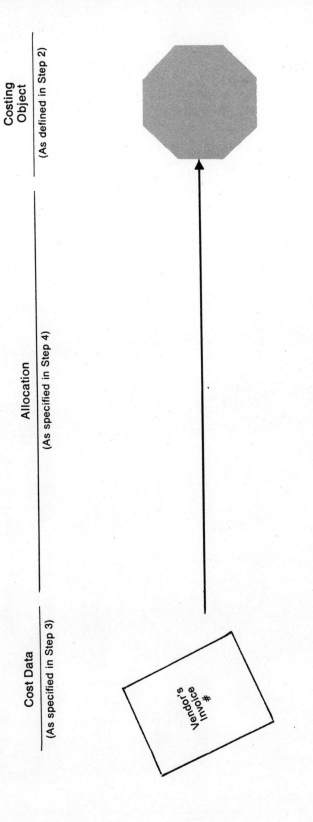

Cost Data

(As specified in Step 3)

Allocation

(As specified in Step 4)

Costing Object

(As defined in Step 2)

Vendor's Invoice #

Figure 3.8—Vendor's Invoice—Direct Transfer to Costing Object

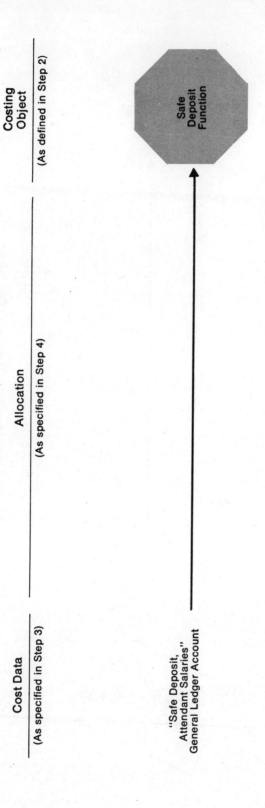

Figure 3.9—General Ledger Account As a Direct Transfer to a Costing Object

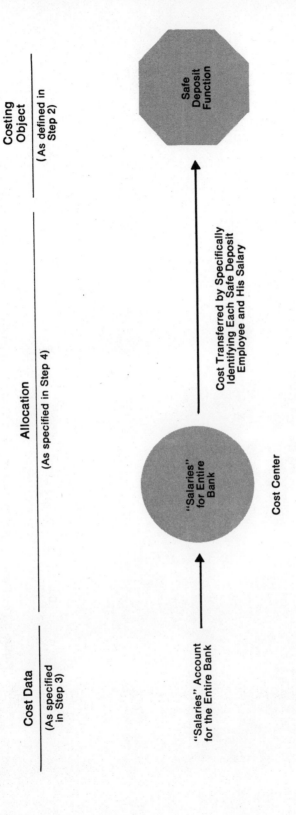

Figure 3.10—Individual Employee As a Transfer Unit

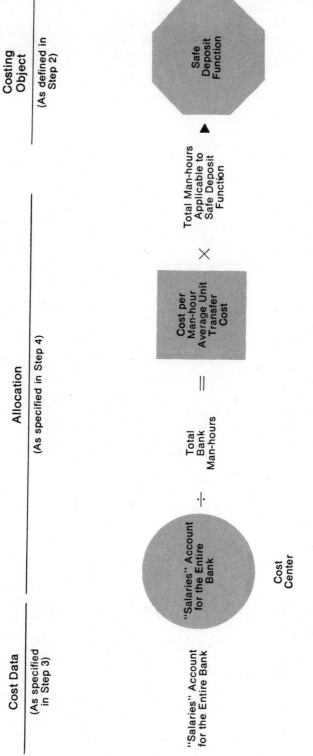

Figure 3.11—General Ledger Account As a Cost Center and Man-hour As a Transfer Unit

assuming that employees with varying assignments tend the safe-deposit vault and that no one group or single employee is assigned to the task full time (Figure 3.11). The allocation basis is the service provided to the safe-deposit function by various employees. In this situation a transfer unit (man-hours) will be used to transfer costs from the "salaries" account (the cost center) to the safe-deposit department. In this case, the unit's transfer cost used was an average unit transfer cost.

SUMMARY

It has been shown that the costing process involves the determination of cost to be used in planning and control for the analysis of alternatives and for both communicating plans and measuring results. When cost is to be used for analyzing alternatives, the cost for each alternative must be determined. When cost is to be used for communicating plans and measuring results, costs must be determined that convey management's action requirements to the bank's organization and, at the same time, provide a reasonable measure of results obtained after action has been taken.

Cost for both of these major purposes is determined by carrying out five costing steps. A thorough understanding of these steps, as well as the exercise of care in carrying them out, is necessary to produce cost information that will be valid for planning and for control. The five costing steps will be used in the remainder of this book in conjunction with the specific uses of cost data.

4

ACTIVITY
MEASUREMENT

It was pointed out in Chapter 3 that measurement of activity played a significant role in the following two costing steps:

- Step Three of the costing process requires, for some costing purposes, a knowledge of resource capacity and utilization so that the effect of past, present, or future actions upon those resources can be determined. Measurement of activity is often required to determine capacity and the utilization of that capacity.

- Step Four of the costing process in some cases requires the use of a transfer unit to allocate costs. Activity measurements are needed to determine the number of transfer units to be used in the allocation process.

USE OF ACTIVITY MEASUREMENT TO DETERMINE CAPACITY AND UTILIZATION

The resources used in a bank have been categorized as funds, people, and facilities. These resources provide benefits that enable management to carry out the objectives of the bank, however, the ability of these resources to produce benefits is not limitless. Each resource can be considered to have a benefit limit that cannot be exceeded even at maximum efficiency. The efficiency with which it is used by management affects the amount of benefit obtained from that resource.

For purposes of this discussion, it will be assumed that benefit limits and maximum efficiency can be determined. As a practical matter, however, this is one of management's most difficult problems since, with perhaps a few exceptions, benefit limits and maximum efficiency cannot be defined with complete precision.

Benefit limits can be thought of as having two dimensions: (1) an amount of benefits provided, and (2) a time span. These two dimensions provide a basis for expressing the capacity of the resource. To illustrate this concept, a few specific resources, and combinations of resources, are shown along with an expression of their capacities:

Resource(s)	Benefits Provided	Expression of Capacity
Funds	Revenue generated	Revenue generated during a time period
People		
Executive Vice President	Administration	Administrative work during a time period
Teller	Transactions handled	Transactions handled during a time period
Facilities		
Premises	Space	Space provided during a time period
Check sorting machine	Checks sorted	Checks sorted during a time period

In each case, the resource provides a benefit that can be identified as an activity. Capacity, therefore, consists of activity performed over a time period, and the determination of capacity involves the measurement of these two factors.

To determine capacity, it is necessary to (1) establish the time period with which activity is to be associated, and (2) determine the amount of activity that can be produced during the time established (month, eight-hour day, etc.). Of the two kinds of data required to determine capacity, developing activity data presents the greater difficulty.

Activity capacity can be determined in two ways:

1. Measure the amount of activity being produced during the time period established to express capacity.

2. Determine how much activity *should* be produced during the time period established to express capacity.

The use of activity being produced as a base for determining capacity incorporates into the capacity measurement any inefficiencies present in carrying out the activity. Any inefficiency that is present uses up resource capacity, since more activity presumably could be produced during a given time period if efficiency were improved.

In some costing situations it is important to know how much capacity could be available rather than how much is available under existing conditions. For example, if the costing situation calls for determining the cost effect of an increase in some particular activity, a significant cost may be required for additional capacity. If the calculation of capacity has been based on an inefficient activity process, however, it is possible that improved efficiency could create additional available capacity in the existing resource and eliminate the need for buying more capacity. In this situation, therefore, it would be important to determine how much activity could be carried out if efficiency were improved.

In reviewing the limited number of resources listed above to illustrate benefits and related activities, it becomes evident that some activities are easier to measure than others. Activity measurement is usually confined to those activities that can be easily measured, for example, transactions, space, and checks sorted.

As to funds, activity in terms of revenue generated can be measured, but the determination of how much revenue *could* be generated under more "efficient" conditions is not susceptible to the type of activity measurement being discussed here.

In addition to determining capacity, the measurement of activity provides a means for determining utilization. The same type of activity that would be used for expressing capacity is measured: the amount and the time required. Although utilization can be measured without determining capacity, for costing it is frequently useful to know the percent of capacity used. In order to determine the percentage, utilization and capacity are determined and compared. The results of the comparison permit calculation of the percent of capacity utilized. The efficiency with which activities are carried out is also an important consideration in determining utilization.

USE OF ACTIVITY MEASUREMENT TO DETERMINE TRANSFER UNITS

The objective of the allocation process is to carry out the transference of cost to a costing object. In some cases, either the general accounting system may have accomplished the allocation or the entire cost of the cost center can be transferred directly. In those cases where the general accounting system has not already accomplished allocation and where only a portion of the cost center is to be transferred, a transfer unit is required. The transfer unit is used to apportion a part of the cost center to the costing object. (A detailed discussion of transfer units will be found in Chapter 3.)

In order to use the transfer unit to apportion the costs of a cost center to a costing object, it is necessary to determine the total number of transfer units applicable to the cost center and the total applicable to the costing object. Activity measurement is used to make these determinations.

The same resources (people and facilities) used in the discussion of capacity and utilization can serve to illustrate the use of activity measurement to determine transfer units. It will be assumed that these resources also are cost centers.

Resources	Allocation Basis	Transfer Unit
People		
Executive vice president	Administration	Arbitrary unit
Teller	Transactions handled	Transaction
Facilities		
Premises	Space occupied	Square foot of space
Check sorting machine	Checks sorted	Check

For each resource, an allocation basis and a transfer unit is shown.

The allocation basis is an expression of the benefits provided whereas the transfer unit is a unit of the allocation basis. Benefits provided, like the benefit limits discussed in relation to capacity, has two dimensions: (1) the amount of benefits provided, and (2) a time span. Since, for our purposes, benefits can be identified as activity, the transfer unit used in allocation also can be identified as a unit of activity. The measurement of activity, for purposes of allocation, therefore involves measuring the number of transfer units over a time span (a week, month, year, etc.) for both the cost center and the costing object.

A transfer unit is not shown for the executive vice president because it is difficult to determine a measurable unit that represents both the benefit provided by the resource and the benefit received by the costing object. Consequently, an arbitrary unit, such as the proportion of total bank expenses incurred by a costing object, would be used. As to the other resources, the transfer units are measurable activity units and activity measurement would be used to determine the number of transfer units to be used in carrying out the allocation process.

For allocation purposes it is necessary not only to determine the number of transfer units both in the cost center and in the costing object, but also to assign a cost to the units. The costs to be assigned would be those incurred for the same time span during which the activity occurs.

ACTIVITY MEASUREMENT

There are a number of ways that activity measurement can be accomplished. Each approach involves:

- Defining the activity unit.
- Counting the number of activity units.
- Associating time with the activity (work measurement).

Defining the Activity Unit

The teller function provides a good illustration of the problems involved in defining activity units:

- Counting drawer cash.
- Recording cash added to the drawer.
- Making change for customers.
- Handling savings deposits.
- Recording savings interest.
- Cashing checks.
- Handling loan payments.
- Preparing certified checks.
- Preparing interest billings.
- Answering customer inquiries.
- Handling interest payments.
- Handling Christmas club deposits.
- Preparing past due notices.
- Handling savings withdrawals.

The preceding list is not exhaustive, but it does illustrate the diversity of activity that can be associated with a bank unit. The important problem at this point is to determine the activity units that will be used to represent the benefits provided or "productivity" of the resource or resources. The units chosen should:

- Represent a significant portion of the total activity of the organizational unit. (For example, since counting drawer cash is probably not a significant part of activity, the time it requires can be absorbed by the more significant activities in proportion to their occurrence).
- Be susceptible to measurement. (For example, since it would probably be difficult to measure answers to customer inquiries because of their variety and random character, it would seem reasonable to absorb their time into that of other more measurable activities).

Figure 4.1 lists typical activity measurements for the organizational units generally found in banks. It is representative and not intended to be all-inclusive. In most instances the activities listed are measured as item counts—"number of collateral records issued"—etc. In certain instances (such as the "time spent on coin work, etc.," in the commercial teller area) the effort cannot be easily expressed in item counts and time is used as a measure.

Methods for Counting Transactions

Activity measurement can be accomplished by counting the number of transactions handled by a department, and the following methods are most frequently used:

- *First and last in a sequence of serial numbers.* For example, if the first serial number used was 1285 and the last number used was 1390, a total of 106 forms was used during the period.
- *Length of adding machine tape listings.* For example, the number of inches of adding machine tape can be equated with a certain number of transactions recorded on the tape.
- *Readings of counters attached to machines.* A counter can be set at zero each day or it may be continuous, in which case starting and ending numbers can be used to determine the total. This method is useful for determining the number of deposits and withdrawals and for measuring proof operations.
- *Hand counters.* Hand-operated counters can be used for simple measurements, such as number of customers served at teller windows, cars passing through the drive-in, etc.
- *Height of document stacks.* This requires the number of items per inch and the height of a stack of documents. This method is used when large quantities are involved, particularly for punched cards.
- *Weight of documents.* This method assumes that all the docu-

ments are approximately the same weight, and it is based on the number of documents (checks, for example) per pound.

- *Tally worksheets.* With this method, the operator must record each activity transaction at the time it takes place. It is the most time-consuming method of obtaining activity counts and should be used only when the other methods cannot be used or when it is desirable to relate the activity to a time period.

Figure 4.2 shows a pro-forma tally worksheet that was filled out by a teller showing the tally of his various activities at half-hour intervals. A miscellaneous column ("other work") is provided to record time required for those activities where units are inconvenient to measure. (The time span selected for a survey could be any period of time, but it would probably be four or more weeks.) This work sheet not only shows the transaction counts but the distribution of transactions over the banking hours. The summary total gives the activity volume for all tellers over the period of the sampling.

Work Measurement

Several methods are used to measure time and activity (referred to here as work measurement for brevity). In general, these methods can be categorized into two groups: (1) those that measure actual time and activity, and (2) those that measure what the time and activity should be in the light of the attributes of the particular resource involved. The latter methods can be used for establishing bench marks against which to measure actual time and activity to determine efficiency.

To illustrate those methods that measure actual time and activity, the self-logging and work sampling methods will be discussed. Three frequently used work measurement methods that lead to a determination of what time and activity should be are the stopwatch time study, micromotion study, and predetermined time standards methods. Their use requires properly qualified technicians.

Self-Logging Method. This method uses self-logging data sheets on which the individual performing an operation records starting time and ending time. Interruption times of a minute or longer also are recorded. This method requires some effort but it has the advantage of being relatively economical and, if diligently carried out, accurate. It has been widely used in banks, and manuals issued by the Bank Administration Institute have suggested its use for studies of various operations. Figures 4.3 and 4.4 illustrate two different approaches to self-logging. The method is best used when there are relatively few

Bookkeeping Department
No. of:
Checks "on us" posted, microfilmed, and filed
Deposits posted, microfilmed, and filed
Monthly statements issued
Weekly statements issued
Special statements issued
Insufficient fund checks paid or returned
Stop payment orders received

Credit Department
No. of:
New loan applications processed
New financial statements processed
Old loans reviewed
Telephone credit inquiries answered
Written credit inquiries answered

Customer Service Department
No. of:
Accounts opened
Accounts closed
Accounts reconciled
Customer inquiries answered

Data Center
No. of:
Punched cards processed
Lines printed
Characters processed
Time Spent On:
Internal processing as measured by the internal clock of the central
processing unit
Input preparation
Programming

Loan Division
No. of:
New loan applications received—by types of loans
New loans made—by types of loans
Loans renewed—by types of loans
Past due notices signed—by types of loans

Personnel Department
No. of:
Applicants interviewed
Persons tested
Persons hired
Separations handled

Proof and Transit Department
No. of debits processed
Checks "on us"
Clearing house checks
Transit checks
Cash items
Official checks
General book debits
Teller cash tickets

**Figure 4.1—Typical Activity Measurements for Organizational Units
Within a Bank**

No. of credits processed
    Deposits
    General book credits

Safe Deposit Department
No. of:
    Boxes rented
    Leases cancelled
    Boxes entered
    Inventories made of box contents
    Rental billings made
    Rental payments handled

Tellers Department
No. of:
    Deposits received, checks only
    Deposits received with cash
    Deposits, cash returned
    Checks cashed
    Loan payments received (including partial and final payments)
    Interest billings prepared
    Interest payments handled
    Past due notices issued
Time spent on:
    Coin and currency work
    Resolutions, authorizations, and endorsement stamps
    Signature control

Trust Division
No. of:
    Receipt and delivery of securities
    Securities income collections
        Coupon entries
        Dividend entries
    Bookkeeping entries prepared
    Investment reviews made
    Mortgages
        Received
        Disposed of
        Payments received
    Real Estate transactions:
        Properties received
        Properties disposed of
        Rent payments received
        Invoices paid
    Disbursements made (other than real estate expense)
    Accounting reports furnished
    State and Federal income tax returns prepared
    Trust accounts analyzed for service charges
    New wills received
    New trust accounts established
        Guardianships
        Administratorships
        Voluntary trusts
        Pension trusts
        Agency trusts
        Corporate trusts
        Other trusts
        Safekeeping accounts
Time trust officers spent on individual accounts

Figure 4.1 (Continued)

Demand Deposits

	Deposits Received			Cash Returned	Checks Cashed	Savings Deposits		Other Counts		Other Work	(Noncount)
	Checks Only	Cash Only	Checks and Cash			Dep.	Withdrawal	Count	Description	Description	Minutes
8:30- 9:00										Supermarket Deposit	30
9:00- 9:30										Supermarket Deposit	30
9:30-10:00										Supermarket Deposit	30
10:00-10:30										Change Order	30
10:30-11:00										Change Order	30
11:00-11:30										Change Order	15
11:30-12:00	⊬⊬ ⊬⊬	⊬⊬ ⊬⊬	⊬⊬ ⊬⊬	///	⊬⊬ ⊬⊬			1	Traveler's Checks		
12:00-12:30	⊬⊬ ⊬⊬ ⊬⊬ ⊬⊬	///	⊬⊬ ⊬⊬		⊬⊬ ⊬⊬	⊬⊬	⊬⊬				
12:30- 1:00	⊬⊬ ⊬⊬ ⊬⊬ ⊬⊬	/	⊬⊬	///	⊬⊬ ⊬⊬	////	/			Returned Item	5
1:00- 1:30	⊬⊬ ⊬⊬ ⊬⊬ ⊬⊬	⊬⊬		⊬⊬ /	⊬⊬ ⊬⊬	///		1	Traveler's Checks	Returned Item	5
1:30- 2:00	⊬⊬	/	///		⊬⊬ ⊬⊬	⊬⊬					
2:00- 2:30	////	/	⊬⊬ ⊬⊬		⊬⊬ ⊬⊬ ////		⊬⊬			Returned Item	5
2:30- 3:00	//	//	/	////	//					Returned Item	15
3:30- 4:00										Obituary / Vault Cash	25 / 5
4:30- 5:00										Vault Cash / Balancing	10 / 20
Total One Window for One Day	71	23	39	16	66	17	11	2 Traveler's Checks		Various — Total Hours Worked 8.0	255 = 4.3 Hours
Total 4 Weeks All Windows	17,900	13,060	10,900	18,960	50,100	10,749	3,639			Total Hours Worked 1,802.0	186.0 Hours

Figure 4.2—Tally of Teller Transactions

Teller Department—Time Distribution by Type of Activity

Demand Deposits			Time Deposits			Loans			Other Activities				Stand By		
Start	Stop	Elapsed	Start	Stop	Elapsed	Start	Stop	Elapsed	Function	Start	Stop	Elapsed	Start	Stop	Elapsed
9:31	9:40	10	9:01	9:30	30				Vault cash	8:31	8:45	15	8:46	9:00	15
10:01	10:15	15	9:41	10:00	20				Utility bills	12:31	12:45	15	10:26	10:30	5
10:31	10:40	10	10:16	10:25	10				Money orders	3:41	3:55	15	2:26	2:35	10
12:46	12:53	8	10:41	11:30	50										
1:49	1:55	7	12:54	1:48	55										
3:56	4:25	30	1:56	2:25	30										
4:46	4:55	10	2:36	3:40	65										
			4:26	4:45	20										
			4:56	5:30	35										
Total Minutes		90			315							45			30
Converted to Hours		1½			5¼							¾			½
Total Hours For the Month 40					100							10			15

Figure 4.3—Self-Logging Work Sheet

Name JOHN SMITH	Position VICE PRESIDENT					
Division, Department, Section or Unit					Date OCTOBER 6, 19—	

Description of Activity	Frequency* D W M I				Estimated Volume Per Month	Approx. Hours Per Month
LOAN COMMITTEE MEETINGS		✓				10
CUSTOMER CONFERENCES	✓					20
NEW BUSINESS CALLS	✓					16
BAI COMMITTEE MEETINGS				✓		7
SUPERVISING COMMERCIAL CREDIT DEPARTMENT	✓					40
REVIEWING LOAN APPLICATION						40
ROTARY			✓			4
DIRECTORS			✓			6
GENERAL ADMINISTRATION						18
						160

*Frequency:
D = Daily
W = Weekly
M = Monthly
I = Irregularly

Figure 4.4—Self-Logging Activity Questionnaire

categories of activity to be counted and the breaks between them are distinct. The self-logging worksheet can be time-consuming, however, and it becomes cumbersome when there are many varied transactions occurring within a short period.

Work Sampling. In this method, which is based on the use of probability theory, many random observations are taken of operators performing their assigned activities. What the operator is doing at the time the observation is made is recorded specifically. This method assumes that the sample data obtained is representative of the total activity. In effect the total activity, or job, is broken into its elements, and the observer determines how frequently each element is being performed. The frequency of the elements is expressed as a percentage based on the total work hours. This method can be learned in a short period of time.

Stopwatch Time Study. In this method, a job is analyzed by its various work elements, each of which is timed. A stopwatch is used to record time in hundredths of a minute. As the observer records time values for each element of work, the difference in work performance between the person being observed and a theoretically average worker must be recognized. This difference is accounted for through a "leveling" adjustment, by which the observed worker's performance is adjusted to what is considered normal. Before the advent of predetermined time systems (see below) this was the basic method used in industry. Because "leveling" of observations is somewhat judgmental, the use of the stopwatch method may not be as objective as the other methods. The use of the stopwatch has the additional disadvantage of possibly affecting an employee's work-pace while he is being observed.

Micromotion Study. This method takes the same approach as the stopwatch time study method except that the raw timing is accomplished by taking motion pictures of the operations. The speed of the camera is set so that it takes a predetermined number of frames per minute. The time for each element in the operation is calculated on the basis of the number of frames required to photograph the operation. The advantage of this method is that the resulting time values lend themselves easily to analysis and judicious leveling, but it is an expensive method for measuring time. Generally it is used only for large-scale activities such as proofing, teller operations, etc., where there is sufficient opportunity for cost savings to justify the costs and inconvenience involved.

Predetermined Time Standards. This method relies on data derived from stopwatch, motion pictures, and other devices that analyze basic body motions. The data is used to develop basic standard time values for each motion, which are put into tables of predetermined time standards. Once the motions for an activity have been analyzed, the time for any transaction is then computed by reference to the tables. This method is best applied to cyclical or repetitive operations. Some of the time measurement systems used are: Methods Time Measurement (MTM), Motion Time Analysis (MTA), Master Clerical Data (MCD), and Work Factor. The advantage of these systems is that they provide objective time values and allow the observer of the operations to be trained to concentrate on the effectiveness of the methods used in the operation rather than on timing the operation. As a result, these systems are very popular and widely used.

The methods described in the three preceding paragraphs usually will entail analyzing an operation according to basic elements of motion (hand, eye, body, etc.) . The skilled technician can review the elements and rearrange them in different sequences that eliminate redundant motions. This can result in improvements in procedures and is probably the major justification for using these more complex methods.

SUMMARY

The measurement of activity is an important requirement in the costing process. It enables management to determine capacity and utilization for planning and controlling resource use, and it is also a vital requisite for determining the unit costs of resources. In addition, activity units are frequently used as transfer units for costing purposes. Activity measurement provides the necessary data concerning the number of transfer units to be used in carrying out the allocation process.

THE CHARACTERISTICS
OF BANK COSTS

E ach industry is characterized by its own peculiar cost composition
and patterns which, in turn, create costs and cost flows unique to
it. Similarly, the banking industry has its own cost characteristics. An
understanding of these characteristics is essential to the development
of effective cost data for decision-making.

Costs in banks should be considered from two points of view: first,
their composition, and second, their unique characteristics.

COMPOSITION OF BANK COSTS

Bank costs that are related to the primary banking function
(acquisition of deposits and making loans) when compared with costs
incurred in a manufacturing organization can help to illustrate some
essential differences in cost composition that have important costing
consequences. Much of the existing literature on costing has been
written in a manufacturing context, and, although the principles
underlying the costing process are the same both for manufacturing
and banking, their application differs. The following comparison provides a generalized summary of comparative costs for a manufacturing
plant and a bank. Although the cost elements in cost of sales may vary
according to the type of plant, the total cost of sales percent is fairly

representative. The banking costs are averages for 240 banks in the 50-200 million dollar range.[1]

Comparative Composition of Total Operating and Banking Cost

	Representative Manufacturing Plant		Costs of Banking
Material	63%	Interest	50%
Labor	14	Noninterest Cost of Funds	30
Manufacturing Overhead	13	Cost of Funds Total	80
Cost of Sales Total	90	Other Costs	20
Other Costs	10	Total Banking Costs	100%
Total Operating Cost	100%		

In this illustration, the noninterest cost of funds is chiefly the expense of handling deposit accounts, such as tellers, proof and transit, posting accounts, and other related activities. Other costs are primarily the expenses incurred in the loan and investment function.

The cost of funds in a bank is very similar to the costs of sales of a manufacturing plant in that it represents the costs required to obtain and sell a product (funds). There the similarity ends, however, because in manufacturing there tends to be a reduction in cost per unit of production as volume increases. This is due to the economies frequently realized in purchasing larger quantities of raw material and the more efficient use of labor and manufacturing facilities. In banking, on the other hand, although interest cost is a substantial part of the "cost of sales," the amount of loans made does not directly affect the interest cost per dollar of funds obtained. Reduction in unit cost, therefore, must come from better utilization of resources categorized as noninterest cost of funds. Further, since factors outside the bank, such as the money market, influence interest cost, it is important in managing and costing to take into consideration both trends in interest cost and the general effect of being locked into a fixed price for a fixed period of time.

Another significant costing consequence resulting from the composition of bank costs is the difficulty in allocating funds costs to specific revenue areas. Unlike a manufacturing enterprise, a bank has difficulty identifying the specific uses of its major raw material (funds). Every dollar is like every other dollar, but not every dollar costs the same to obtain. The source of dollars for a particular loan,

[1] Federal Reserve System: *1969 Functional Cost Analysis For 11 Federal Reserve Districts.*

and consequently the cost of funds for that loan, are difficult to identify. Management must therefore recognize the costing problems inherent in allocating the cost of funds and the effect on profit calculations used for evaluating pricing and marketing strategy. This problem of the cost of funds is dealt with in some detail in Chapter 11.

CHARACTERISTICS

There are four conditions in the banking industry that significantly influence cost characteristics. Although they may vary in degree from one bank to another, they are, nonetheless, characteristic of the industry as a whole:

1. *Variable Transaction Volume:* Wide fluctuations during a given period (daily, weekly, and seasonal) in the volume of transactions processed.

2. *High Fixed Expenses:* A large portion of noninterest expenses that do not vary with volume.

3. *Predictability:* Payday and holiday patterns that influence the volume of transaction activity.

4. *Traceable Costs:* Significant portions of administrative and clerical expenses that can be directly identified with lending and other revenue producing functions.

Variable Transaction Volume

A large portion of bank expenses are for personnel and equipment directly or indirectly involved in processing checks and other documents. In all banks, however, the daily volume of checks handled fluctuates widely from one day of the week to the next, from month to month, and from one season to another (Figures 5.1 and 5.2).

Because of these fluctuations, there must be sufficient capacity (personnel and equipment) to accommodate service demands during peak periods. Between these periods, however, much of this capacity would remain idle if it were maintained at the same fixed levels. Therefore, it is important to carefully examine the determination of capacity requirements and the scheduling of personnel.

High Fixed Expenses

Because bank activities are of a service nature, a substantial portion of noninterest expenses for the bank as a whole is for buildings, equipment, and full-time personnel. These expenses are generally fixed because of the need for constantly maintaining a capability to handle at least a certain portion of peak activity.

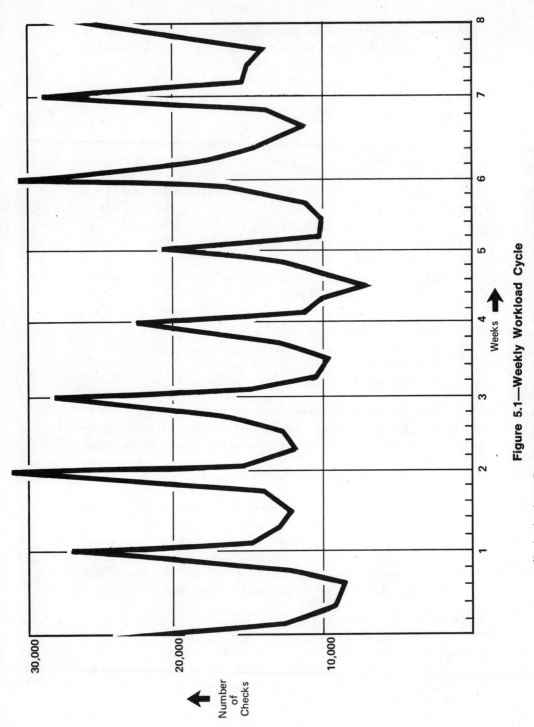

Figure 5.1—Weekly Workload Cycle

(Inclearing Items Processed in Proof and Transit Department Per Day At Sample Bank)

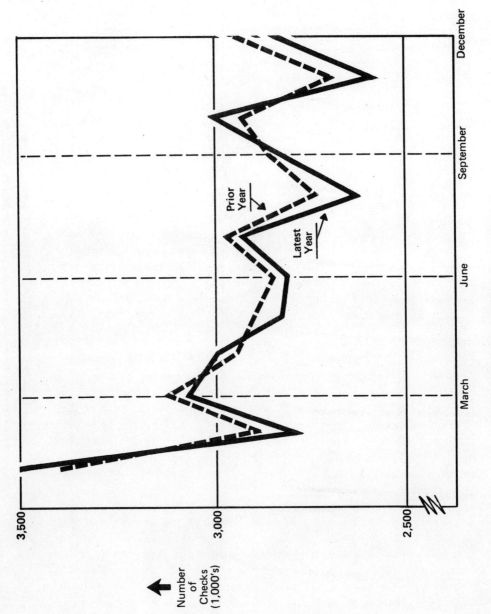

Figure 5.2—Monthly Workload Cycle

(Inclearing Items Processed in Proof and Transit Department Per Day At Sample Bank)

Figure 5.3, which illustrates the components of noninterest expense in a particular small bank, shows that fixed expenses are a substantial portion of the total. A larger bank could reasonably experience different percentage breakdowns. The most noticeable change probably would be percentage increases in "supplies and other" (variable expense) and decreases in salary expenses for tellers and administration (fixed expenses).

Predictability

Certain days of the week, month, and year (paydays, holidays, etc.) produce predictable patterns of check activity, which is, of course, the major transaction activity of the bank. These patterns, which are illustrated in Figures 5.1 and 5.2, permit banks to forecast fluctuations in the volume of their check transactions with a reasonable degree of accuracy by applying current trend information to historical data.

The predictability of check volume fluctuations has enabled many banks to schedule portions of their payroll costs to coincide with the anticipated volume of activity, by using part-time clerks in the operations affected by check activity (proof and transit, key punching, tellers, etc.). Thus, certain expenses that otherwise would have been fixed can become variable.

Traceable Costs

Most bank costs are easily associated directly (i.e., are traceable) to either a fund-providing activity, a fund-using activity, or a nonfund activity. As a result, the allocation process in a bank usually has available a reasonable basis for allocating costs. For example, tellers, proof and transit clerks, and bookkeepers usually can be associated directly with the deposit function; file clerks and credit analysts usually can be associated directly with the lending function; and the data center can be associated with specific activities on the basis of the tasks it performs for those activities.

Thus, all but an insignificant portion of bank costs can be allocated to particular units, functions, activities, etc., with reasonable accuracy. There is little need to use arbitrary bases of allocation, unless problems of internal organization make it necessary to do so. Instances will be found in which the relationship of administrative cost to specific banking functions cannot be clearly identified because of the way authority and responsibility have evolved around particular individuals. For example, the authority for making commercial loans may reside among several different officers, each of whom may have a separate group of customers. Each officer may have a departmental or

Fixed Expenses

Salaries and fringe benefits[1]		
Tellers	28.6%	
Administration	25.1	
Statement and clerical	17.6	
Janitorial and other building maintenance	1.7	
Total salaries and fringe benefits		73.0%
Insurance, depreciation, rent, taxes, etc.		11.0
		84.0%

Variable Expenses

Data processing fees charged by correspondent	6.9	
Postage and telephone	4.7	
Supplies and other	4.4	
Total Variable Expenses		16.0
Total Noninterest Expenses		100.0%

[1]These expenses are for the most part fixed, but a portion of them are potentially variable (e.g., part-time salaries and overtime).

Figure 5.3—Summary of Fixed and Variable Noninterest Expenses for a Small ($10,000,000) Bank

functional operating responsibility as well. In such cases, if the purpose of a cost calculation requires allocation of officer salaries, this allocation probably would need to be made on an arbitrary basis.

COSTING CONSEQUENCES

The significant costing consequences related to the characteristics described above are as follows:

- Because of the high degree of fixed costs, coupled with variable transaction volume, it is important to measure resource capacity and utilization accurately before costing.

- Because transaction volume is variable, the capacity of resources provided by the fixed costs may sometimes stand idle, and if this idle capacity is to be a part of the average unit costs, the period over which the average is computed must be long enough to cover the major fluctuations.

- Because transaction volume is largely predictable, average unit costs computed on the basis of past experience can be projected into future periods with reasonable accuracy.

- Because bank costs are traceable, the need to use arbitrary bases of allocation is minimal.

Further, the high fixed cost characteristics of banks affect their use of costing for planning and control purposes. The commitment to sustain high fixed costs in order to have capacity available places heavy emphasis on maximizing the use of those resources once they have been obtained. The associated costing consequences are more fully explored in Chapter 7.

SUMMARY

The characteristics of bank costs shape the nature of the remaining discussion in this book. Particular attention is paid to the importance of resource use because of the relatively high proportion of fixed costs that represent payment for capacity.

Specific attention also is given to allocation problems in banks, particularly those involving cost of funds. The latter is a substantial bank cost and is important to the determination of profitability by profit area.

Further, the high proportion of fixed costs gives rise to a substantial requirement for allocating costs in order to determine the profitability of the various services provided. In accomplishing this allocation, however, the coster is aided by the fact that many of these fixed costs are reasonably predictable and traceable.

6

COST PERFORMANCE

Because the following chapters of this book will deal with specific uses of cost information in a bank and the costing processes related to those uses, it is appropriate at this point to relate those uses to the problems management must deal with in carrying out its planning and control responsibilities. Chapter 3 showed how costing assists management in analyzing alternatives for planning as well as in communicating plans and measuring results for control purposes. Within this planning and control framework, the particular uses of cost relate to "cost performance," i.e., the performance expected and required of bank resources in relation to costs incurred for them. This definition of cost performance is the key to understanding much of this book.

For planning and control, management must establish adequate performance levels for resources and follow up to ensure that these levels are achieved when costs have been incurred. The function of cost in helping to plan and control the performance of a resource has two aspects:

- Cost performance in terms of maximizing resource use or minimizing resource cost.
- Cost performance in terms of the revenues and profits related to the costs incurred. (This includes pricing, which is a special cost/profit determination.)

When approaching cost performance in terms of resource use, the emphasis in costing is on maximizing cost performance by using resources to the maximum extent. Thus, emphasis is placed on utilization without reference to the revenues generated. If the utilization of resources cannot be increased, emphasis will be placed on reducing the resource in order to minimize its cost.

Cost performance in relation to revenues and profits, on the other hand, is viewed in a more generalized way than cost performance in terms of resource use. Since a basic purpose for incurring costs is to create revenues, the extent to which revenues exceed the related costs becomes a reasonable measure of cost performance for management to use. However, it is difficult to identify any specific item of cost with any specific item of revenue generated. Therefore, costs must be grouped in some way (e.g., by function, organizational unit, etc.) By contrast, when the objective is to minimize costs it is possible to determine cost for one specific resource, such as a machine.

In practice, management frequently shifts emphasis in its approach to control. For example, as profit decreases, the emphasis is often placed on maximizing the use of specific resources available or on minimizing their costs. In a period of increasing profit, however, it is common for management to add costs with the reasonable expectation that they will help to generate additional revenue that will either maintain profitability or increase it.

Despite these periodic switches in emphasis for the bank as a whole, it is also possible that in specific bank areas both approaches to cost performance will be used concurrently. Management must understand the difference between the two in order to use cost information effectively in planning and control.

MAXIMIZING RESOURCE USE/MINIMIZING RESOURCE COST

When emphasis is placed on resource use in considering cost performance, the objective is to keep costs at a minimum, which makes it necessary to either (1) plan to make better use of current costs or anticipated costs, or (2) reduce current or anticipated costs.

In order to maximize the use of resources, it is first necessary to determine the capacity of a resource and then to measure the utilization of that capacity. Cost indicates the magnitude of benefits available to the bank through maximizing the use of a resource, whereas activity indicators supplement cost by providing the necessary measures of capacity and utilization.

Resource costs are minimized through reduction in resources where possible. The determination of what is a minimal level of cost can be highly judgmental, since it is often difficult to determine the overall effect on a bank of a reduction in certain resources. Consequently, the approach often taken by management is to reduce costs whenever it is believed that doing so will not have a detrimental effect on the generation of revenues (and thus of benefits). This is most often done by increasing the efficiency of personnel, with different or additional supporting equipment, eliminating any marginal work that was being performed, etc.

The maximization of resource use and the minimization of resource cost is best planned and controlled through organizational units. Generally, bank organization is represented by units for which responsibility has been assigned to particular individuals. These individuals are responsible for efficiently using the resources assigned to them in carrying out their objectives. Consequently, an effective approach to minimizing cost and maximizing resource use is to associate costs with responsibility units, since cost responsibility is placed on individuals who also are responsible for the efficient use of resources. They must reach their objectives at costs that are reasonable in the light of planned targets or budgets.

PROFITABILITY

Profit is probably the most widely used measurement of cost performance, since it is generally assumed that cost performance is adequate when profits have reached a satisfactory level and are either being held at that level or are increasing. Even under these circumstances, however, there may be opportunities to reduce costs without concurrent losses of revenue. Since the ultimate goal of the bank is to develop profits, satisfactory profit performance is a valid measurement of cost performance.

To measure profitability, costs must be related to revenues for a period of time, not only for the bank as a whole but also for its revenue-generating units (such as the trust division and the branches). It is difficult, however, to associate specific groups of costs with specific revenues when dealing, not with organizational units, but with functions, the revenues of which are generated by the efforts of many organizational units.

Profitability can be measured by using one of two basic approaches:

- The contribution approach (the excess of revenue over costs directly related to the resource).
- The net profit approach (excess of revenue over all costs).

The contribution approach associates costs with the resources that generate the revenues and by so doing determines profit. For example, costs generated within the trust division can be directly associated to its revenues as a whole. Although some costs—generated at the top level of the bank—assist the trust division in generating revenues and without which it could not function, they cannot be directly related to that division. Consequently, the contribution approach develops profit on the basis of revenues minus directly related costs. This results in an amount representing the portion of profit contributed by a particular resource (or combination of resources) to cover the administrative expenses of the bank and to contribute to its overall profit. This information can be helpful in estimating the effect of curtailing any revenue-generating activity.

The net profit approach, on the other hand, assigns a portion of all bank costs to a particular revenue-producing resource. However, there are some disadvantages to using the net profit approach. For example, general overhead costs (those costs that are incurred for the bank as a whole and not for any particular unit) must frequently be associated with revenues on a somewhat arbitrary basis. This creates the possibility of a degree of error, which in turn affects the credibility of the results. Unless the nature of the costs associated with revenues is well understood, the process of developing plans and exercising control on the basis of this kind of information could lead to erroneous decisions.

Planning and control of profit also is done through organizational units, but profit responsibility may be more difficult to define. Care should be taken to properly locate this vital responsibility in the organizational structure.

PRICING

Cost information also is used in the planning and control system to assist in developing pricing strategy. Although the immediate measure of price effectiveness is the volume of market response, cost information can assist in developing prices and is necessary for measuring the ultimate effect of prices on profits.

Cost is one of several determinants in establishing price, but frequently there is a tendency to disregard it and to consider only market conditions. Even if a bank is unable to influence market price, it runs the risk of considering less than an optimum choice of action when it does not have cost information. Moreover, undue emphasis can be unintentionally placed on unprofitable services.

Costs have to be accumulated for pricing subject to the circumstances under which prices are being developed. Management generally wants to determine whether a price covers related expenses, all bank overhead, and also allows a provision for profit. Usually, the costing process must deal with all costs (both directly related and general overhead).

In some situations, however, costs for pricing a service appropriately include only those costs incurred as a direct result of providing the service. One such situation occurs when capacity that would otherwise be idle is available to provide the service. Hence, a price that provides an excess of revenue over direct costs generates a profit contribution that would otherwise not exist.

SPECIAL DECISIONS

This chapter on cost performance has dealt with costing as though the resource involved (e.g., a machine, a loaning function, etc.) were to be used over a long period. However, there are situations in which costing is used to determine the effect of a specific action at the particular time the action occurs. They usually involve a decision to add, expand, contract, or eliminate a resource, a function, or an activity, etc.

In considering whether to add or drop a service or unit, for example, it is necessary to determine what costs might be added or reduced. Generally, costs have a tendency to be "sticky," with the result that when a service is eliminated some present costs will not be affected, since they are relatively fixed. On the other hand, costs that are incurred directly to provide such services could very well be eliminated, so it is essential that they be properly identified for sound decision-making.

SUMMARY

Cost performance results from action taken by management in carrying out its planning and control responsibilities. It is the effect of resource use (either of individual resources or combinations of resources) on cost. The use of resources results in benefits that can be measured as productivity, and the measurement of the productivity against the costs incurred is the principal use made of cost information by management.

Resource "productivity" must be viewed from the vantage point of the ability of a resource (or of a combination of resources) to carry out an intended role. For those resources that must produce something measurable as "production" (e.g., checks processed, loans made, etc.) management emphasizes either maximizing their use or minimizing their cost. Other resources (usually more complex combinations, often

including those noted above) have as their productive role the generation of revenues, and cost is used to measure their productivity
through the determination of profitability.

Although pricing and special costing considerations, such as adding or eliminating resources, also have to be taken into account, they
are in effect manifestations of cost performance in specific situations.

Cost performance is the key to the remaining sections of the book,
and the use of costing in carrying out the planning and control of cost
performance provides the framework for specific discussions of costing.

Part III

COST FOR PLANNING AND
CONTROL OF RESOURCES

Bank Costs for Planning and Control

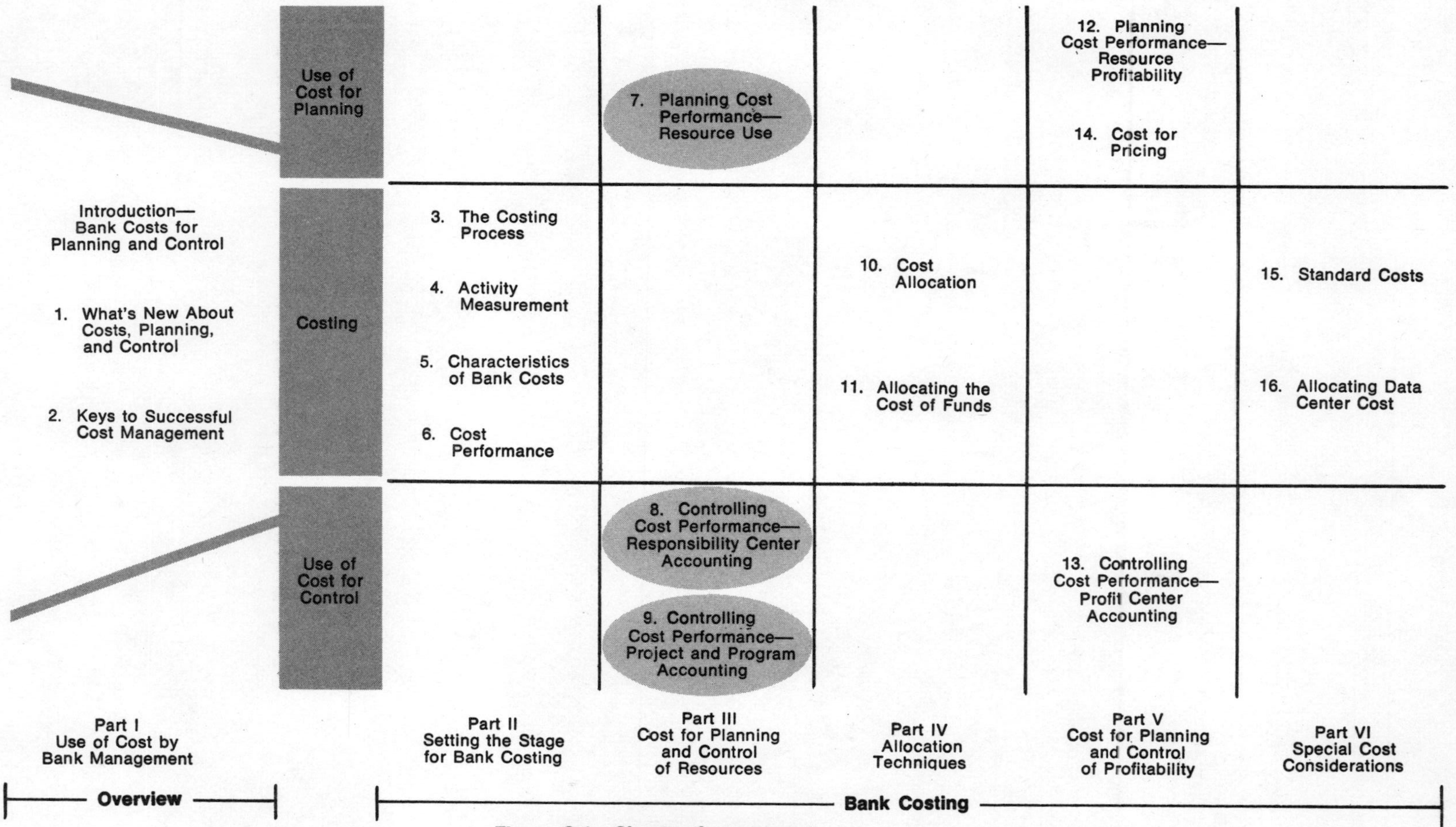

Figure O.1—Chapter Arrangement

Overview

Part I
Use of Cost by
Bank Management

Introduction—
Bank Costs for
Planning and Control

1. What's New About
Costs, Planning,
and Control

2. Keys to Successful
Cost Management

Use of
Cost for
Planning

Costing

Use of
Cost for
Control

Bank Costing

Part II
Setting the Stage
for Bank Costing

3. The Costing
Process

4. Activity
Measurement

5. Characteristics
of Bank Costs

6. Cost Performance

Part III
Cost for Planning
and Control
of Resources

7. Planning Cost
Performance—
Resource Use

8. Controlling
Cost Performance—
Responsibility Center
Accounting

9. Controlling
Cost Performance—
Project and Program
Accounting

Part IV
Allocation
Techniques

10. Cost
Allocation

11. Allocating the
Cost of Funds

Part V
Cost for Planning
and Control
of Profitability

12. Planning
Cost Performance—
Resource
Profitability

14. Cost for
Pricing

13. Controlling
Cost Performance—
Profit Center
Accounting

Part VI
Special Cost
Considerations

15. Standard Costs

16. Allocating Data
Center Cost

Part III

COST FOR PLANNING AND CONTROL OF RESOURCES

Management's planning and control responsibility is concerned with the effective acquisition, creation, use, and, if necessary, discarding of resources. These resources in the form of funds, people, and facilities embody the functions and departments of a bank. They are the basic components of the costing objects whose costs are measured by the costing process. Management's concern when costing, therefore, is to develop cost information that is useful in making decisions about resources. These costs can be viewed from two vantage points: (1) costs related to the performance of resources where capacity and utilization are being considered, and (2) costs related to the performance of resources where profitability is of concern.

This section is concerned with resources that are being considered only from the standpoint of capacity and utilization. The costing techniques required here are relatively simple and straightforward because the costs are the directly related or incremental costs (added costs) that are incurred when resources are acquired, created, enlarged, or reduced. Part V, *Cost for Planning and Control of Profitability,* will consider profitability where more complex costing, including allocation, is required because of the relatively more complex combinations of resources required to produce revenues. Part IV, *Allocation Techniques,* describes the allocation techniques necessary to determine profitability.

Chapter 7 reviews the use of costing for planning where cost alone is the major consideration. The facilities and departments considered from this point of view are those where maximizing use or, conversely, minimizing cost is the primary objective.

The other chapters of Part III treat the costing used for controlling costs incurred by the bank's various functions and departments. Chapter 8 reviews the responsibility center concept and the costing associated with controlling costs through the organization structure. Chapter 9 treats the control of costs using special projects or programs established for a one-time purpose.

7

PLANNING COST PERFORMANCE— RESOURCE USE

Bank resources (funds, facilities, and people) represent productive capabilities all having certain cost characteristics. This chapter examines the process by which management uses costing to analyze alternatives and measure cost performance when it seeks either (1) to maximize the use of resources, or (2) to minimize their cost. In both cases, management may implement its decisions by either changing the utilization level of resources or by adding, eliminating, expanding, or contracting resources.

In operating an organizational unit (e.g., a division, department, or branch) or a function (a collection of resources devoted to a common purpose), or a specific resource (such as a building or a computer), management may seek to do so at minimum cost, while obtaining the maximum productivity. Stated simply, management is concerned with getting the most for its money.

Cost performance in relation to resources is the theme of this chapter for two reasons: First, this relationship reflects one of the important bank cost characteristics that was described in Chapter 5— the combination of high fixed costs with a variable volume of business. This combination forces management to study not only the capacity of resources to provide services but also the effective utilization of their capacity. Second, the costing requirements in such circumstances are relatively simple. Chapters 8 and 9 will discuss management's exercise of control once decisions have been made on resource utilization and cost.

This chapter will demonstrate the cost effects that follow from maximizing the use of any resource or set of resources and the cost effects of minimizing the cost of resources. It will then discuss the effects on the various units of a bank when one of them experiences a change in resources—i.e., what may be called the "chaining effect."

The discussion will concentrate on those bank units that use resources to provide services to other units or functions, for example, a data center, a bookkeeping department, or a teller's department. The principles discussed in this chapter apply equally to any single resource of the bank that has a productive capability (e.g., a teller, a bookkeeper, a microfilm machine, a wing of the building) or to any possible combination of productive resources.

Many of these units, or parts of them, participate in functions that generate bank revenue (e.g., a lending function or a trust function). This participation introduces a new set of complexities, because the resources involved must be defined and considered in their most complicated form, that is, as functions or activities that produce revenue. Cost performance related to revenue-producing functions is measured by profitability. Revenue-producing functions will be examined more closely in Chapter 12.

MANAGING THE UTILIZATION AND COST OF RESOURCES

Techniques for controlling resource utilization and cost will be discussed in Chapter 8. It is important that the steps management must take to analyze alternatives for resource utilization and for cost are understood because they are the foundation for subsequent control.

In analyzing alternatives for resource use and cost, management must first identify the situations that present significant opportunities to reduce costs or increase productivity in terms of planned resources or resources currently used. Thus, it is important to know:

- Current or planned utilization.
- Resource capacity, and
- Resource cost.

If resource management is to have maximum impact on improving bank profitability, the first consideration is the cost of resources, since it provides some estimate of the magnitude of profit improvements that can be made either through better utilization or through cost minimization. In this context, costing is relatively simple and in many cases will already have been accomplished by the bank's accounting system. The cost information required is the magnitude of cost related to a particular resource, such as a machine, the cost of which can easily be determined from accounting documents. The cost of an organizational unit, on the other hand, is somewhat more complex, since costs must be accumulated for salaries, equipment, and supplies. This data also is likely to be available from accounting records. It is management's general knowledge of resource costs that makes it possible to establish priorities for resource management, and specific costing therefore is generally not required at the outset.

When an informal set of priorities have been developed for resources, it becomes necessary to determine their capacity and the degree to which this capacity is being utilized. To do this, the unit of measure (or units) required to state capacity must be determined. Thus, the capacity of a machine that has only one function (e.g., reading the magnetic ink characters on a check) can be stated in terms of the number of characters or checks it can read. It is necessary, however, to decide whether its capacity measurements should be stated in terms of maximum possible productivity (such as three operating shifts, totalling 24 hours, less two hours per day for maintenance) or in terms of what might be considered a more practical measure of capacity, such as the productivity that could be attained during a two-shift operation (less an allowance for setting up the machine, maintenance, operator fatigue, etc.).

It is more difficult, however, to determine the capacity of more complex resources (such as clerical personnel). Work measurement techniques are helpful in measuring the capacity of resources of this type as well as the capacity of certain types of operator-paced equipment.

"Practical" capacity has the widest application in resource management. Once this capacity has been determined, it is necessary to determine actual utilization. Work measurement techniques are useful for measuring actual time used to carry out a task and for deciding whether the time is being used efficiently. It is not the purpose of this chapter to treat capacity determination in detail, but it should be understood that it is necessary, at least to some reasonable extent, when management is analyzing alternatives that affect the acquisition of new resources or the use of existing resources.

When management has this information (cost, capacity, utilization, and the efficiency of utilization), the next step is to determine the action to be taken. The two alternative courses of action that apply to the acquisition of new resources or the use of existing resources are:

- Maximizing the use of a resource.
- Minimizing its cost.

MAXIMIZING USE OF RESOURCES

As pointed out in Chapter 5, two outstanding cost characteristics are the high degree of fixed costs and the degree to which routine transaction volume varies. If capacity is to be available to handle peak loads, there will be times when it is not fully used. Since this unused capacity has already been paid for, it represents an opportunity for management to obtain further productivity without significantly increasing costs.

A data center is an excellent example of maximizing resource use. It can increase its utilization (assuming it has capacity available) by expanding applications for its services within the bank, by increasing services to correspondent banks, or by selling services to additional outsiders. The three graphs shown in Figure 7.1 illustrate cost performance when the utilization of resources increases. Graph A illustrates that once a resource cost has been incurred, it tends to remain constant. Examples would be the rental or depreciation expense related to a computer or to premises, or the salary cost of loan department employees. To the extent that the capacity shown in Graph A is not used, the portion of cost shown in Graph A that applies to that unused capacity could be called the cost of unused capacity. This is illustrated in Graph B, which shows that the cost of unused capacity diminishes as use reaches capacity. Graph C illustrates the result of the characteristics illustrated in Graphs A and B, and it shows that unit cost is reduced as the number of units produced approaches capacity. Unit costs are reduced as resource use increases, because the fixed resource costs are spread over a greater number of units.

When resource use is being maximized, increased productivity is obtained without a corresponding increase in cost. Of course, there must be productive work to be done, and the costs involved in making increased use of the resource must be minimal or at least reasonable in amount. When resource use is being maximized and additional capacity is being made available through improved efficiency, the costs of implementation can create a problem. The action taken may require substantial procedural redesign, which in itself creates costs.

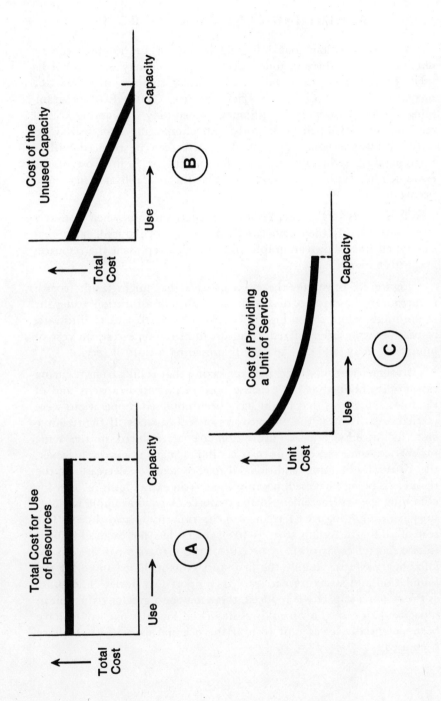

Figure 7.1—Maximizing Resource Use

MINIMIZING COST OF RESOURCES

It is very seldom that 100% utilization of any resource can be obtained, and so there is almost always some capacity that cannot be used. Furthermore, the amount of unused capacity often may be increased through heightened efficiency (e.g., better EDP programming, better personnel or equipment scheduling, promoting use of mail deposits to lessen peak loads, and eliminating nonessential details). To the extent that unused capacity can be reduced with a corresponding reduction in cost, the current or future cost of the resource can be minimized, assuming that the available capacity is not needed.

The charts in Figure 7.2 show the effect on costs when resources (and consequently their associated capacities) are reduced. Note that the dotted lines shown in graphs in Figure 7.2 represent the resources graphed in Figure 7.1.

Figure 7.2 illustrates the effect on cost that might result from a reduction in the capacity of a resource, a unit, or a function, using the assumptions set forth in Figure 7.1. Graphs A, B, and C illustrate, respectively, the effect of reduction on total resource cost, on cost of unused capacity, and on the cost of providing a unit of service.

In some cases, however, the cost saving that results from reducing capacity is obtained at the expense both of potential capacity and of the lower unit costs that might have been obtained if operations were carried on at or near the old measure of full capacity. If the resource cost, its capacity, and its utilization are all reduced in the same proportion, the effect on unit costs is nil. For many resources, however, the costs of obtaining additional capacity tend to decrease as the resource is being increased, because there is an extra "built-in" cost for obtaining the first increment of the resource. A good example is a one-story bank building that has an ultimate capacity of two stories. The cost of adding a second story is likely to be less for each additional square foot of capacity than the cost of the first story (if there is no inflationary effect), because the first story costs included those for the foundation and structure necessary to support two stories. Therefore, as the resource capacity is reduced, there may be a greater reduction in capacity than cost. This would result in the loss of what would have been potentially lower unit costs if the original capacity could have been used.

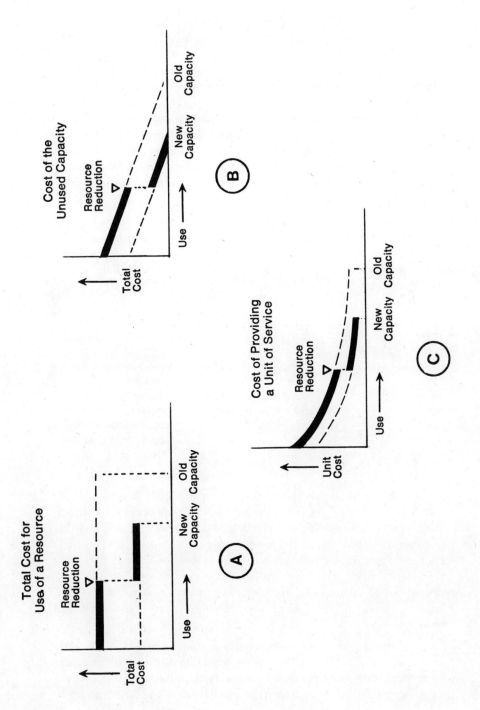

Figure 7.2—Minimizing Resource Cost

MAXIMIZING USE AND MINIMIZING COST
OF RESOURCES—AN EXAMPLE

To illustrate the preceding principles, it will be assumed that management has been concerned about the cost of its data center. A substantial cost has been incurred for computer equipment, acquisition and training of personnel, systems design and conversion, and space. Yet the data center seems to have time available, because its current uses (an occasional run of data for "interest only" purposes, etc.) do not seem productive. As a result, a brief study has been made of data center capacity and utilization with the following results (presented in simplified form) :

	Capacity	Utilization
Computer equipment and operating personnel	Assuming two shifts six days per week with allowance of 25% for maintenance, testing, etc. = 72 meter hours per week	50 hours (excluding nonessential processing)
Systems design and programming	Four people five days per week at eight hours per day = 160 hours per week	Program maintenance —40 hours System design and programming for an application—120 hours for the next three weeks

The results of the study indicate that about 30% of the time (22 meter hours per week) is available for additional processing; this percentage seems conservative, since it would be possible to add another processing day per week and, if necessary, a third shift. Either of these steps raises special personnel problems, however, and so only two shifts six days per week were assumed in determining capacity. The determination of utilization did not take into consideration special computer runs, since management decided that they were not essential.

In addition, the systems and programming capability of the data center will have additional capacity available for use three weeks hence. Since one full-time programmer is required to keep existing programs updated, the available time after three weeks will amount to

120 hours of system and programmer time per week. The computer application being designed and programmed at the present time is expected to use approximately five percent of computer capacity, with the result that the present 30% of available capacity will be reduced to 25% at that time.

In considering what action to take, management has considered two alternatives:

- Reduce the capacity of the data center.

- Find additional work for the data center that could be done without increasing cost within the data center (or with a minimal increase) and that would either reduce costs elsewhere or make it unnecessary to develop additional capacity elsewhere.

Management has concluded that reduction in data center capacity does not seem to be a reasonable alternative because:

- Cost reductions resulting from reduction in computer equipment would be minimal.

- In management's judgment, continued growth of the bank will require computer capability to such an extent that any capacity reduced would have to be restored within a short time. A reduction in the highly trained systems and programming staff would cause particularly difficult restaffing problems.

Certain existing manual operations were found to have the attributes necessary to make good computer applications, that is, repetitive activity volumes and records susceptible of conversion to data processing and computer-maintained files. It was then decided to determine the cost effect of converting the work of the bookkeeping department to the computer, and the following cost analysis was prepared. (The five costing steps are clearly applicable, but because of their relative simplicity when resource use is being considered, they are not presented here).

Reduced Costs in Bookkeeping (Monthly)		Added Costs in Data Center (Monthly)	
Salaries of clerical staff	$1,728	Printed forms	$600
Printed forms	400		
Total	2,128		
Added costs in data center	(600)		$600
Net monthly cost savings	$1,528		

There are a number of assumptions behind every such analysis, and in this case a major assumption had to be made as to the propriety of showing clerical staff salaries as a cost reduction. It was determined that during the time required to convert bookkeeping to the computer, personnel no longer needed could easily be transferred to other productive activities. This cost savings therefore represents a permanent reduction in personnel cost.

Forms costs of the bookkeeping department will, in effect, be transferred to the data center, where they will be higher because forms suitable for computer use are more complex.

As to the data center, it is assumed that the 120 hours of systems and programming time it has available will be adequate to permit conversion within ten weeks, after which the staff would be available to work on other new applications. Since the expected computer time required will amount to approximately 15% of capacity, sufficient capacity is available.

In drawing conclusions from this analysis (admittedly simplified), management must carefully assess the overall effect of a decision to computerize the work of the bookkeeping department. One obvious effect would be the reduction of unused computer capacity in the data center to ten percent. If there are other applications that management wishes to computerize, the remaining capacity may become insufficient, thus possibly requiring a substantial increase in cost to provide the additional capacity.

THE CHAINING EFFECT

The foregoing example showed the cost effect on only the two bank units that were involved in a transfer of work from one unit to another. What would have been the total cost effect to the bank if 20 employees had been released? What would the cost effect have been on the units that serve bank employees (e.g., cafeteria, personnel department, payroll section, etc.)? When decisions are made affecting any given resource, consideration must be given to the impact of the change on all related resources. It must be expected that there will be a chaining effect, and this must be calculated as part of the cost change. Each of the related units or functions must be examined individually to see if they will be subject to this chaining effect.

The possible effect on bank activities of using up available computer capacity to process bookkeeping section work was discussed. The bank's cafeteria can be used to further illustrate the point. If 20 employees are released as the result of reducing the capacity of several bank units, cafeteria utilization is likely to be affected. But whether the chaining effect causes cost reduction in the cafeteria depends on the level of utilization of the cafeteria before the change. If this was low, the fact that there are 20 less lunches to serve may require a cutback in cafeteria personnel. On the other hand, if the cafeteria was already being used to near maximum capacity, there may be no significant effect on operations.

If, instead of reducing capacity, a new unit is added or an existing one is expanded, the chaining effect is more difficult to determine. The new activity levels and resource requirements are based entirely on projected data, probably developed without the benefit of experience. With an increase in activity levels, the question becomes: can the unused capacity of current resources absorb the increase?

To answer this question, the cost data required is the cost of any additional capacity needed. Would adding 20 persons call for additional cafeteria staff? If present personnel are already strained, then the "straw-that-broke-the-camel's-back" principle might apply, and the added demand might necessitate at least one more person in the cafeteria. Of course, for a cafeteria the consequence of error is not considerable, but it would be substantial for a data center if a new computer application is being contemplated at a time when present utilization is already approaching capacity. The incremental cost of additional capacity may be substantial (Figure 7.3), and may even exceed the immediate benefits anticipated from the course of action under consideration. The analysis must be based on bank-wide assessment of costs and benefits, and a final decision should be made at the executive level.

Since the chaining effect involves dealing with a series of cause-and-effect relationships, each of these relationships can be analyzed in much the same manner as the data center and bookkeeping department were in the foregoing example. The result of analyzing each relationship is then combined to determine the aggregate result.

SUMMARY

The interaction of costs with the performance of resources that have productive capacity is of primary concern to management in deciding whether to maximize the use of resources or minimize the cost of resources required to perform any specified activity. The interdependence of bank costs is illustrated by the chaining effect that actions taken with respect to one resource have on another resource. The cost

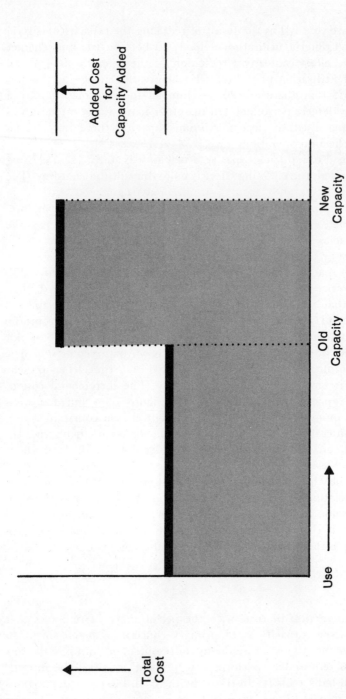

Figure 7.3—Stair-step Nature of Capacity Costs

data required for analysis is relatively simple to determine and includes the costs of the resource being considered as well as the added costs or reduced costs that are associated with increases or decreases in resources. All five costing steps are involved but due to the uncomplicated form of the resources involved, the allocation and cost calculation steps are relatively simple to carry out.

8

CONTROLLING COST
PERFORMANCE—
RESPONSIBILITY CENTER
ACCOUNTING

Chapter 7 was concerned with the costing required to assist management in analyzing alternatives for the maximization of resource use and the minimization of cost related to resources. Once the required analysis has been completed and the alternative selected, it is necessary to communicate the resulting resource plans to the organizational unit that will be responsible for the efficient use of them. The type of cost information used in the plan to communicate with the organizational unit also will be used to measure the results of action taken by that unit for purposes of controlling cost performance.

The role played by organizational units here is vital from two standpoints: (1) organizational units are the most effective mechanisms for controlling costs since they are responsible for the use of resources, and (2) the manager of each organizational unit also plans the use of those resources assigned to him and participates, or should participate, in the decisions concerning selection of the most effective alternatives for resource use. Organizational units that are assigned these roles in planning and control of cost are referred to as responsibility centers.

The costing required when managers of organizational units assist in planning resource use was explained in the previous chapter. Costing for control, however, requires relating costs to those organizational units responsible for the efficient use of resources. An organizational structure that is defined in terms of responsibility centers provides effective control of resource use. Accounting by responsibility associates costs that relate to resources with those centers.

A responsibility center is any organizational grouping of activities the objectives of which have been made the responsibility of one individual. These objectives may be stated by management in terms of specified activity, cost, revenue, profit, resource commitment, etc. A responsibility center may be as large as an entire bank (the president's responsibility) or as small as one individual (a loan function handled entirely by one loan officer).

A responsibility center manager may be held responsible for costs, for costs and revenue, or for profit (revenue after expenses). He also may be held responsible for meeting such nonfinancial criteria as loan volume, new customers obtained, volume of activity, etc. The factors that determine the responsibility of the manager are (1) the manner in which the organization structure is defined or, stated another way, the activity or function performed within the center, and (2) management policy.

STRUCTURING THE ORGANIZATION

In the development of a responsibility center accounting system it is essential to have a reasonably well-defined organizational structure that provides for logical groupings of activities to be supervised by specific persons. This structure also should establish the responsibility relationships between organizational units and levels of management in a pyramid fashion so as to permit the proper assignment of responsibility down to the operating level and the flow of summarized information back up to top levels for review and control.

It is beyond the scope of this book to cover the various techniques of organization planning, but a few general comments will be presented here concerning the structure of a bank organization.

Without some formal evaluation of the bank's organization structure, top management should not assume that it is sufficiently well defined to permit the establishment of a system of accounting by responsibility center. For example, many banks do not even have a formal organization chart. The specific areas of responsibility and authority may be vague, there may be overlapping in responsibilities, and there may be no clear chain of command.

In order to transfer costs effectively to responsibility centers for the purpose of planning and control, there must be clarity of organization, responsibility, and authority. This clarity also is required for the logical assignment of responsibility and delegation of authority, as well as to facilitate reporting the results of operations to appropriate management levels.

A commonly encountered bank organization structure is shown in Figure 8.1. It is intended only to be illustrative, however, since the organization of specific banks can differ significantly, with no one organizational structure being appropriate for all.

ROLE OF THE RESPONSIBILITY CENTER

Any activity performed in a responsibility center will incur costs because resources are used. Therefore, all responsibility centers can be charged with those costs appropriate to their own operations. Some functions (which are a collection of separate activities, such as instalment loans) will generate direct revenue. Whether the responsibility center managers are held responsible for costs, revenues, or both will depend on the desires of top management. If the latter has assigned only the responsibility for cost control to a center manager, then only cost data for that center will be collected by the accounting system and reported. Cost control responsibility is the most frequently encountered type of responsibility, and in such situations it is assumed that responsibility for revenue generated has been retained by higher levels of management.

If, on the other hand, management also wishes to assign responsibility for revenue to a responsibility center manager, revenue data must be collected and reported for that center. For example, the trust division manager could be given responsibility for all trust revenues. In essence, management is assigning to him the responsibility for attaining certain revenue goals. To perform effectively, the center manager also must have the authority to initiate any action that he feels would increase trust revenue, such as instituting programs to attract new customers or to increase services to existing customers.

In some instances, the bank may also wish to assign profit responsibility to certain responsibility center managers. This places an added dimension of responsibility on a center manager that he did not have even if he had responsibility for both cost and revenue control. When the center manager is given responsibility for profit, he also has full responsibility for cost and revenue, but the primary measure of his performance is profit (revenue after expenses).

In assigning profit responsibility bank management is saying, in

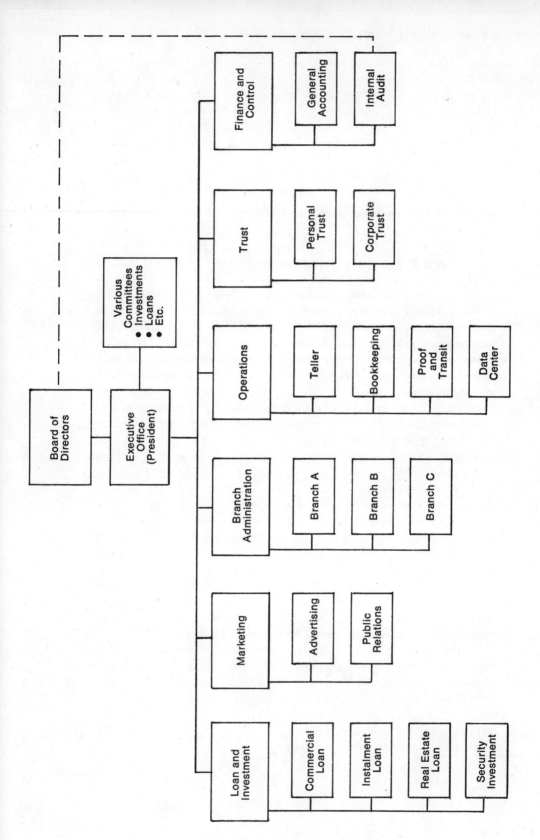

Figure 8.1—Typical Functional Organization

effect, that the center manager has the authority to initiate action that will increase profitability. Again using the trust division as an example, the manager can now go beyond the kinds of action open to him when he had only responsibility for revenue control, such as getting new customers or increasing services to existing customers. He should now be able to consider new trust services or new pricing structures. In other words, he now has responsibility to see that profit is maximized, and the levels of cost and revenue, in themselves, are of secondary significance. This assumes that the center manager will be able to exercise his profit responsibilities over a period long enough to discourage him from making decisions for reasons of short-run expediency that might adversely affect the center's profitability over the longer term.

In addition to measuring the results of responsibility centers in financial terms, bank management also measures results in terms of nonfinancial criteria. For example, a loan department's activities might be judged on the number and type of loans outstanding and on activity volume. The nonfinancial measures of responsibility center results are more appropriate when the center is small, or when it has few controllable direct costs. When nonfinancial measures are used, the responsibility for costs, revenue, and profits must necessarily reside at some higher responsibility level.

Accounting measurement becomes progressively more complex as one moves from the general accounting system that considers the bank as a whole to accounting for costs by responsibility center, for costs and revenue by responsibility center, and, finally, for profit by responsibility center. Since the purpose of this chapter is to discuss the concepts of a system that has as its primary objective the control of costs through cost information, it will be assumed that responsibility center managers are responsible only for cost performance, and not for revenue, profit, or nonfinancial factors. Revenues are excluded only for the sake of brevity, but the allocation of revenues to responsibility centers follows the process established for allocating costs. Therefore it does not create additional conceptual or mechanical problems. The use of responsibility centers operating as profit centers creates unusual costing complexities, which are discussed in Chapter 13.

RESPONSIBILITY CENTER ACCOUNTING

A general accounting system records the financial transactions of the bank as prescribed by statute or convention. Funds deposited in a bank are accounted for as liabilities to customers, and money invested in the bank's capital stock is shown as stockholders equity. Similarly, expenditures are classified as expenses or fixed assets depending upon whether or not the acquired resource is used in the current accounting period or deferred to future accounting periods. For example, salaries are classified as expenses for the period in which they are earned, while an expenditure for office furniture is classified as a fixed asset and is amortized (depreciated) over its useful life. The depreciation is an expense of a subsequent accounting period or periods. Banks record their financial transactions daily and produce a daily statement of condition and a corresponding income statement. The statement of condition is published daily while the income statement is usually published once a month, after the necessary month-end adjustments have been made.

The general accounting system is a primary source of information, but this information is not always useful for management in its general accounting form, since the system is concerned with the bank as a whole. If management is to be carried out through organizational units operating as responsibility centers, the general accounting system must be extended to reflect the activities of these units separately.

A responsibility center accounting system not only classifies expenses in the same way the general accounting system does, that is, by their natural categories (salary expense, supplies expense, depreciation of office furniture, etc.), but it also groups those expenses by the appropriate responsibility centers.

Controllable and Noncontrollable Cost

A "controllable" cost is one type of cost that can be significantly affected by the action of a responsibility center manager. Once management has decided that the bank shall engage in, say, a trust function, the responsibility center manager has the job of using resources (funds, people, and facilities) in the most effective manner.

Thus, the costs reported for a responsibility center by the accounting system should be those over which the manager is expected to exercise a significant degree of control. Salaries of employees in a responsibility center are a good example of controllable costs, since the responsibility center manager is responsible for the efficient use of those employees. He also can change their salary level by his appraisal of their performance.

The classification of costs by responsibility center is not always clearcut because of the interrelationships of bank activities where a number of diverse activities may have an impact on the same cost. For example, trust department transaction activity and efficiency of data center keypunch activity both have an impact on data processing costs. The responsibility centers responsible for control of such costs are defined in the planning stage and results are then reported to that center. Usually, it is not difficult to define an appropriate center to charge with the costs.

The traditional general ledger classification of accounts has been adequate to satisfy the needs of regulatory authorities and for annual reports to the stockholders. As noted above, however, they have limited usefulness for effective internal management, because accounting by responsibility center requires the association of an expense with individuals responsible for its incurrence. In order to make this association, it is necessary to integrate the natural expense categories of the general ledger chart of accounts (discussed in Appendix B) with the organizational division of responsibilities within the bank.

PLANNING BY RESPONSIBILITY CENTER

Adoption of the responsibility center concept carries with it the need to involve responsibility center managers in the planning process. Since each manager is responsible for the costs incurred by his organizational unit, he will feel a greater commitment to exercise his control responsibilities if he has been involved in planning the costs of his center.

The planning process involves the analysis of alternatives by which planned objectives can be carried out through the use of resources. In Chapter 7 the important part played by cost information in this analysis was covered in detail. For purposes of this chapter, therefore, it is assumed that management has decided on one particular alternative course of action and that the next step is to implement the plan. To do so, it is necessary to state an objective or objectives in terms of the bank's organization. For example:

- The objective of the bank's plan
  . . Increase savings deposits by 15%.

- The action to be taken in illustrative responsibility centers of the bank to implement this plan

  . . Advertising and public relations department
  Carry out an advertising program in newspaper and other media with provisions for weekly follow-up to assess effect.

  . . Branch administration
  Implement special savings plan for personal accounts with weekly follow-up to assess results.

Data center

Use one programmer full time for three months to modify existing programs so as to accommodate additional savings accounts and to track effects of advertising program on increases in accounts.

This simplified example illustrates how the bank's objectives must be translated into specific action steps that can be implemented by responsibility center managers. The managers are then able to develop the details of their plans to accomplish their portion of the stated objective by identifying specific resources to be used and levels of activity to be maintained.

Measures of activity and accomplishment are frequently required in addition to cost data in order to plan levels of expense and productivity. The number of checks processed, loans handled, and teller deposits handled, etc., are an important source of information for planning, communicating, and controlling.

Thus, accounting by a responsibility center system provides an effective means for translating overall long-range objectives into short-range plans to be implemented by specified organizational units and it is also an effective means for measuring the performance of those units. Since the accounting system is built around the organization units that are required to carry out plans, it becomes an integral part of the bank's planning and control system.

The responsibility center manager's role in the planning cycle and his relations with the chief executive officers and the accounting department are illustrated in Figure 8.2, which shows that the responsibility manager responds to the long-range objectives by developing plans in management areas under his control. He implements the plans by employing specific resources to conduct specified activities within a certain period of time. He is also continuously involved later on in measuring activity results, comparing them to the plan, and identifying any unacceptable variances. The manager changes the use of resources or the type of resources being used so as to compensate for variances and thereby produces results that will conform with the plan.

REPORTING BY RESPONSIBILITY CENTER

When plans are developed by a responsibility center, reports on the results of its operations should be made by the same organizational responsibility units. For "pure" responsibility reporting, only those items that are directly controllable by each manager should be re-

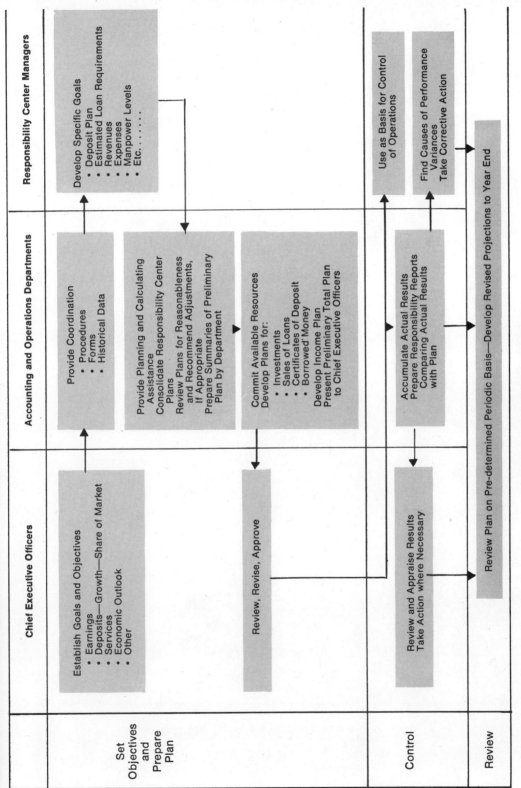

Figure 8.2—The Planning Cycle
Incorporating Responsibility Center Concepts

ported for him. In this chapter, however, it is assumed that every item of cost will be made the responsibility of some individual in the organization. Further discussion of this problem is included in Chapter 13.

Reporting Procedures

The pyramiding concept is generally used for responsibility reporting (Figure 8.3). For example, the lowest level manager receives a detailed report of his actual operating results compared to his approved plan. Each higher level manager receives a report that is a *summary* of the plans and actual operating results of all managers

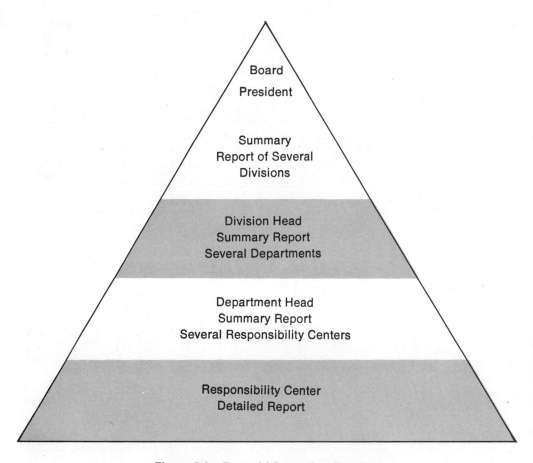

Figure 8.3—Pyramid Reporting Structure

reporting to him. The pyramiding continues until the highest level summary report is prepared for the president and the board of directors. This report describes the operating results of the whole bank.

The reports prepared for each level of management highlight performance that is "off target" and facilitate the use of "management by exception" techniques. Thus each level of management is able to concentrate its attention on matters that require corrective action. Illustrative responsibility center reports are shown in Appendix B.

When reports that show a variance of actual from plan are being evaluated, the original plan should be reviewed to determine whether it has continuing validity. The original assumptions may have been in error, or the assumptions may have been outdated by events that are beyond the control of the responsible planning officer. The first few times a bank prepares a formal plan the actual results may show wide variance from plan. This variance will be due to inadequate or inaccurate historical information and inexperience on the part of the planners.

SUMMARY

The control of a bank's cost performance is best accomplished by using a system of accounting by responsibility center and the comparison of actual operating results with plans. Management's ability to control bank operations effectively depends on its ability to associate particular results with specific individuals. Accounting by responsibility center provides a structure for planning, a vehicle for communication, and a mechanism for control as plans are put into action.

A system of accounting by responsibility center may be implemented by a bank in phases over a period of time, in accordance with its needs and capabilities. A responsibility center accounting system serves as a basic data collection and cost (and if appropriate, revenue) control mechanism for a bank, and it can be refined, sophisticated, and extended as management desires. Appendix B sets forth the general design of a responsibility center accounting and reporting system for a small-to-medium-size bank.

9

CONTROLLING COST PERFORMANCE— PROJECT AND PROGRAM ACCOUNTING

Control of cost performance by each of the bank's organizational units was discussed in some detail in the previous chapter. There are many activities, however, for which control of cost performance is important, but they are nonroutine in nature and frequently cross organizational and functional lines. These activities require either varying degrees of effort from many diverse organizational units or the efforts of specially created organizational units. They are frequently referred to as programs or projects.

In the banking community there are many examples of activities that can be established as formal programs: opening branches, installation of a data center, adding new services, and various community activities such as minority assistance. The concept of program management is similar to that of responsibility center management, and it provides a useful supplementary technique for planning and control of resources. But, since programs are concerned with controlling non-recurring activities that take place, in some cases, over a span of years, the application of the concept takes a different form.

Programs are those efforts for change that normally have their own management structure and they have one or all of the following features:

- Formal planning, budgeting and controlling systems.
- Heavy total resource commitment.
- Strategic change to bank operations.
- Longer range time frame for execution.
- Broad impact on the bank.

Projects generally have the same features of programs, but they are normally smaller in scope and scale. Examples would be the development of a specific computer application, remodeling a teller facility, etc. This chapter will refer only to programs, but the same general principles are applicable to projects.

A bank preparing to engage in a program should state the objective, determine the resources required to carry out the program, determine the cost and/or revenue justification, and then formalize the organization steps and timing required to accomplish the program. It might even consider establishing a special organizational unit to plan, coordinate, and monitor the events required to carry out the program. An organizational unit created specifically for the management of change highlights management's interest in the desired change. By setting this unit apart from the normal functional organizational structure of the bank, management is able to preserve the basic strengths of the existing organization and the continuity of its operations.

Because of the breadth, scope, and duration of a program, neither the ordinary general accounting system nor the responsibility accounting system provide all the information necessary for adequate program planning and control. This chapter, therefore, introduces an approach to program costing to ensure adequate information for planning and control. The approach is applicable to those programs for which the expense and effort can be justified either by their overall importance or by the cost of the resources committed to them. Before discussing program costing, however, it is necessary to review program initiation and the development of detailed plans for carrying out the program.

PROGRAM INITIATION

Management initiates action based on its formulation and interpretation of objectives. Many of these objectives can be accomplished through the routine operation of the bank's organization units. In some cases, however, it is evident that the nature of the objective (increasing market penetration through establishing a branch, for example) calls for planning and controlling the actions required as a program.

Once a preliminary decision is made to establish a program, it is then necessary to outline the actions and related resources required to carry it out. Based upon these resource requirements the estimated costs, and revenue if applicable, should be calculated for use in determining the feasibility of the contemplated program. The costing required to determine the feasibility of the program as it relates to resources to be used is discussed in Chapter 7. Chapter 12 discusses the costing required when profitability is the criterion for determining program feasibility.

The establishment of a program should be formally announced by management. Objectives, specific activities to be carried out, and the expected date of completion should be clearly indicated. Milestones (significant decision points in the program) and related target dates should also be specified if the program is particularly long or complicated. The milestones selected by bank management should be natural "go" or "no go" decision points in the life of a program; for example, a point at which a major commitment of resources is required, or a point where progress and future prospects should be assessed.

The probability of success and assurance of a cooperative attitude can be enhanced if management clearly indicates (1) the relationship of the activities to be performed in the program to the other bank functions, and (2) the authority and responsibility of the designated program manager. To a practical extent, the authority and responsibility of the program manager should not conflict with those of other managers. Some indication of personnel, facilities, and funds being committed to the program can also be made at this time. The milestones, target dates, resources to be committed, and benefits expected of the program will, of course, be more fully defined as it progresses.

The organizational structure for execution of a program may be "within" the current organizational structure or it may be a separate one "outside" the present structure. Figures 9.1 and 9.2 indicate alternative organizational structures for managing a program.

To illustrate briefly where the organization structure (Figure 9.1) might be used, assume that the bank wishes to establish a program to assist minority group businessmen. Further, assume that the objectives of such a program are to improve the financial management ability of

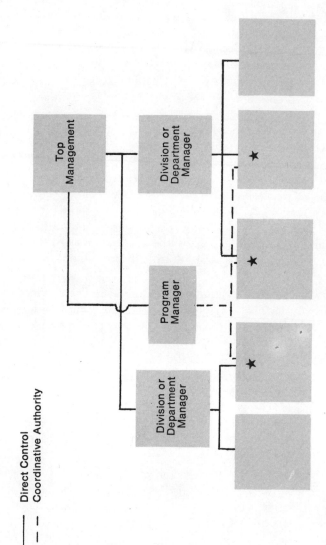

— Direct Control
- - - Coordinative Authority

★ Organizational units performing activities under the department manager's direct control for the benefit of the program and monitored by the program manager

Figure 9.1—Program Organized "Within" Existing Structure

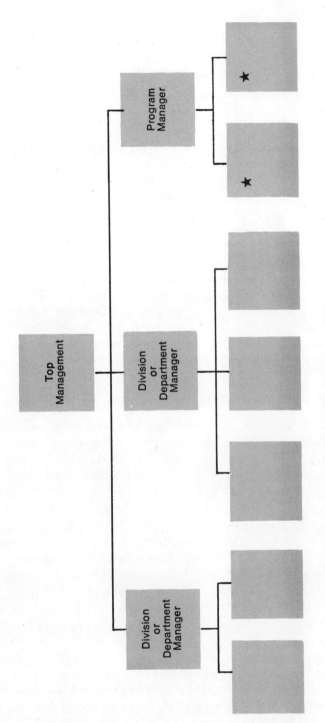

★ Organizational units established for the expressed purpose of carrying out program activities under the direction of the program manager

Figure 9.2—Program Organized "Outside" Existing Structure

the minority businessman and the financial structure of his business. This can be accomplished by

- Assisting with preparation of financial plans.
- Advising on the need for and type of financial records.
- Assisting with financing of the business.

In order to carry out the program, the program manager will receive assistance from designated persons in the loan and investment division and the finance and control division.

By contrast, a new banking activity, such as branch banking, would probably be organized in the manner shown in Figure 9.2. Branches would be physically established and set into operation in the development phase of the program, but the success or failure of the branching program may not be certain for several years. The advantage of the organization form shown in Figure 9.2 is that when the branching program is completed, the program organizational units may become the nucleus of a permanent branch organizational unit to be established in the future. Or, if the program fails, the various resources used in the program can be returned to the bank's regular activities and the program organizational units can be dissolved with minimal disruption of normal bank routine.

PLANNING THE PROGRAM

After bank management has designated the program objective and selected the organizational structure, the appointed program manager assumes the burden of program execution—achieving the objective by the deadline established with the resources made available to him.

The program manager begins his work by determining the steps required to be accomplished to attain the objective of the program. These steps are, in turn, divided into detailed tasks or substeps in such a manner that the program objective is partitioned into small, manageable segments with deadlines for the accomplishment of each. This is illustrated in Figure 9.3, in which the bank's objective is to improve its market position by establishing a new branch.

There are a number of techniques for planning the program. All involve a definition of steps and the tasks required to carry out each step, a determination of the relationship between tasks, and an estimate of the time required to complete each task. If a target completion date has been set, the detailed tasks are worked backward from that date to determine a reasonable starting date. If a completion date has

Program Objective

Establish a branch in new town within 24 months

Program Steps	Milestones	End of Month Target Dates
• Determine organizational arrangements and assignment of authority and responsibility		• Month 1
• Prepare the detailed plan and budget	• Approve plan	• Month 2
• Conduct a study of customer needs and recommend banking services	• Approve banking services	• Month 4
• Develop branch banking strategy and policies		• Month 8
• Review and select a site for the branch	• Approve site	• Month 15
• Determine personnel requirements and develop hiring and internal personnel transfer plans		• Month 16
• Prepare a forecast of funds to be provided and used and recommend initial funds required	• Approve fund requirements	• Month 22
• Prepare marketing plans and specific target date for opening		• Month 24

Tasks and Target Completion Dates (For Branch Site Selection Step)

- • Locate possible branch sites —end of 12th month.

- • Estimate the costs and benefits associated with each of the possible sites—end of 14th month.

- • Select the site for the new town branch—end of 15th month
  (Tasks should be sufficiently detailed to identify all significant actions required to carry out the program step and reach the milestone).

Figure 9.3—Illustration of Program Steps, Milestones, and Tasks

not been given, planning can begin with the first task to determine the estimated completion date.

To illustrate the development of a detailed, step-by-step plan, it will be assumed that a completion date of June 1, year 2, has been established. First, all of the tasks required for the accomplishment of the objective are graphically portrayed using arrow diagrams to show their sequential relationships. This is an example:

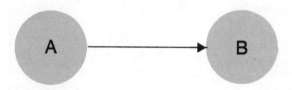

Tasks A and B are related; Task A must precede Task B and be completed before Task B can commence. If there are three tasks involved, then the following diagram

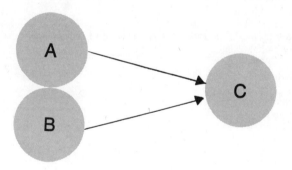

would mean that all three tasks are related, that Task A and B must precede Task C, and that *both* must be completed before Task C can commence. To permit more rapid understanding, the arrows are only drawn to show the flow of action from left to right, and occasionally vertically. Figure 9.4 uses the arrow diagramming technique to portray a possible branch banking program.

Since a completion date has been established, the detailed planning entails starting with the last task of the program and the program target completion set by management. The time required to complete that last task is estimated so as to determine the deadline(s) for the task (s) immediately preceding it, for example:

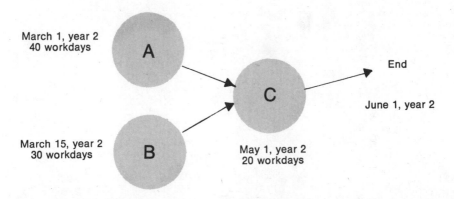

March 1, year 2
40 workdays

A

March 15, year 2
30 workdays

B

C

May 1, year 2
20 workdays

End

June 1, year 2

Task C is estimated to require 20 workdays (about one month) to complete and must be completed no later than June 1, year 2 if the program target completion date is to be met. Therefore, Task C must be started no later than May 1, year 2, prior to which *both* Task A and Task B must have been completed. If Task A requires 40 workdays for completion, it must be started any time before March 1, year 2 to be completed before the required starting date of Task C. If Task B requires only 30 workdays for completion, it can be started any time before March 15, year 2. The time estimates for each task should be realistic to ensure that the objective is met by its assigned deadline.

Once the step, milestone, and task descriptions have been prepared and the target completion dates and resource requirements determined, the plan should be communicated to the bank staff for coordination and implementation. The bank staff should also be informed about the overall program plan and time schedule for the purpose of assigning responsibilities.

As the tasks in the plan are being carried out, there will be cases when the time required to complete a task will either be greater or less than that estimated. The program manager will likely want to rework his detailed schedule showing tasks and related target completion dates. If he has prepared an arrow diagram, the relationships between tasks will have been defined and he may be able to prepare new task completion date estimates readily. For very complex programs, a computer can be used to help rework the estimates.

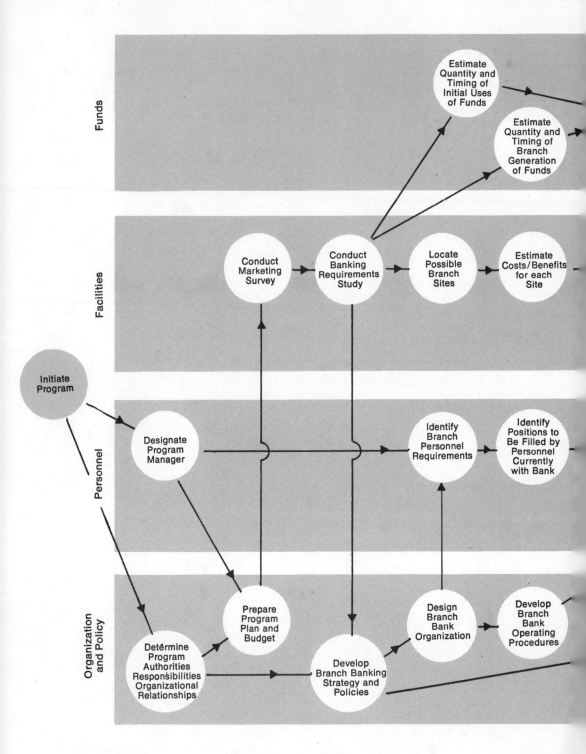

Figure 9.4—Illustration of Arrow Diagramming for a Program

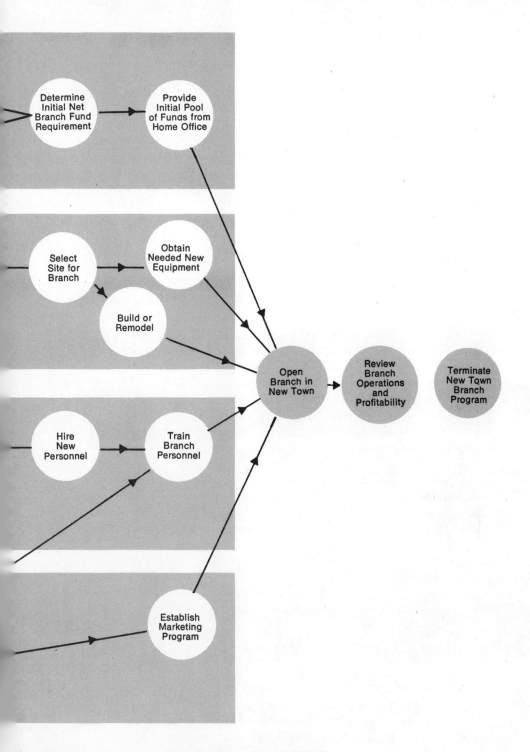

(A Simplified Network for Establishing a Branch Bank)

PROGRAM ACCOUNTING SYSTEM

Program objectives are usually expressed in terms of establishing new operations or services for the bank, and all costs incurred and any revenues obtained during the course of carrying out the program must be accounted for. Although all costs and revenues may be currently accounted for and reported to the bank's various responsibility center managers, many of those same revenues and costs (or parts of them) are the result of activities undertaken in connection with various programs.

The general accounting and responsibility accounting systems discussed thus far are inadequate for this new recording and reporting requirement. Therefore, a program accounting system is frequently necessary to record and report appropriate cost and revenue items to the program manager so that he and the bank's management can judge the effectiveness of program execution and can exercise control when necessary.

If a responsibility accounting system is in use, a program accounting system can cause the legitimate dual reporting of some items of cost or revenue. For example, the time spent by a loan officer on a loan application connected with a new or experimental loan service program can be reported both to the loan department manager and to the program manager. The program accounting system becomes a complement to the responsibility center accounting system, helping to show bank management just how well the program is fulfilling its original objective and budget commitments.

Since many accounting periods may pass between the start and completion of a program, the program accounting system must be capable of handling the costs and revenues of several accounting periods. It must do so without confusing such costs and revenues with those accounted for in the bank's regular accounting system. The program accounting system should not only account for any necessary capital and start-up costs, but it should also consider each program as a separate entity and report the costs of funds, personnel, facilities, and other supporting services used until the program is terminated.

ACCOUNTING FOR PROGRAM COSTS AND REVENUES

The program manager together with the bank's controller can develop the accounting techniques necessary to record and report all costs and revenues relevant to the execution of the program.

The resulting program accounting system may require special coding to provide program identification and to permit proper recording, classifying, summarizing, and reporting of program data. If the bank has a responsibility accounting system and if costs and revenues can be incurred for the program by an organizational unit not under the control of the program manager, a suffix or a prefix can be added to the bank's existing account and organizational unit code structure. This will permit accumulation of costs and revenues both by organizational unit and by program. (An account and organizational unit code structure is discussed in Appendix B and illustrated in Figure B.4.)

There may be cases when special coding of costs and revenues by program is not practical, such as when the cost of such accounting and reporting is excessive. An alternative accounting method is to periodically reallocate to the program the costs (and where necessary, revenues) already recorded in the general accounting system. Although using this method of program accounting is acceptable, it can present some problems:

- The resulting cost and revenue data may not be as accurate as it could be if the data were specifically coded within the accounting system.
- The reallocation may have to await preparation of reports from the bank's accounting system and, as a result, the program manager may not receive the timely information he needs to evaluate and control fast-moving events.

Whether each item of cost and revenue is specifically coded within the accounting system or is periodically reallocated, the program information can be developed in at least two ways. Cost data can include all costs and revenues allocable to the program or only the additional (incremental) costs and revenues incurred and received as a direct result of the program activities. Figure 9.5 briefly illustrates the total cost and incremental cost approach.

In making a choice between total and incremental costing of programs the purpose of the costing must be considered. The incremental method is appealing because it approximates cash outlay. But if this method is used, the program manager is not able to see all the costs of resources being utilized in behalf of his program since only the cost of resources required in addition to the normal resource capacities are reported. Further, incremental costs could be misleading if, for example, the program is a pilot operation of what might later be a routine bank service.

The program costing process continues until bank management declares that the program has achieved its objectives or declares that the objectives and the program are to be abandoned. If the objectives

Monthly Costs	Total Cost Approach	Incremental Cost Approach
Program 1		
Salary of full-time program manager (A) from investment department	$2,100	
Salary of new investment department manager hired to replace manager (A)		$1,600
Costs charged to Program 1	$2,100	$1,600
Program 2		
Salary of full-time program manager (B), hired from the outside for this program	$1,500	$1,500
Salaries of clerical assistants, one each from investment, marketing, and data center departments (monthly salaries of $500, $600, and $500, respectively; program requiures 50% of their time and results in overtime equal to 10% of their salaries)	250 300 250	50 60 50
Costs charged to Program 2	$2,300	$1,660

Figure 9.5—Illustration of Total and Incremental Program Costing

are achieved, the program will be dissolved and any ongoing costs and revenues resulting from the execution of the program (such as a new banking activity) will now be recorded and reported by the bank's accounting system. There will be no further need of the program subcoding used earlier, and any dual reporting of costs and revenues that existed because of the program would be eliminated.

PROGRAM CONTROL AND EVALUATION

A program manager would normally have the responsibility for his entire program and the authority to expend any of the resources at his disposal to carry out the program objective. Although program organization and chain of command may change somewhat as the program is carried out, the program manager would still be held accountable for budget performance, work quality, and progress towards the timely accomplishment of the overall program objective. If the performance of the program begins to slip, it is important that the program manager

- Detect the slippage.
- Measure the slippage and its potential danger.
- Decide on the remedial action.
- Coordinate corrective action to be taken.
- Communicate the slippage and remedial action to top management.

This detected slippage could be

- Late completion of one or more tasks.
- Failure to meet performance standards on one or more tasks.
- Excessive costs incurred anywhere.
- Less revenues received than expected.

The continuing need for timely and accurate information to detect problems and to take action to correct them makes the program approach more than just a system of accounting—for it involves all the traditional functions of management. This view is presented in Figure 9.6.

The program manager should control his program by comparing reports of actual results against objectives and plans. Figures 9.7, 9.8, and 9.9 illustrate some useful reports. Figure 9.7 shows the schedule and cost status for each task, step, and milestone. For those tasks, steps, and milestones that are not yet completed a budget amount is calculated by multiplying the original budget by the percentage of completion. This is compared against actual costs incurred to date. Schedule

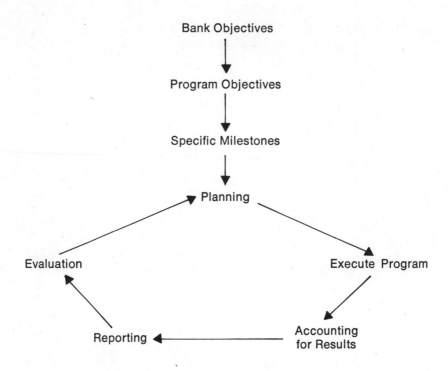

Planning and executing of programs creates a cycle. This cycle must be completed before the process can be effective. It also must continue throughout the life of the program until the program objectives have been accomplished.

Figure 9.6—Program Management—A Complete Cycle

and cost status that the program manager believes to be outside of acceptable limits are highlighted in the "alert" column. Figure 9.8 illustrates the use of a chart to show planned and actual cumulative costs and revenues for a program. Costs are measured from the inception of the program, with the greatest amount usually incurred in the beginning. If revenues are to be part of the objective, they may not be generated until the program has reached a more advanced stage of

Program Status Report

As of April 1, 19___   Prepared April 15, 19___

	Department Responsibility[1]	Schedule Status			Cost Status			Remarks
		Budget	Date Complete/ Percent Complete	Alert	Budget	Actual	Alert	
Task 111	PM	Mar. 1	Feb. 27		$ 500	$ 550		
Task 112	PM	Apr. 15	80%		*4,000*[2]	*3,850*[3]		Task 112 Ahead of schedule
Task 113	PM	Apr. 28	0%		—	—		
Step 11	PM	Apr. 28	70%		*4,500*	*4,400*		
Task 121	PM	Feb. 20	Mar. 1	●	1,500	2,500	●	Task 121 Delayed by weather
Task 122	CL	Mar. 1	Mar. 10		6,800	6,200		
Task 123	CL	Apr. 15	60%	●	*8,000*	*9,200*	●	Task 123 Additional personnel employed to speed task
Task 124	CL	May 1	0%		—	—		
Step 12	CL	May 1	80%		*16,300*	*17,900*		
Task 131	ML	Apr. 1	Mar. 15		3,400	3,250		Task 131 Started early at no additional cost
Task 132	ML	Apr. 28	80%		*6,300*	*6,600*		
Step 13	ML	Apr. 28	90%		*9,700*	*9,850*		
Milestone 1	PM	May 1	80%		*30,500*	*32,150*		
Task 211								
Task 212 → etc.								
etc.								
etc.								

All tasks, steps, and milestones grouped, numbered, and listed down in similar fashion

1 PM—Project Management Office
CL—Commercial Loan Department
ML—Mortgage Loan Department
2 Costs in the budget column with asterisks are the budgeted costs prorated to the task using the estimated percentage of completion.
3 Costs in the actual column with asterisks are the costs through April 1 for those tasks not yet completed.

Figure 9.7—Illustration of a Program Progress Report

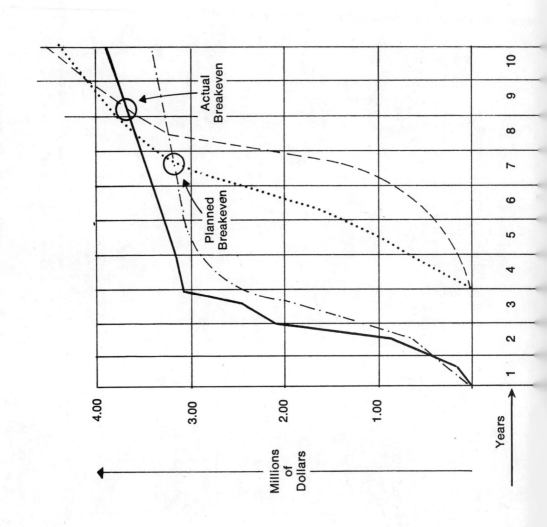

Millions
of
Dollars

Actual
Breakeven

Planned
Breakeven

4.00

3.00

2.00

1.00

1   2   3   4   5   6   7   8   9   10

Years

Years	1	2	3	4	5	6	7	8	9	10	Chart Symbols
Costs — Plan — Annual	.45	.80	1.35	.35	.15	.10	.10	.05	.05	.05	—·—·—
Costs — Plan — Cumulative	.45	1.25	2.60	2.95	3.10	3.20	3.30	3.35	3.40	3.45	————
Costs — Actual — Annual	.45	1.65	1.00	.10	.10	.10	.10	.10	.10	.10	··········
Costs — Actual — Cumulative	.45	2.10	3.10	3.20	3.30	3.40	3.50	3.60	3.70	3.80	– – – –
Revenue — Plan — Annual	—	—	—	.50	.90	1.30	.60	.45	.40	.35	
Revenue — Plan — Cumulative	—	—	—	.50	1.40	2.70	3.30	3.75	4.15	4.50	
Revenue — Actual — Annual	—	—	—	.15	.25	.55	1.35	1.35	.50	.50	
Revenue — Actual — Cumulative	—	—	—	.15	.40	.95	2.30	3.65	4.15	4.65	

Figure 9.8—Plan vs Actual Costs and Revenues

Periodic Status Report of _____ Program to Bank Management[1]

Reporting Period—Month of March, 19____

Program Progress

Tasks programmed to be completed during this reporting period	111,122
Tasks programmed for prior completion—not yet completed	None
Tasks completed in this period	
• Completed early (from this period)	111
• Completed early (from later periods)	131
• Completed on time (from this period)	None
• Completed late (from prior periods)	121
• Completed late (from this period)	122
Tasks not completed as scheduled in this period	None

REMARKS: Action Step 12 currently behind schedule but acceleration efforts in Task 123 are expected to recover lost time and keep Milestone 1 on schedule.

Program Budget

	This Period	Year to Date	Program to Date	Estimated Cost to Complete	Total Estimated Cost at Program Completion
Costs budgeted	$28,500	$30,500	$30,500	$1,344,500	$1,375,000
Costs incurred	29,100	32,150	32,150	1,350,000	1,382,150
Budget variance—favorable (unfavorable)	$ (600)	$ (1,650)	$ (1,650)	$ (5,500)	$ (7,150)
Revenues budgeted (if any are to be generated)			None generated or budgeted to date.		
Revenues generated					
Budget variance					

REMARKS: Savings realized in execution of Task 122 were offset by the added cost incurred by using more personnel on Task 123 so as to accelerate its completion and bring action Step 12 and Milestone 1 back on schedule.

Potential Problem Areas

The personnel availability survey has determined that few employees are available in NewTown and that prevailing compensation levels are above those established for the bank. A study is now being made of possible transfer of current employees to the new branch.

[1] Report based on information from Figure 9.7.

Figure 9.9—Illustrative Program Report for a Calendar Period

development. The evolution of the program's costs and revenues should be projected and actual results controlled against that projection.

A report also can be submitted periodically (e.g., monthly or quarterly), showing the program progress for a period. Figure 9.9 illustrates such a report. Such reports can serve as formal records of program progress.

Formal oral presentations should be given to top management at preselected major milestones. These are the natural "go" or "no go" decision points within the program. The presentations ensure that the program does not continue unchecked, but that it is continually evaluated. At these presentations, the program manager can review the plan for the program, progress to date, problem areas, and the time and costs required to complete the program. It may be necessary to re-evaluate the specific objectives in light of the probable benefits, costs, time, and risks involved in continuing the program. The outcome of such a presentation could be renewal, abandonment, or modification of the program; provision for resource commitment to carry the project through to its next milestone; and the issuance of managerial guidance on the manner of completing the program (quality of work expected, architectural style, etc.) .

SUMMARY

The bank will very often initiate activities that require broad participation throughout the bank. The use of the program technique for managing such activities can contribute significantly toward a successful result.

Programs are directed toward specific objectives, are nonrecurring, and are usually of such cost magnitude that they represent major economic ventures. Programs also can extend over many accounting periods and very often cross present and future organizational lines. For these reasons programs present some unique planning and control problems.

Where management has decided to use the program technique for planning and control

- Authority for the program should be vested in a program manager.
- Special program accounting should be instituted to provide program cost and revenue information.
- Programs should be controlled by comparing actual results against projected plans.

Part IV
ALLOCATION TECHNIQUES

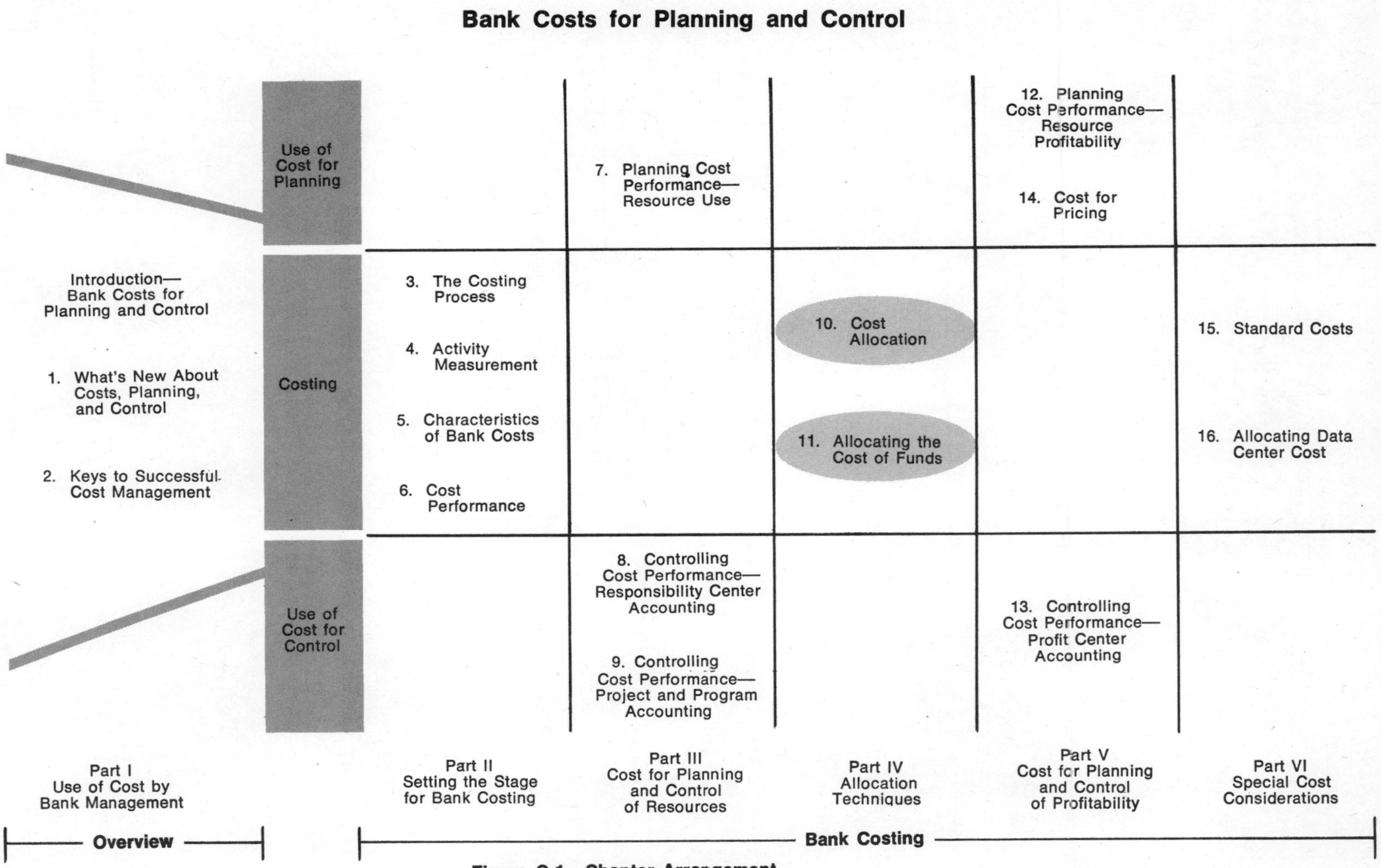

Bank Costs for Planning and Control

Use of Cost for Planning

Costing

Use of Cost for Control

Introduction—
Bank Costs for
Planning and Control

1. What's New About
Costs, Planning,
and Control

2. Keys to Successful
Cost Management

3. The Costing
Process

4. Activity
Measurement

5. Characteristics
of Bank Costs

6. Cost Performance

7. Planning Cost
Performance—
Resource Use

8. Controlling
Cost Performance—
Responsibility Center
Accounting

9. Controlling
Cost Performance—
Project and Program
Accounting

10. Cost Allocation

11. Allocating the
Cost of Funds

12. Planning
Cost Performance—
Resource Profitability

14. Cost for
Pricing

13. Controlling
Cost Performance—
Profit Center
Accounting

15. Standard Costs

16. Allocating Data
Center Cost

Part I
Use of Cost by
Bank Management

Part II
Setting the Stage
for Bank Costing

Part III
Cost for Planning
and Control
of Resources

Part IV
Allocation
Techniques

Part V
Cost for Planning
and Control
of Profitability

Part VI
Special Cost
Considerations

Overview

Bank Costing

Figure 0.1—Chapter Arrangement

Part IV

ALLOCATION TECHNIQUES

The purpose of this section is to discuss the more complex considerations involved in allocation.

Part III discussed costing for the use of resources where management had to concentrate on getting the most for the cost incurred. The costing techniques employed were rather simple and straightforward. Part V reviews costing where cost performance is being considered in terms of profits generated from costs incurred. The nature of resource organization, utilization, and control (such as in the loaning function, trust function, etc.) is complex and the costing required can likewise be complex. This section is intended to prepare the reader for these more complex costing requirements.

The most essential requirement for the more complex costing is an understanding of cost allocation. Chapter 10 discusses cost allocation and builds upon the brief discussion of allocation in Chapter 3. Chapter 11 reviews cost allocation from the point of view of a special problem for banks—the allocation of costs of funds.

10

COST ALLOCATION

Special attention is devoted to the allocation process in this chapter for two reasons: (1) it represents a level of costing complexity that must be well understood before costing to determine profitability can be discussed; (2) allocation (cost transference) is at the heart of the costing process.

The allocation process is Step Four of the costing process and consists of two major steps:

- Determination of allocation basis and definition of transfer unit; and
- Specification of allocation method (direct, step, or reciprocal).

This chapter enlarges upon Step Four as described in Chapter 3. Criteria will be developed for selecting an allocation basis so that a reader can judge for himself whether a particular basis is appropriate under given circumstances.

Examples of cost calculation (Step Five of the costing process) are included in this chapter to illustrate the allocation methods. Unit transfer cost is discussed as part of the discussion of calculation. Unit transfer price, being somewhat similar to unit transfer cost, also is discussed in this chapter.

ALLOCATION BASIS

The completion of the three preliminary costing steps (defining the purpose, defining the costing object, specifying the cost data) brings the costing process to the point where the coster must determine how the cost is to be transferred to the costing object. This is the allocation process. The basis for allocation is selected by identifying the dominant benefit passed on to the costing object.

The identification of the benefit is not difficult, because it is usually inherent in the purpose for which the benefit-providing unit was created. A few examples are:

Benefit-Providing Units and Resources	Examples of Benefits Provided
Data center programming section	EDP program preparation and maintenance
Bookkeeping section	Deposit tickets and cancelled checks filed
Deposit function	Investable funds
Occupancy cost center	Working space
Administrative function	Supervision and administration
Computer equipment	Data processed
Clerk	Transactions handled

The benefit provided by one unit to another also is presumed to correspond to a flow of cost that is incurred to provide that benefit. Thus, when the benefits provided have been identified, they become the basis for allocation and costs are assumed to flow in direct relationship to the flow of the benefit.

To carry out the allocation process and thus to transfer cost in accordance with benefit provided, the allocation basis must be reduced to a unit of measure (transfer unit) to which costs can be assigned (unit transfer cost). The unit transfer cost is then used to transfer the cost from the benefit-providing unit or resource to the cost center or costing object. (*Note:* A review of Figures 3.4 and 3.5 may be helpful to the reader.)

TRANSFER UNITS

The transfer unit to be used in allocating should ideally be one that is easily quantified in terms of benefits provided and one that is also a reasonable measure of the costs incurred to provide these benefits. EDP programming is a good illustration.

The programming section of the data center provides benefits by updating existing programs for the operations section and preparing special programs for various users throughout the bank. The benefits provided can be measured in several ways:

- Market value of the programs.
- Cost savings derived from their use.
- Time expended in writing them.

Market value might be acceptable for cost allocation, but only if better methods are not available. Market value not only depends on factors and conditions external to the bank, but it has to be determined for all programs prepared or being prepared so that the proportion of cost applicable to any one program can be determined properly.

Cost savings implies a measure of benefit that is passed along, but it presents a difficulty similar to the market value measure. Each program prepared or being prepared has to be associated with cost savings, and this often becomes a cumbersome activity.

The costs of the programming section are substantially salaries and fringe benefits. Thus, when time is used to measure benefits of the programming section it provides an ideal transfer unit, because the benefit and the attendant costs have time as a common denominator.

Sometimes a benefit may be derived from a variety of costs that have a variety of measures. The occupancy cost center is a case in point. It comprises a collection of costs that arise from a variety of factors: insurance is based on replacement cost, depreciation on original cost, taxes on assessed valuations, rent on floor space, the salary portion of maintenance on time, etc. Only one of these factors (rent) corresponds to the unit measure (square foot) normally used to measure the benefits from occupancy. Square footage is used because it is a good measure of the benefits provided (space occupied). It also represents a reasonable measure of a major portion of occupancy costs, namely, rental.

Contrast this with the problem of measuring the benefits produced by senior administrative officers. These benefits are intangible and very likely cannot be associated with the officers' time or salaries, unless a time report is kept. A measure of benefit that can logically apply to the receiving unit is therefore difficult to find, and in these cases an arbitrary transfer unit is used.

For convenience of discussion, the type of transfer unit referred to above that provides a logical measure of the benefits will be referred to as a "natural transfer unit," while one that is arbitrary in nature will be referred to as an "arbitrary transfer unit."

Natural Transfer Unit

When the unit of measure of the allocation basis is easily determined—both in terms of the number of units (activity) associated with the cost center and the number of units associated with the costing object—the transfer unit is a "natural" unit. This means that it is "natural" to the incidence of benefits provided and benefits received.

A frequent "natural" transfer unit is some unit of time, such as a man-hour or machine hour. Examples of other transfer units that can be referred to as "natural" are number or amount of

- Transactions (checks processed, deposits processed, etc.) .
- Loans made.
- Square feet occupied.
- Demand deposit accounts.
- Savings accounts.
- Average daily balance.

Arbitrary Transfer Unit

A transfer unit is arbitrary when it is not feasible to measure the benefits provided and received in terms of the same units.

Administrative costs are a good example of the need to use an arbitrary transfer unit, since it is more difficult to determine a transfer unit for them than for any other group of costs. The difficulty can be minimized, however, by minimizing the amount of administrative costs that must be allocated, defining them to include only expenses of the directors, the president, the controller, and the auditor, and perhaps, other senior officers. The time senior officers spend on specific responsibilities can be estimated with reasonable accuracy and may be a logical basis of allocating their time to specific organizational units or activities, thus reducing the portion of administrative cost that must be allocated arbitrarily. When administrative expenses are defined narrowly, they do not comprise a significant portion of the total operating costs of the bank, since much of the allocation has already been done through the accounting system.

When arbitrary allocation of administrative cost is necessary, a number of transfer units are available:

- Average balances both of deposits and of loans and investments. If desired, these balances may be weighted to allocate more cost either to fund sources or to fund users.
- Estimated time spent on different functions.
- Noninterest expenditures of the various cost centers throughout the bank.
- Judgmental percent of administrative expense based on degree of senior management responsibility.

In any event, administrative expenses should be allocated only to the major bank activities, especially in pricing services, since no useful purpose would be gained by allocating these expenses to minor activities.

In some cases, the transfer unit may be dictated more by the philosophy of management toward planning and control of cost than by any natural affinity to the benefits provided and received. Allocating the auditing portion of administrative expenses furnishes a good example of the problem. In this case, there are at least three transfer units that could be used: time spent in various departments being audited, noninterest dollars expended by all departments, and predetermined amounts to be allocated to customers' deposits, loan and trust accounts. Time would be a natural transfer unit, but some argue that, since the audit is conducted for the good of the bank as a whole, its cost should be borne by all departments, not just by those that require the greatest amount of time. Therefore, some other transfer unit is sometimes used, and frequently its choice is arbitrary.

In the preceding examples, the circumstances do not point to one basis that is obviously more appropriate than the others, so a choice must be made that is largely judgmental or arbitrary, and arbitrary cost allocation creates special difficulties. When allocation is made on an arbitrary basis, it is important to understand how the resulting cost information will be affected. If the costs so allocated are of material significance, the resulting cost information should be accompanied by a statement that specific costs were arbitrarily allocated and that caution should be exercised in drawing conclusions from the resulting information.

TRANSFER UNIT WEIGHTING

There are occasions when use of the transfer unit to simply divide up a cost center into average costs per transfer unit would not result in a fair allocation of cost. EDP programmer time will be used to illustrate the need to weight the transfer unit to assure proper assignment of cost to the transfer unit.

Figure 10.1 shows the distribution of programmers' time in preparing programs for several different functions. The time has been expressed in man-hours. The total time for each employee is shown in Column I and the distribution of actual time by bank function is posted in the appropriate column to the right (Columns II through VI). Total man-hours for all programmers and total man-hours distributed to functions are shown on line 1. The unidentified hours are eliminated at line 2 and Column VI. Net man-hours are shown on line 3. A percentage of net man-hours distributed to each function is

Distribution of Man-hours by Bank Function

Programmers	Total I	Demand Deposits II	Time Deposits III	Loans IV	Trust V	Unidentified VI
John Jones	165	40	100			25
Mary Smith	160	40	40	80		
George Brown (part-time)	42	7	7	7	7	14
Tom Johnson	160			40	100	20
1. Total man-hours	527	87	147	127	107	59
2. Eliminate unidentified man-hours	(59)					(59)
3. Net man-hours	468	87	147	127	107	-0-
4. Percent distribution	100.0%	18.6%	31.4%	27.1%	22.9%	

**Figure 10.1—Distribution of Programmer Man-Hours
Four-Week Period**

computed on line 4. If the value of one hour is approximately the same for each programmer, then the percent distribution of time (shown on line 4), as well as the number of man-hours (shown on line 3), would provide acceptable transfer units.

A simple distribution of time is satisfactory when the transfer units are all of equal weight (Figure 10.1). If they are not equal, the determination of an appropriate transfer unit becomes more complex. For example, if one of the programmers is paid four times as much as the others, then man-hours alone may not be an equitable transfer unit. To provide a more equitable transfer unit, the actual hours spent should be weighted by the various pay rates (Figure 10.2).

The total programmer hours in Column I of Figure 10.2 are the same as those in Figure 10.1. These hours are weighted according to the various salary levels of each programmer in Column II, and new weighted total hours are determined (Column III). These are distributed in the same manner as in Figure 10.1, except that weighted hours are used (Columns IV through VIII). Unidentified weighted hours are eliminated in Column VIII and line 2 to arrive at net weighted hours on line 3. The hours on line 3 or the corresponding percentages developed on line 4 could be used as the transfer units.

Similar inequities existing in other situations can be corrected by using the weighting technique. For example:

Department or Activity	Inequity	How Weighted
Occupancy	Area occupied may have different values (banking floor, corner offices, upper floors, etc.)	Weights assigned to rates per square foot for each area
Tellers	Various types of deposits, each requiring different execution time	Time-weighted transaction counts
Credit	Time required for credit analysis will vary by type of customer	Time-weighted credit analysis counts

In connection with occupancy cost, some managements apply a weighting factor to the transfer unit in order to recognize the difference in value applicable to different floor areas. The area of the

139

Distribution of Weighted Man-hours by Bank Function

Programmers	Total Man-hours I	Weight* II	Weighted Total Man-hours III	Demand Deposits IV	Time Deposits V	Loans VI	Trust VII	Unallocated VIII
John Jones	165	1.0	165	40	100			25
Mary Smith	160	.8	128	32	32	64		
George Brown	42	4.0	168	28	28	28	28	56
Tom Johnson	160	1.5	240			60	150	30
1. Total man-hours	527		701	100	160	152	178	111
2. Eliminate unidentified man-hours			(111)					(111)
3. Net weighted man-hours accounted for			590	100	160	152	178	-0-
4. Percent distribution			100.0%	16.9%	27.1%	25.8%	30.2%	

*Based on Salary Rate

Figure 10.2—Weighted Distribution of Programmer Man-Hours Four-Week Period

banking floor sometimes receives special consideration. It may be weighted and allocated to those cost centers that make use of the banking floor, or it may be ignored in the allocation of bank occupancy cost on the theory that the cost of maintaining the banking floor area should be shared by the entire bank.

The library and central files also present a problem of equitable distribution for costs associated with space devoted to storage and for the time devoted to information retrieval. One approach is to use an inquiry count weighted, if necessary, by the space dedicated to storing material identified with specific departments.

When benefits provided consist of more than one type of transaction (such as frequently occurs with the teller function), a single type of transaction cannot function as a transfer unit because each requires a different time to process and thus a different cost. One approach to developing a transfer unit in this situation is to assign a time factor to each type of transaction and to use weighted time as the transfer unit. This approach is illustrated for a teller function in Figure 10.3.

In Figure 10.3 the actual number of transactions handled by the tellers (Column I) represent benefits provided to various functions throughout the bank. These counts are of transactions that differ widely in the estimated time required for each. In order to time-weight the transactions, standard minutes required for each different type of transaction are used (Column II). The standard minutes used have been developed by Bank Administration Institute and are included in Appendix C. The results of multiplying the standard minutes by the actual number of transactions are shown in Column III. Column III represents a time-weighting of the actual transactions and it is used to distribute the actual hours required to process all transactions to each type of transaction processed as shown in Column IV.

In order to show a realistic example, Figure 10.3 also lists some activities that are measured by elapsed time rather than by counting transactions. These activities account for 186 man-hours (Column IV). Since the hours do not relate to those transactions counted, they do not enter into the weighting calculation.

The actual man-hours shown in Column IV are then distributed to benefit-receiving units in Columns V through IX. Those activities that require minor amounts of time are carried to Column X and are eliminated from the allocation percentage calculation.

	Transaction Count[1] I	Time-Weighting Factors—Standard Minutes Per Transaction[2] II	Time-Weighted Count Standard Minutes III
Items Counted:			
Demand Deposits Received			
Checks Only	17,900	.28	5,012
Cash Only	13,060	.41	5,355
Checks and Cash	10,900	.62	6,758
Cash Returned	18,960	.53	10,049
Checks Cashed	50,100	.29	14,529
Savings Deposits Received	10,749	.65	6,987
Savings Withdrawals	3,639	1.30	4,731
Certified Checks	1,579	.98	1,549
Utility Payments	3,814	.51	1,945
Travelers Checks	640	2.42	1,549
Commercial Loan Payments	6,243	.51	3.184
Real Estate Loan Payments	9,276	.51	4,731
Instalment Loan Payments	9,970	.51	5,085
			71,464

Activities Timed—Not Counted:

Supermarket Deposit

Change Orders

Safe Deposit Payments

Filing Checks

Checking Obituary Notices

Return Items

Balancing

Miscellaneous

Total items timed

    Total Man-hours Worked

       Less unallocated time

           Man-hours used for allocation basis

           Percentage allocation

[1] From Figure 4.2

[2] From Appendix C

[3] Man-hours spent on counted transactions	1,616
÷ Weighted count	71,464
= Weighted-time conversion factor	.02261

Distribution of Actual Hours Based on Weighted Time at .02261[3] IV	Demand Deposits V	Savings Deposits VI	Commercial Loans VII	Real Estate Loans VIII	Instalment Loans IX	Unallocated X
113	113					
121	121					
153	153					
227	227					
329	329					
158		158				
107		107				
35	35					
44	44					
35	35					
72			72			
107				107		
115					115	
1,616						
33	33					
20	20					
11						11
14						14
9						9
8						8
73						73
18						18
186						
1,802	1,110	265	72	107	115	133
(133)						(133)
1,669	1,110	265	72	107	115	—0—
100.0%	66.5%	15.9%	4.3%	6.4%	6.9%	

Figure 10.3—Time-Weighting Teller Transaction Counts

ALLOCATION METHOD

The transfer unit discussed in the preceding section provides the unit of measure required to transfer cost from one cost center to either another cost center or the costing object. A further consideration in transferring cost is the sequence of cost centers required to simulate the flow of costs from the benefit-providing units to benefit-receiving units. As noted briefly in Chapter 3, allocation methods attempt to represent cost flow. The methods can be summarized as follows:

Cost Flow	Allocation Method
Direct flow from benefit-providing units to benefit-receiving units	Direct allocation
Compound flow from one benefit-providing unit to another and finally to a benefit-receiving unit	Step allocation
Complex flow where reciprocal relationships between benefit-providing units are recognized before allocation to benefit-receiving units	Reciprocal allocation

Direct Allocation Method

The direct allocation method involves an allocation of each benefit-providing unit's costs directly to the ultimate user cost center or functions. This is a simple method that produces an adequate cost calculation, particularly for smaller institutions. It has the additional merit of being easily understood because of the straightforward cause-and-effect relationships that are assumed in the allocation.

Figure 10.4 illustrates the use of the direct allocation method to allocate costs of benefit-providing units to benefit-receiving units. Benefit-providing units are considered to be those organizational units, functions, activities, etc., whose purpose is to provide service to other bank units. The benefit-receiving units are assumed to be those that provide or use funds, and the trust department. Since, in this illustration (and also in Figure 10.5), the costs of all benefit-providing units has been allocated, general overhead has been included both to complete the total annual cost column (as has interest cost) and to permit allocation of all costs of the benefit-providing units. Cost of capital has been included for the latter reason. The capital costs refer to such current expenses as stockholder meetings and printing annual reports, and do not necessarily represent the total cost of obtaining bank capital.

The costs used in Column I are for a 12-month period, and the source of data is the responsibility center accounting system. All the costs of each benefit-providing unit are allocated directly to the benefit-receiving units (Columns II through IX). Whether or not all costs would be allocated in a particular costing situation as shown in the illustration will depend upon the purpose for the calculation. The transfer units used for each benefit-providing unit are at the foot of Columns II through IX. Column X represents the total cost of the benefit-receiving units after allocation of the costs of benefit-providing units.

Direct allocation has limitations that restrict its use for bank costing. For example, occupancy cost in Figure 10.4 was directly allocated to demand and savings deposits and to the various lending departments because each of these departments was assumed to have its own teller windows. If the practice of universal tellers had been followed, it would not have been possible to allocate occupancy costs on the basis of square feet alone. An initial allocation of occupancy cost would be made to the universal teller function and other units. A second allocation would then be necessary. In this second allocation, the universal teller costs, including the allocated occupancy cost, would be apportioned to the ultimate user function. This is what occurs in the step allocation method.

Step Allocation Method

The step allocation method recognizes that there are several levels of cost allocation. Occupancy cost, for example, applies to administrative expense, which in turn applies to the data center, which in turn applies to other cost centers. Figure 10.5 illustrates a sequence for closing out benefit-providing units to benefit-receiving units.

The annual costs of organizational units, functions, and activities used in Figure 10.5 (Column I) are generally the same as those in Figure 10.4, except that universal tellers' expenses have been shown as a separate benefit-providing unit. Each benefit-providing unit is allocated both to other benefit-providing units where applicable and to benefit-receiving units (Columns II through X). Note that as each benefit-providing unit is allocated, its total cost includes costs allocated from those units that preceded it.

The sequence in which the costs of the benefit-providing units are allocated is important, the general rule being that the units that serve the greatest number of other units are distributed first. Thus, Figure 10.5 shows that occupancy cost, communications costs, and administration costs are allocated first.

	Annual Costs I	Occupancy II	Communications III	Administration IV
Benefit-Providing Units				
Occupancy	$ 150,000	$(150,000)		
Communication	57,600		$(57,600)	
Administration	447,200			$(447,200)
Data Center	192,400			
Proof and Transit	131,600			
Bookkeeping	63,600			
Credit Files	125,000			
Credit Analysis	147,000			
Benefit-Receiving Units				
Demand deposits:				
Cost	133,400	52,000	4,600	51,900
Service charge revenue	(102,000)			
Savings Deposits	51,700	8,000	3,450	11,700
Commercial Loans	111,500	24,000	10,350	101,000
Real Estate Loans	58,800	16,500	10,350	60,800
Instalment Loans	119,400	21,000	10,350	77,400
Credit Card	38,400	6,000	5,760	4,000
Investment	34,000			10,100
Trust	72,000	22,500	6,980	81,800
Cost of Capital				8,100
General Overhead	116,000		5,760	40,400
Interest	2,012,400			
Total	$3,960,000	—0—	—0—	—0—

Transfer Units	Square Foot	Toll Charges and Number of Instruments	Man-hour
Number of Transfer Units	25,000	Various	20,000
Average Unit Transfer Cost	$6.00	Various	$22.36

	Allocation				Total Cost of Benefit-Receiving Units (Including Allocation From Benefit-Providing Units)
Data Center V	Proof and Transit VI	Bookkeeping VII	Credit Files VIII	Credit Analysis IX	X
$(192,400)					
	$(131,600)				
		$(63,600)			
			$(125,000)		
				$(147,000)	
144,700	110,000	63,600			$ 560,200
					(102,000)
20,400	11,400				106,650
5,200	3,200		49,000	86,900	391,150
3,300	3,200		16,900	15,800	185,650
3,300	3,800		42,300	28,500	306,050
6,300			16,800	15,800	93,060
1,600					45,700
6,900					190,180
					8,100
700					162,860
					2,012,400
—0—	—0—	—0—	—0—	—0—	$3,960,000
Time-Weighted Item	Document	No Transfer Unit Required Entire Cost Center Transferred	Time-Weighted Inquiry	Man-hour	
5,000,000	6,580,000		250,000	8,000	
$.04	$0.02		$.50	$18.37	

Figure 10.4—Direct Allocation of Costs to Benefit-Receiving Units

	Annual Costs I	Occupancy II	Communications III
Benefit-Providing Units			
Occupancy	$ 150,000	$(150,000)	
Communications	57,600	900	$(58,500)
Administration	447,200	34,000	18,000
Data Center	192,400	7,700	5,200
Tellers (Universal)	136,800	42,400	4,100
Proof and Transit	131,600	7,000	1,300
Bookkeeping	63,600	5,800	1,000
Credit Files	125,000	10,000	5,000
Credit Analysis	147,000	7,000	7,000
Benefit-Receiving Units			
Demand Deposits—Regular Checking:			
Cost $ 32,400			
Less Service Charge Revenue (72,000)			
Net	(39,600)		
Demand Deposits—Special Checking:			
Cost $ 7,000			
Less Service Charge Revenue (30,000)			
Net	(23,000)		
Other Demand Deposits	3,000		
Regular Savings	25,000		
Club Savings	1,000		
Certificates of Deposit	4,000		
Commercial Loans	105,600	6,800	2,600
Real Estate Loans	50,000	5,000	3,000
Instalment Loans	110,000	6,000	2,000
Credit Card	38,400	2,000	3,000
Investments	34,000		600
Trust	72,000	15,400	5,700
Cost of Capital			
General Overhead	116,000		
Interest	2,012,400		
Total	$3,960,000	—0—	—0—

Transfer Units	Square Foot	Toll Charges and Number of Instruments
Number of transfer units	36,800	Various
Average unit transfer cost	$4.09	Various

Administration IV	Allocation Data Center V	Tellers VI	Proof and Transit VII	Bookkeeping VIII	Credit Files IX	Credit Analysis X	Total Cost of Benefit-Receiving Units (Including Allocation From Benefit-Providing Units) XI
$(499,200)							
13,000	$(219,200)						
5,000		$(188,300)					
5,000	25,800		$(170,700)				
	13,900			$(83,400)			
8,000					$(148,000)		
25,000						$(186,000)	
51,400	99,000	115,300	124,800	60,000			$ 410,900
	36,700	10,000	17,900	23,400			65,000
1,000							4,000
10,000	19,200	29,400	14,800				98,400
		600	200				1,800
500							4,500
100,000	4,800	8,000	4,000		58,000	110,000	399,800
60,000	3,000	12,000	5,000		20,000	20,000	178,000
76,600	3,000	13,000	4,000		50,000	36,000	300,600
3,900	6,000				20,000	20,000	93,300
10,000	1,500						46,100
80,900	6,600						180,600
8,000							8,000
40,000	600						156,600
							2,012,400
—0—	—0—	—0—	—0—	—0—	—0—	—0—	$3,960,000

Man-Hour	Time-Weighted Item	Man-Hour	Document	Time-Weighted Item	Time-Weighted Inquiry	Man-Hour
20,000	5,000,000	21,697	6,580,000	7,000,000	250,000	8,000
$24.96	$.04	$8.706	$.0259	$.01191	$.59	$23.25

Figure 10.5—Step Allocation of Costs to Benefit-Receiving Units

Allocation Method	Advantages	Disadvantages
Direct allocation method	Simplicity, shows cause and effect more plainly, better for control purposes	May not reflect realistic allocation of benefit-providing units when such costs as occupancy and administration are a material part of the cost of other benefit-providing units
Step allocation method	More precise than direct allocation, best used to compute the noninterest cost of funds on an occasional basis	Cumbersome—to some extent obscures cause-and-effect relationships
Reciprocal allocation method	A refinement of step allocation, best suited to purposes other than planning and control, such as cost reimbursement, tax computation, or legal proceedings	Complex—obscures cause-and-effect relationships, generally not applicable to banking purposes

Figure 10.6—Comparison of Allocation Methods

Reciprocal Allocation Method

It is possible to have units that render substantial services to each other. The larger the bank and the more complex the organizational structure, the more frequently this will occur. For example, if the commercial loan function is divided into regional subfunctions, it is quite likely that these subfunctions will assist each other in developing customer relationships. Under some circumstances, there may be a desire to reflect reciprocal cost relationship between units, and there are several methods that can be used. Each of them involves multiple close-out allocations of costs of benefit-providing units to benefit-receiving units. Principal methods are:

1. *Trial and error.* This method applies allocation factors to reciprocal cost center costs and repeats the close-out procedure until the last trial produces an insignificant change in results from the previous trial.

2. *Continued distribution.* This method applies successive distributions of the amounts allocated to the reciprocal centers until the change is negligible.

3. *Simultaneous equations.*

4. *Matrix algebra.*

The use of these methods does not appear to be appropriate for planning and control purposes because they tend to obscure cause-and-effect relationships, and therefore they will not be treated further. However, they can be useful when costing is being done for other purposes, such as the preparation of legal defenses, cost reimbursement, etc. They are more fully described in the *Accountants' Cost Handbook.*[1]

A summary comparison of the three allocation methods discussed in this chapter is presented in Figure 10.6.

UNIT TRANSFER COST CALCULATION

Figures 10.4 and 10.5 show completed cost calculations that were made using average unit transfer costs that were in turn used to transfer the costs. Average unit transfer costs reflect the allocation as an average cost per unit of the allocation basis. That is, the cost center cost is expressed as dollars per unit of activity (man-hour, transaction, square foot, etc.).

In Figures 10.4 and 10.5 the average unit transfer costs were calculated and used to transfer costs as part of a historical cost allocation carried out at a particular point in time. These average unit transfer costs also can be used to allocate costs recurringly in future periods as the actual activity of the costing object becomes available. A typical example of this use of average unit transfer costs would be the allocation of teller costs to a profit center each month for management reporting purposes. Since the number of transfer units handled by the teller is only determinable as it occurs, allocation using average unit

---

[1] Robert I. Dickey (ed.), *Accountants' Cost Handbook,* 2nd ed., New York: The Ronald Press Company, 1967, p. 8.31.

transfer cost is held in suspension awaiting determination of activity (Figure 10.7).

Average unit transfer costs used in this way are predetermined costs in that the cost is calculated for future use. Standard costs, which will be discussed in Chapter 15, are another type of predetermined cost. In using any predetermined cost, it is important to review the underlying calculation to be certain that the costing decisions are in keeping with the immediate purpose for which the cost is being used. When using average unit transfer costs as predetermined costs, it is especially important that their original calculation is based on a period of sufficient duration to eliminate the effects of short-term fluctuations in volume and activity mix.

The calculation of average unit transfer cost to allocate costs of the teller function is illustrated in Figure 10.8. In Figure 10.5 the allocation of annual teller expense of $188,300 is shown using a man-hour as the transfer unit and the applicable rate of $8.706 per hour. However, to meet the needs of future allocations and to provide management with unit costs that reflect specific teller activities, average unit transfer costs are calculated in Figure 10.8 for each of the basic activity units. This calculation is done by dividing the dollar amount applicable to the activity by the total number of activity units. The resulting average unit transfer costs can be used for subsequent allocations and other cost calculations such as handling a demand deposit account.

UNIT TRANSFER PRICE

A special type of allocation is carried out through the use of transfer pricing. Whereas average unit transfer costs are developed in order to allocate cost of services to benefiting departments, transfer pricing not only results in the allocation of those costs but it can also provide an element of profit for the benefit-providing unit.

Transfer pricing might be used where a bank organization is structured by profit center and services are performed for the various profit centers within the bank as well as for outside customers. A data processing facility that provides services to the public and also performs record-keeping services for other bank units is one example. The investment analysis group within the trust department is another.

When developing transfer prices, the size of the permissible profit element in the transfer price is a matter that must be decided on at the top management level in order to maintain an equitable relationship

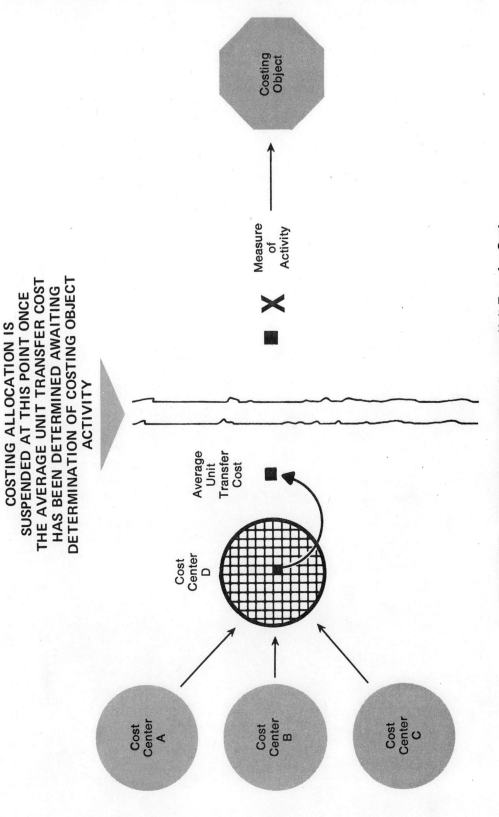

COSTING ALLOCATION IS
SUSPENDED AT THIS POINT ONCE
THE AVERAGE UNIT TRANSFER COST
HAS BEEN DETERMINED AWAITING
DETERMINATION OF COSTING OBJECT
ACTIVITY

Costing
Object

Measure
of
Activity

Average
Unit
Transfer
Cost

Cost
Center
D

Cost
Center
A

Cost
Center
B

Cost
Center
C

Figure 10.7—Suspended Allocation: Average Unit Transfer Cost

Computation of Average Unit Transfer Costs for Teller Function

	Four-Week Distribution of Time[1]	Percentage	Annual Amount Allocated	Annual Number of Activity Units[2]	Average Unit Transfer Cost
Receive Demand Deposits:					
Checks only	113	6.8%	$ 12,800	232,700	$ .055 per deposit
Cash only	121	7.2	13,600	169,780	.080 per deposit
Checks and cash	153	9.2	17,300	141,700	.122 per deposit
Cash returned	227	13.6	25,600	246,480	.104 per deposit
Deposit average	614	36.8	69,300	790,660	.088 per deposit
Checks Cashed	329	19.7	37,100	651,300	.057 per check cashed
Other Demand Deposit Transactions	167	10.0	18,900	2,171	8.706 per man-hour
Savings Deposits Received	158	9.5	17,900	139,737	.128 per savings deposit
Savings Withdrawal	107	6.4	12,100	47,307	.256 per savings withdrawal
Commercial Loan Payments	72	4.3	8,000	81,159	.098 per commercial loan payment
Real Estate Loan Payments	107	6.4	12,000	120,588	.100 per real estate loan payment
Instalment Loan Payments	115	6.9	13,000	129,610	.100 per instalment loan payment
Total	1,669	100.0%	$188,300	All activity	8.706 per man-hour

[1]Hours from Figure 10.3
[2]Based on counts in Figure 10.3 (Four week count x 13 periods)

Figure 10.8—Calculation of Average Unit Transfer Cost

among the bank units. The selected final "price" can be based on cost, cost plus profit, an external market price, or an arbitrary rate.

Although transfer pricing may have some applicability to banks, it can be difficult to use effectively unless there are clear lines of demarcation between "selling" and "buying" units. Further, the difficulty in setting a "price" that all parties can accept as equitable places limits on its usefulness.

SUMMARY

Allocation is the heart of the costing process, and it raises more difficult technical problems than all the other costing steps combined. The determination of the allocation basis, transfer unit, allocation method, and average unit transfer cost can under some circumstances be difficult or highly judgmental. Therefore, it is important that they be carried out thoughtfully and carefully.

Each manager using cost information should also realize the difficulties inherent in the allocation process. An appreciation of the process can help him evaluate the cost information he receives and assist in its use. In particular, he should not be deluded into thinking that the refinement of cost amounts that may be required necessarily represents ultimate precision. There are no "true" costs, but rather costs that are representative of benefits received, and they have been assembled to form a basis for a particular type of decision.

11

ALLOCATING
THE COST OF FUNDS

The activities of a bank that have to do with deposits, loans, and investments (i.e., its deposit functions, lending functions, and investment functions) are customarily described as "banking operations." This distinguishes them from such "nonbanking operations" as trust activities. Although the exact proportion of the total activities that is represented by these banking operations will vary from one bank to another, it will always be high. In many cases it will represent almost the entire activity of the bank.

Predominant in the total costs of banking operations are the costs of interest and operating activities connected directly with deposits (e.g., teller costs and bookkeeping costs). These costs are frequently called collectively the "cost of funds."

A survey published in 1970 by the Federal Reserve System indicated that for 240 banks having deposits of between $50 million and $200 million the average "cost of funds," as defined above, would account for almost 80% (78.1%) of annual "banking" costs (i.e., of the costs of banking operations). This would include roughly 50% (49.2%) for interest and 30% (28.9%) for operating costs. The remaining "banking" costs would be portfolio expense (19.3%) and unallocated general and administrative costs (2.6%). These figures break down as follows[1]:

[1] Federal Reserve System. *1969 Functional Cost Analysis for 11 Federal Reserve Districts.*

**Average
Annual Banking Cost**
(For 240 banks with deposits of $50,000,000-$200,000,000)

		Percent of Total
1. Noninterest cost		
Demand deposits	$1,027,887	23.2%
Time deposits	254,716	5.7
Total Noninterest Cost	1,282,603	28.9
2. Interest cost	2,182,023	49.2
Total Cost of Funds	3,464,626	78.1
3. Portfolio expense	858,150	19.3
4. Unallocated costs		
(general and administrative)	115,305	2.6
Total	$4,438,081	100.0%

In allocating the cost of funds, however, it is necessary also to take into account other funds (not just deposits) and their costs. These funds include, for example, capital, other bank liabilities, and Federal Reserve funds purchased. Thus, the total cost of funds to be allocated is even greater than the total cost of funds for deposits.

Apart from the fact that the cost of funds is important because of the percentage it represents of banking costs, it is essential to review the procedures to be followed in its allocation because those procedures are more difficult than the ones applied in allocating other bank costs. This is true because of the special complexities involved in attempting to trace the flow of benefits of particular funds (and therefore of their associated costs) to the loaning or investing functions that receive the benefits.

FUNDS MANAGEMENT

Because of this difficulty in tracing the flow of funds, it is necessary to make assumptions as to flow for purposes of costing. The method selected for allocating the cost of funds is heavily influenced, though not necessarily restricted, by the philosophy that guides a bank in managing its funds—which may be called its "funds management philosophy."

In managing its funds a bank must necessarily be guided by the fact that "banking operations" tend to produce narrow profit margins.

As a result, the bank must carefully manage the uses it makes of its funds (i.e., loans and investments) and its sources of funds (i.e., deposits, capital, etc.). It also must weigh several factors:

- The nature and amount of costs and revenues associated both with obtaining funds and with using them.

- Laws and regulations that establish reserve requirements and those that also influence lending practices and investment policies.

- Risks involved both in lending and in investing.

- "Volatility" of the funds that are available to the bank for investment. One of the indicators of volatility is the turnover of funds. Turnover is the number of times the average daily deposit balance can be divided into the total deposit flow coming into the bank in a period.

- "Liquidity" of the loans and investments for which funds are used. Liquidity is a measure of the ability of the bank to convert its loans and investments into cash both quickly and without loss.

Of these factors, volatility and liquidity are considered prime determinants of the flow of funds.

Fund Volatility/Liquidity

In weighing the factor of "volatility," banks will rank funds according to the length of time they expect to have them at their disposal. Those likely to be withdrawn in a short period of time are considered the most volatile, and those likely to remain the longest time the least volatile. For example, fund types can be ranked according to volatility as follows:

Most Volatile ⟶ Federal Reserve funds purchased
Tax receipt demand deposits
Payroll account demand deposits
Regular demand deposits
Certificates of deposit
Savings deposits
Capital funds ⟵ Least Volatile

In weighing the "liquidity" factor, a bank might rank its loans and investments as follows:

Most Liquid ——▶ Federal Reserve funds sold
U. S. Treasury Bills
Municipal bonds
Demand loans
Term loans
Instalment loans
Real estate loans ◀—— Least Liquid

The bank manager may think of his deposits (which are liabilities) and capital in terms of strata of volatility. His loans and investments (which are assets) might be thought of in terms of corresponding strata of liquidity. For purpose of this discussion, three strata of volatility will be used—high volatility, medium volatility, and low volatility.

Stratification of deposits, capital, and loans and investments by degree of volatility and liquidity provides an effective way to view funds management. Banks have frequently determined the low volatility stratum from trend lines developed in the familiar form of the graph shown in Figure 11.1. In this example, the low volatility stratum is defined as that amount of funds below a trend line charted against the monthly averages of deposits; the trend line is drawn to approximately equal the lowest deposit amounts. The definitions of medium and high volatility strata are not clear using this method. The definition of the most liquid (high liquidity) stratum is also familiar to funds managers, but the low and medium liquidity strata are perhaps vague. In order to describe the three strata used in this discussion, deposits and capital will be classified according to their turnover; loans and investments according to their maturity.

Volatility. The turnover guidelines are as follows:

High volatility—That portion of a deposit account or aggregate of accounts that is expected to flow in and out of the bank within approximately ten days. Deposits in this group include for example, a payroll imprest account, the noncompensating portion of a deposit account of a heavy borrower, and an escrow deposit nearing the time the money is to be withdrawn for its escrow purposes, etc. Turnover —six times a month (assuming deposits are available for an average of five days).

Medium volatility—That portion of a deposit account or aggregate of accounts that is expected to be retained less than a year but more than a short period of approximately ten days. Turnover—two times

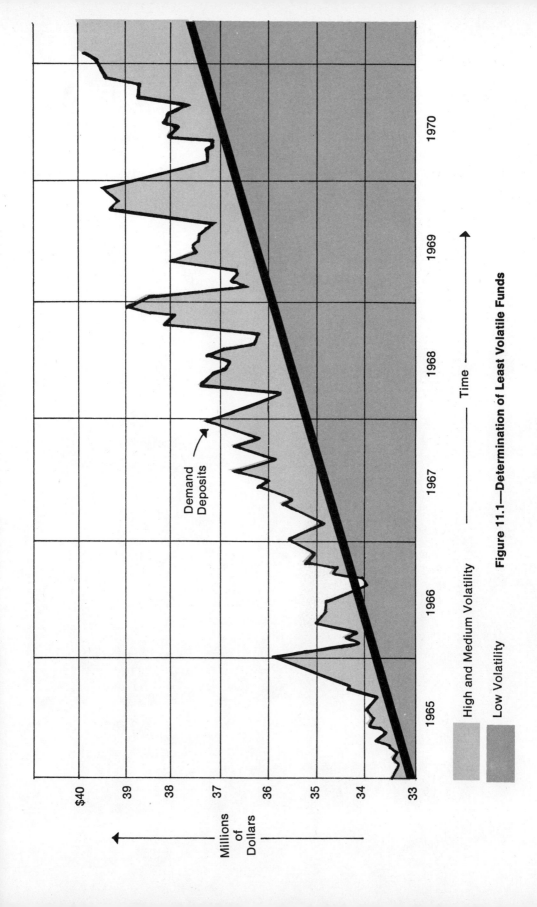

Figure 11.1—Determination of Least Volatile Funds

High and Medium Volatility

Low Volatility

a year (assuming deposits are available for an average of six months).

Low volatility—That portion of a deposit account or aggregate of accounts that is expected to remain in the bank for a year or more. Capital and long-term liabilities also would be included in this group. Turnover—not more than once a year.

Liquidity. The maturity guidelines are as follows:

High liquidity—Those loans and investments that can be converted into cash quickly without loss. Loans and investments in this group include treasury bills and immediately maturing portions of loans.

Medium liquidity—Those loans and investments that are expected to mature within one year; except those in the high-liquidity category.

Low liquidity—Those loans and investments that are not expected to mature for at least a year. Loans and investments in this group include portions of loans maturing after one year.

There is a pool of funds (Figure 11.2) linked and related to loans and investments by corresponding strata of liquidity and volatility (high, medium, and low). A bank's objective would be to arrange the mix of its loans and investments over time periods so that the amount falling into one stratum of liquidity (e.g., those that are least liquid) will be approximately the same as the amount of deposits and capital falling into the corresponding stratum of volatility (i.e., those that are least volatile). For example, those funds that are most likely to be withdrawn quickly (most volatile) would then, theoretically, have fund uses that can be converted quickly to cash (most liquid) in order to meet the withdrawal requirements as they arise.

In making the adjustments to his mix, the funds manager is affected by changes that occur in the money markets, customer demands, and the availability of funds. He must measure the character and extent of these changes in order to make compensatory adjustments in the mix of his loans and investments as quickly as possible, doing so with an eye not only to profitability but to good customer relations. Changes occur frequently in the money markets and funds managers are obliged to make their adjustments within short periods of time. The consideration of profitability gives rise to a necessity for considering funds costs.

There are two primary approaches to the problem of allocating the cost of funds to fund uses. The first of these, which is called the

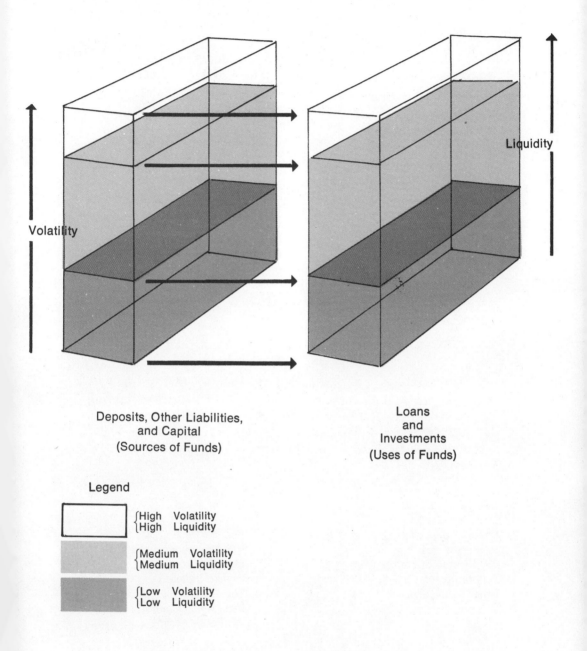

Volatility

Liquidity

Deposits, Other Liabilities,
and Capital
(Sources of Funds)

Loans
and
Investments
(Uses of Funds)

Legend

{High   Volatility
{High   Liquidity

{Medium   Volatility
{Medium   Liquidity

{Low   Volatility
{Low   Liquidity

Figure 11.2—Funds Management—A Matching Process

"specific method" (or, alternatively, the "multiple pool method"), recognizes the volatility of fund sources and the liquidity of fund uses by designating portions of each category of fund sources as being available for certain specified categories of loans and investments.

Because it is quite difficult to accurately designate specific funds sources used for specific categories of loans and investments, some bankers prefer to assume that all funds, regardless of their source, come from a common pool. When this approach is taken, the method for allocating the cost of funds to uses is referred to as the single pool method.

Each of these methods compiles fund costs in cost centers (referred to in this discussion as "pools") for subsequent allocation to fund uses. Some of these costs are being transferred to these pools from cost centers previously compiled.

Because of its simplicity, the single pool method will be discussed in detail first, and the more complex specific method next. A third method, the market-oriented method, which has distinctive features, will be treated at the conclusion of this chapter.

SINGLE POOL METHOD FOR ALLOCATING THE COST OF FUNDS

When the single pool method for allocating the cost of funds is used, it is assumed that funds from all sources are placed into a common pool to be loaned or invested. Figure 11.3 shows the way in which the sources of funds make up a single pool from which funds flow to uses. The sources and uses of funds shown in the Figure are as follows:

Sources of Funds	Use of Funds
Demand deposits	Federal Reserve funds sold
Savings deposits	U.S. Treasury securities
Certificates of deposit	Municipal bonds
Federal Reserve funds purchased	Demand loans
Other liabilities and capital	Term loans
	Instalment loans
	Real estate loans

The procedure by which the cost of funds is calculated using the single pool method is shown in Figure 11.4. The following sources of funds are identified and captioned:

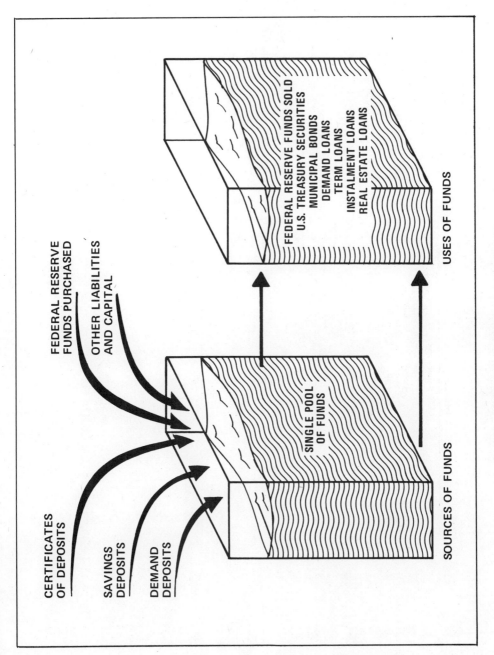

CERTIFICATES
OF DEPOSITS

SAVINGS
DEPOSITS

DEMAND
DEPOSITS

FEDERAL RESERVE
FUNDS PURCHASED

OTHER LIABILITIES
AND CAPITAL

SINGLE POOL
OF FUNDS

SOURCES OF FUNDS

FEDERAL RESERVE FUNDS SOLD
U.S. TREASURY SECURITIES
MUNICIPAL BONDS
DEMAND LOANS
TERM LOANS
INSTALMENT LOANS
REAL ESTATE LOANS

USES OF FUNDS

Figure 11.3—Single Pool Costing Concept

| | Investable Funds | | | | | Cost of Funds | | | |
| | | Less: Deductions | | | | | | | |
Source of Funds	Average Balance[1] I	Float II	Legal Reserves III	Premises and Other Assets IV	Investable Funds V	Non Interest Cost[2] VI	Interest[3] VII	Total Cost of Funds VIII	Annual Cost Rate of Investable Funds IX
1. Demand deposits									
a. Regular demand deposits	$ 33,826,000	$2,368,000	$5,506,000		$25,952,000	$410,900		$ 410,900	1.58%
b. Special demand deposits	3,869,000	271,000	630,000		2,968,000	65,000		65,000	2.19
c. Other demand deposits	521,000	36,000	85,000		400,000	4,000		4,000	1.00
Total demand deposits	38,216,000	2,675,000	6,221,000		29,320,000	479,900		479,900	1.64
2. Regular savings	38,684,000		1,161,000		37,523,000	98,400	$1,291,400	1,389,800	3.70
3. Club savings	825,000		25,000		800,000	1,800		1,800	.23
4. Certificates of deposit	7,337,000		440,000		6,897,000	4,500	350,000	354,500	5.14
5. Federal Reserve funds purchased	5,000,000				5,000,000		371,000	371,000	7.42
6. Other liabilities and capital	11,061,000			$3,061,000	8,000,000	8,000		8,000	.10
	$101,123,000	$2,675,000	$7,847,000	$3,061,000	$87,540,000	$592,600	$2,012,400	$2,605,000	2.98% (single pool average cost of funds)

[1]See Figure B.8
[2]See Figure 10.5
[3]See Figure B.9

Figure 11.4—Illustration of the Cost of Funds Calculation for the Single Pool Method of Allocation

1. Demand deposits
   a. Regular demand deposits
   b. Special demand deposits
   c. Other demand deposits
2. Regular savings
3. Club savings
4. Certificates of deposit
5. Federal Reserve funds purchased
6. Other liabilities and capital

Columns I through V demonstrate the way in which "investable funds" (i.e., funds available for lending or investment) are determined for each category of fund source. The point of departure for this process is the average balance for each type of source, as shown in Column I. When the cost calculation is made, it is essential to exercise care in developing this average daily deposit balance for a period. It would ideally represent an averaging of amounts for each of the liability classes that appear on daily statements of condition for a period of time sufficiently long to represent all possible cyclical variations. As an alternative, selected statements for certain representative days of the month can be used to calculate an average. In doing so, care should be taken to choose days from differing periods of cyclical variation so as to minimize possible distortions.

In Figure 11.4, Column I was derived from the statement of condition that appears as Figure B.8 of Appendix B. While any one statement of condition would not be adequate for the purposes of cost calculation, it is to be assumed for purposes of this discussion that the statement of condition contained in Figure B.8 (and the amounts used in Column I of Figure 11.4) does represent properly averaged liability amounts drawn from an adequate selection of daily statements of condition.

Columns II, III, and IV then proceed to show the deductions that must be made from fund classes in order to arrive at investable funds in Column V. These deductions include investment in premises and other assets in the case of other liabilities and capital, and float (uncollected funds) in the case of demand deposits. Float for savings deposits, normally not material, has not been recognized in the illustration.

Column VI represents the noninterest costs associated with each category of liability taken from the amounts in Figure 10.5, whereas Column VII shows the interest costs (for regular savings, certificates of deposit, and Federal Reserve funds purchased) that are contained (in total only) in Figure B.9 of Appendix B. Costs are totaled in Column VIII, which represents the total cost of funds for each category of funds.

The annual cost rate for each category of investable funds is then developed as a percentage by dividing Column VIII (total cost of funds) by Column V (investable funds). Thus, for regular demand deposits, the annual cost rate is 1.58%, while for special demand deposits it is 2.19%, etc.

The rates shown here serve to illustrate the range of cost rates to be averaged in determining the single pool average rate. Viewing all the funds as a single pool, this rate is developed simply by dividing the total of Column VIII (total cost of funds) by the total of Column V (investable funds) to arrive at a percentage. Thus, total cost of funds of $2,605,000 divided by total investable funds of $87,540,000 yields an average rate for cost of funds of 2.98%. This rate would then be used to calculate the costs to be allocated to all fund uses.

SPECIFIC METHOD FOR ALLOCATING THE COST OF FUNDS

It was noted earlier that the specific method takes into consideration the volatility of fund sources and the liquidity of fund uses. It must be pointed out, however, that most bankers regard this method as being academic in character and too abstract to be of any practical application. There may be situations, however, in which it could be useful, one possible example being the need to prepare a legal defense for a pricing policy.

The use of the specific method requires the designation of all or portions of each category of funds as being available for certain designated categories of loans or investments. In making these designations, management attempts to classify categories as closely as it can according to their volatility (for deposits, capital, etc.) and their liquidity (for loans and investments). Obviously, funds that can be considered available for extended periods pair most naturally with loans and investments covering extended periods. By the same token, funds on hand for short periods pair with funds loaned or invested for short periods. In applying this approach, therefore, a bank would tend to match slow turnover funds such as savings deposits (low volatility) with loans of long-term maturity (low liquidity). Conversely, it would match funds available from demand deposits (high volatility) with short-term loans and short-term investments (both of high liquidity).

Matching of fund sources to uses can be assumed to occur when:

- Each dollar of fund source is specifically designated for a particular loan or investment use.
- Each category of fund source (regular demand deposits, regular savings deposits, etc.) is designated for a category of loan or investment (demand loans, term loans, etc.).

Although the first concept (that of matching each dollar of funds with uses) may appear simple, it would be difficult to apply in practical operations without determining the volatility and liquidity characteristics of each deposit and loan account. The sheer number of accounts would make this difficult to do. Federal Reserve statistics show, for example, that those banks mentioned at the outset of this chapter (240 banks having deposits ranging from $50 million to $200 million) might average over 18,000 demand deposit accounts, 19,000 regular savings accounts, and over 12,000 loan accounts.

As to the second way of matching funds with uses, the constantly changing amounts of each category of fund source and use create extreme difficulties in applying a cost rate to each use. Further, this kind of matching does not recognize the volatility characteristics, which may vary substantially, for each category of fund source.

To simplify the task of matching fund sources with uses, management may use the multiple pool method (a variation of the specific method) described below.

MULTIPLE POOL METHOD FOR ALLOCATING THE COST OF FUNDS

Figure 11.5 demonstrates that in using the multiple pool method, management first recognizes that even within one class of funds (such as demand deposits or savings deposits) there are necessarily gradations as to volatility. Some demand deposits, for example, are extremely volatile, others are not. Although most savings deposits are of low volatility, some can be considered highly volatile.

Having thus identified the strata applicable to the sources of funds and the uses of funds, management is now in a position to relate the two in terms of overall amounts. Thus, the least volatile strata of each class of funds, once joined together, would constitute the pool of funds from which long-term loans would be made. In other words, each volatility level of the sources of funds becomes a general lending pool from which funds flow to a corresponding level of liquidity for loan and investment. The pool of least volatility would become the

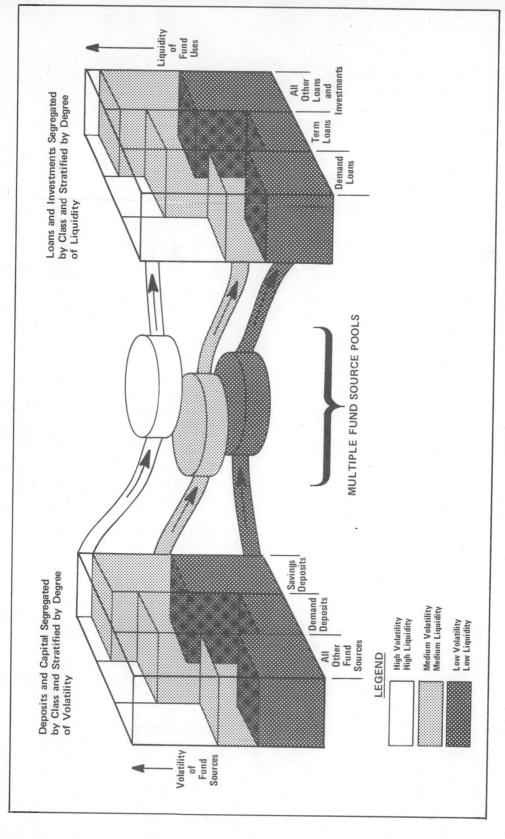

Liquidity of Fund Uses

Loans and Investments Segregated by Class and Stratified by Degree of Liquidity

All Other Loans and Investments

Term Loans

Demand Loans

MULTIPLE FUND SOURCE POOLS

Deposits and Capital Segregated by Class and Stratified by Degree of Volatility

Savings Deposits

Demand Deposits

All Other Fund Sources

Volatility of Fund Sources

LEGEND

High Volatility High Liquidity

Medium Volatility Medium Liquidity

Low Volatility Low Liquidity

Figure 11.5—Multiple Pool Costing Concept

source from which funds would flow to loans and investments of least liquidity.

Naturally the principle of matching volatility with liquidity cannot be followed strictly in cases where the supply of funds of low volatility is greater than the corresponding level of low liquidity uses to which they would normally flow (i.e., when the demand at that level is lower than the available supply of funds). Since the basic objective of the bank continues to be to keep all funds working and creating revenue, an excess of low volatility funds would simply be applied to purposes of higher liquidity than would normally be the case.

In separating funds into levels of volatility, it becomes important to calculate the costs of the funds at these levels rather than in terms of the classes of funds from which they originated. In doing so, the first decision to be made is the number of volatility levels to be recognized, and the second decision is how to distribute each class of funds among these levels. Figure 11.6 illustrates this process of distribution, using the same classes of funds that were shown in Figure 11.4 with the exception that regular demand deposits, special demand deposits, and other demand deposits have been joined together as one figure.

In the case illustrated management chose to recognize three levels of volatility for funds and decided that the amounts of each class of funds at its disposal should be apportioned to volatility levels as follows:

Class	Fund Percentages Assigned to Levels of Volatility		
	Low	Medium	High
Demand deposits	20	40	40
Regular savings	30	40	30
Club savings	—	100	—
Certificates of deposit	—	100	—
Federal Reserve funds purchased	—	—	100
Other liabilities and capital	97	—	3

In deciding how to distribute fund classes among volatility levels, a bank must draw not only on its specific knowledge of each class but also on its own assessments of the economy in general and of the particular business community with which it deals.

Having distributed fund classes to volatility levels, it is a simple task to determine the cost of funds rate for each pool. For example, the investable funds for regular savings amount to $37,523,000 (Columns I

Investable Funds (Figure 11.4) | **Low Volatility Pool** | **Medium Volatility Pool** | **High Volatility Pool**

Source of Funds	Amount I	Cost II	Percent Apportioned III	Amount IV	Cost V	Percent Apportioned VI	Amount VII	Cost VIII	Percent Apportioned IX	Amount X	Cost XI
1. Demand deposits (regular & special)	$29,320,000	$ 479,900	20%	$ 5,864,000	$ 95,980	40%	$11,728,000	$ 191,960	40%	$11,728,000	$ 191,960
2. Regular savings	37,523,000	1,389,800	30	11,256,900	416,940	40	15,009,200	555,920	30	11,256,900	416,940
3. Club savings	800,000	1,800				100	800,000	1,800			
4. Certificates of deposit	6,897,000	354,500				100	6,897,000	354,500			
5. Federal Reserve funds purchased	5,000,000	371,000							100	5,000,000	371,000
6. Other liabilities and capital	8,000,000	8,000	97	7,721,000	7,760				3	279,000	240
Total	$87,540,000	$2,605,000	28%	24,841,900	520,680	39%	34,434,200	1,104,180	33%	28,263,900	980,140
7. Cost rate of pool funds available		2.98%			2.10%			3.21%			3.47%
8. Fund transfers in (out)				(5,024,180)	(105,005)		5,024,180 (9,864,595)	105,005 (302,091)		9,864,595	302,091
9. Funds loaned or invested	$87,540,000	$2,605,000		$19,817,720	$415,675		$29,593,785	$ 907,094		$38,128,495	$1,282,231
10. Average cost of funds rates		2.98%			2.10%			3.07%			3.36%

Figure 11.6—Illustration of the Cost of Funds Calculation for the Multiple Pool Method of Allocation

through V, Figure 11.4), while their cost amounts to $1,389,800 (Columns VI through VIII), which represents a cost of funds rate of 3.70%. If 30% of regular savings is to be distributed to the pool of least volatility (Figure 11.6), then 30% of $37,523,000 (or $11,256,900) will be assigned as the fund amount (Column IV) and 30% of $1,389,800 (or $416,940) will be assigned as the cost (Column V).

Once the classes of funds have been distributed to volatility strata, the figures for each volatility pool (amount of funds and costs) can be totaled, and a rate for the cost of funds of each pool can be determined. When the total costs for the pool of medium volatility ($1,104,180) are divided by the total amount of investable funds ($34,434,200), the result is a pool average rate for cost of funds that is 3.21% (Figure 11.6). The rates would then be used to allocate the cost of funds to various fund uses in accordance with the loan and investment liquidity stratification.

As indicated above, it will naturally sometimes happen that the amounts of money in a given volatility pool will be greater than the normal uses for them. Thus, while the pool of low volatility might customarily be reserved for real estate loans, representing the lowest liquidity, the demand for these loans, nonetheless, might be lower than the amount available in the pool. Since the bank proposes to keep all its funds at work, the portion of funds in the pool of least volatility that cannot be applied to real estate loans (or other long-term uses) will be transferred to the next highest pool of volatility (i.e., the medium pool). Thus, in Figure 11.6 (Columns IV and V), the amount of $5,024,180, representing costs of $105,005, was transferred from the pool of low volatility to the medium pool, while an amount of $9,864,595, representing costs of $302,091, was transferred from that pool to the pool of high volatility.

When funds are transferred in this fashion, it becomes necessary to calculate a new pool rate for the pools affected by the transfers. In line 9, the transfers resulted in new totals for Columns IV, V, VII, VIII, X, and XI, resulting in a change of rate for the medium volatility pool from 3.21% to 3.07% and for the high volatility pool from 3.47% to 3.36%. The rate for the pool of low volatility remained at 2.10% because funds were transferred out of this pool but not into it. Recalculation of these percentages can be a complex procedure because of the constant change in the strata. This is one reason why the specific method and the related multiple pool method for calculating the cost of funds are used only in those situations where this type of precision is considered necessary.

MARKET-ORIENTED METHOD FOR
ALLOCATING THE COST OF FUNDS

For purposes of analyzing alternatives in the planning process, both the single and multiple pool methods for allocating the cost of funds can be used. Some bankers feel, however, that these methods have limited value in communicating plans and measuring results, principally because the rates reflect historical averages, and secondarily because the calculations are complex. Even though projected into the future at increased amounts, the rates may still not reflect the realities of the market place (i.e., substantially higher rates), particularly in a tight money market.

As a result, some bankers prefer to use the market-oriented method to determine the rate at which funds costs are to be charged to fund users. This method uses the current market rates (possibly based on treasury notes or certificates of deposit) to represent the cost of the funds used. (Note: these costs are determined external to the bank's accounting system and are likely to be quite different from those actually incurred.) This method also is referred to as the "incremental" method due to the assumption that the fund cost for a new loan is measured by the rate required to obtain new money in the market place. The cost for the new money is the added (incremental) cost for the added loan.

When management uses the market-oriented method, its philosophy is to motivate loan officers to lend funds at rates that will be profitable, assuming the funds were obtained on the open market. The market-oriented method is therefore used primarily to guide day-to-day decisions rather than for aiding in longer range strategy and planning decisions.

SUMMARY

Funds are one of three bank resources (funds, people, and facilities), but they differ from the other two in that the bank must expend a major portion of its energy and other resources in obtaining funds. Furthermore, funds constitute raw materials that quickly lose their source identity once they are obtained.

The major efforts and resources expended to obtain funds result in a considerable cost—one so substantial that it becomes critical to the meaningful analysis of fund use profitability. The fact that funds quickly lose their source identity means that tracing them to specific uses is difficult if not impossible.

The management of funds is a challenging task that, among other things, must give some recognition to the matching of fund volatility and loan and investment liquidity. These notions and an assumption as to how they either do occur or might occur gives rise to the methods used for allocating fund costs to fund uses.

Probably the most widely used method, due in part to its simplicity, is the single pool method that uses an average cost rate for all funds, including capital. The specific method, which closely follows a somewhat strict interpretation of volatility and liquidity, is impractical for most banking purposes. The multiple pool method is a more practical approach to recognizing volatility and liquidity, although it, too, may have limited usefulness due to the complexity, even at this simplified level, of stratifying funds and their uses and the resultant complexity of calculation.

The market-oriented method, in which a current market rate is used for costing funds, has the merit of simplicity and provides a strong profit motivation. It is, however, most effective when used for communicating plans and measuring results in situations where day-to-day decisions are given emphasis.

COST FOR PLANNING
AND CONTROL OF
PROFITABILITY

Bank Costs for Planning and Control

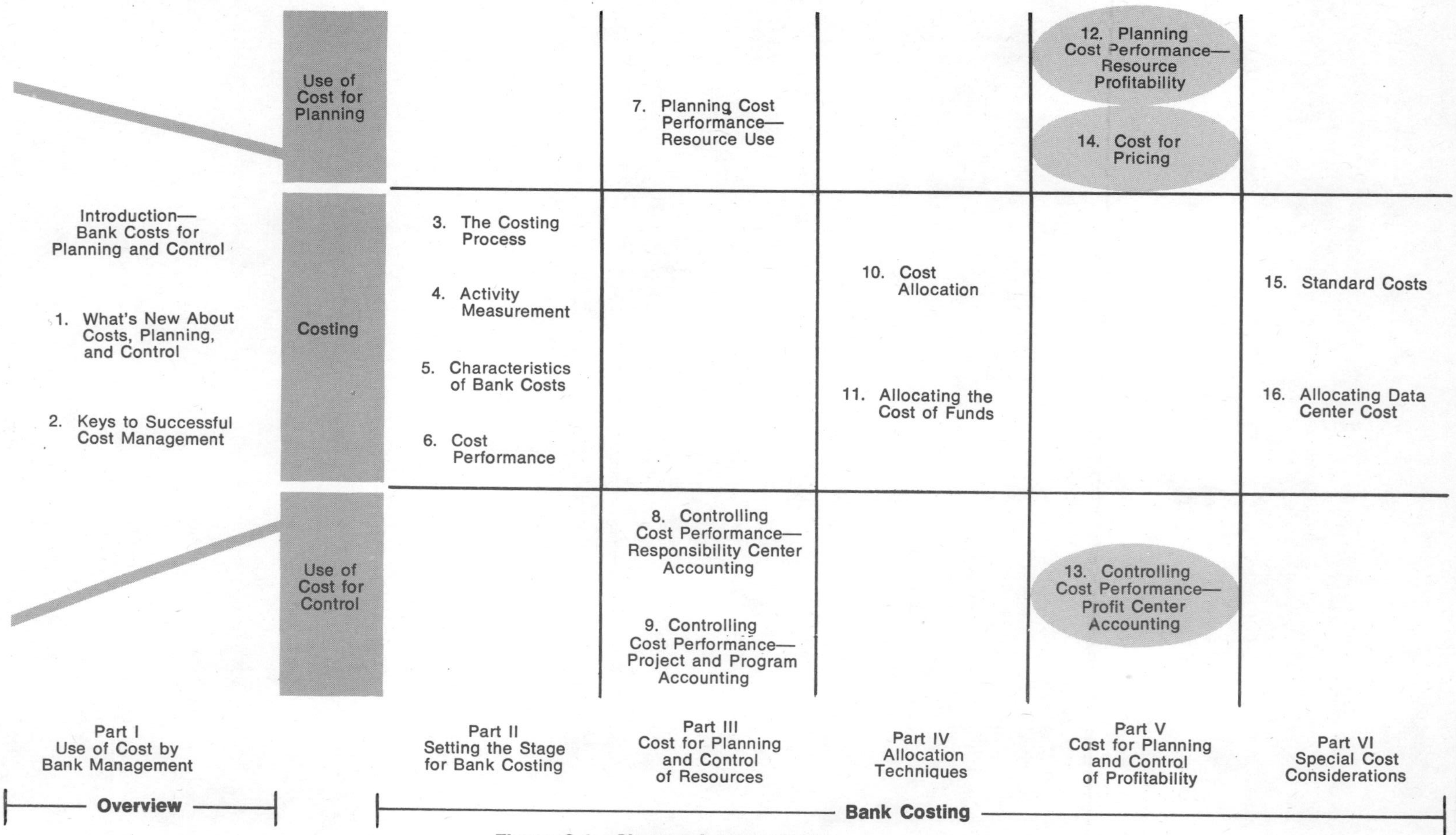

Figure 0.1—Chapter Arrangement

Part V

COST FOR PLANNING AND CONTROL OF PROFITABILITY

Cost performance, in terms of the profits resulting from the incurrence of costs, is probably management's most difficult planning and control problem. Profits often can be elusive and the "causes" are difficult to determine. Costing does not provide the answers to all questions that arise from profit analysis, but its use will permit a better understanding of the planning and control problems involved.

Chapter 12 addresses itself to a range of costing approaches to determining profitability for planning purposes with emphasis on the determination of profit under varying circumstances. Some measures of the quality of profits thus determined are discussed briefly to show how profit can be further evaluated.

With Chapter 12 as background, Chapter 13 discusses at some length the use of profit centers in order to provide organizational control over profit. The conditions that make the use of profit centers effective are discussed along with various approaches to costing for profit centers.

The section concludes with a discussion of costs for pricing. Although there are many considerations other than cost in determining prices, costs can play an effective role. Chapter 14 is built around the concept of "cost-visible pricing" and it approaches the discussion of costs from the point of view that cost visibility can improve management's understanding of the impact of particular pricing strategies.

12

PLANNING COST PERFORMANCE— RESOURCE PROFITABILITY

This chapter enlarges upon the theme of Chapter 7, namely, maximizing resource use and minimizing resource cost as management objectives. Resource profitability is introduced here as an additional and probably the most important objective in the bank's management of its resources.

Regardless of what the bank's other goals or accomplishments may be, it is the ability of the enterprise to make a profit over the long run that permits it to continue in existence. A bank's goals may be expressed in terms of community service, growth, and service to customers, but accomplishment of these goals is meaningless if they are not supported by profit. Profitability analysis is a means to measure the ability of any activity within the bank to contribute to the bank's total profit.

Any sphere of bank activity that may potentially produce a profit is a profit area. It may be any function, organizational unit, or grouping that can generate a revenue or have a revenue imputed to it. The list below shows the many forms profit areas may take:

- Organizational units
  - . . Divisions (e.g., banking, trust)
  - . . Departments (e.g., commercial loans, instalment loans, branches)
  - . . Sections

- Functions
  - . . Fund uses—loans and investments by
    - Type (e.g., commercial loans, instalment loans)
    - Industry
    - Location
    - Customer group
  - . . Fund sources—deposits by
    - Type (e.g., demand deposits, savings, C.D.'s)
    - Industry
    - Location
    - Customer group
  - . . Nonfund Activities
    - Trust
    - Safe deposit
    - EDP services
    - Travelers' checks
    - Bond sales

- Locations
- Industries
- Programs
- Customers, by
  - . . Individuals
  - . . Groups, by
    - Industry
    - Geography

This chapter will describe how profitability is calculated with respect to fund users, fund providers, branches, customers, and non fund activities. The calculation of profitability in these profit areas will require particular care in applying those portions of the costing process described in Chapters 10 and 11.

Management is always faced with the problem: Where can the bank's energy be best directed? In costing terms this problem translates into: What levels of resources shall be applied to the various possible activities of the bank? Each possible application actively competes for management's commitment of available resources. This competition can be seen when decisions are being made on advertising outlays, distribution of available funds, etc.

One way of deciding where resources should be used is to compare the relative profitability of various possible activities. This is a quantitative process. Profitability, once measured, can be subjected to tests of quality: return on assets employed, return on invested capital, and discounted cash flow. These techniques are introduced later in this chapter as a further application of the costing process.

QUANTITATIVE MEASURES OF PROFIT AREAS

In order to measure profitability, it is necessary to match revenues with costs. The costs used in a particular costing situation depend on the specific purpose the analysis is to serve. Several types of costs could be used:

- Directly related (costs related to those resources—funds, people, and facilities—used directly by the profit area) .
- Directly related and traceable costs (traceable refers to those costs incurred by benefit-providing units of the bank in behalf of the profit area being evaluated) .
- Added costs (incremental) .
- Costs reduced or eliminated.
- Fully absorbed costs (directly related costs, traceable costs, and a portion of the general administrative costs of the bank) .

From an overall standpoint, the bench mark against which each profit area should be measured is its ability to produce sufficient revenue to offset fully absorbed costs and provide a profit. There are situations, however, where management may wish to consider directly related or directly related and traceable costs to determine the ability of the profit area to offset those costs which are a result of its activity. There may be other situations where added or reduced costs may be required to determine the effect of any change in profit area activity.

This chapter discusses the costing of those profit areas that are of a fund-using and fund-providing nature as a preparatory step to the discussion of branch and customer profitability. It is in each of these types of profit areas that the profitability calculation unique to banks is encountered because of the necessity to allocate the cost of funds or credit for funds. For this reason, in each detailed case, illustrative examples of the use of the five costing steps are given. The profitability of those profit areas that do not use funds, of which trust is an example, is also discussed, but without detailed illustrations of the costing steps.

Fund-Using Profit Areas

An illustrative calculation of costs for several fund-using functions is shown in Figures 12.1 through 12.3. In determining these costs, the

Step 1. Define the Purpose

- Management wants to determine the emphasis that should be given to the various fund-using functions for the ensuing year.

- The criteria is their comparative profitability using directly related and traceable costs (general overhead costs not to be allocated).

Step 2. Define the Costing Object

- The costing objects are the fund-using functions as follows: commercial loans, real estate loans, instalment loans, credit card operation, other loans and investments.

- They are each made up of the following resources and services received from benefit-providing units:

    - • Invested funds, as follows[1]

Commercial loans	$35,935,000
Real estate loans	11,681,000
Instalment loans	19,299,000
Credit card operation	1,022,000
Other loans and investments (U.S. government securities, municipal and state securities and other)	19,603,000
Total invested funds	$87,540,000

    - • People (employees directly associated with the profit area).

    - • Facilities (space, equipment, and supplies used directly by the profit area).

    - • The resources of the following benefit-providing units to the extent they provide service to the particular profit area:

        Occupancy cost center
        Communication function
        Administrative function
        Data center
        Teller department
        Proof and transit department
        Credit files section
        Credit analysis section
        Bookkeeping department

    The relationships of resources and benefit-producing units to the profit area are shown in Figure 12.2 (illustrative only—there may be other relationships not shown).

[1]The assets shown in the Statement of Condition (Figure B.8) are shown here as if they were the average of 12-month-end balances.

Figure 12.1—Illustration of Calculating the Costs for Fund-Using Profit Areas

Step 3. Specify the Cost Data

Funds

Interest cost

Noninterest cost of funds; (all the costs of demand deposit—regular checking, demand deposit—special checking, other demand deposits, regular savings, club savings, certificates of deposit, capital)

Total cost of funds

People and Facilities

Costs for employees, equipment, space, etc. used directly by each fund-using profit area.

Total Allocated Cost of Benefit-Providing Units:

- Occupancy cost center
- Communication function
- Administrative function
- Data center
- Teller department
- Proof and transit department
- Credit files section
- Credit analysis section
- Bookkeeping department

Step 4. Specify the Allocation Process

Interest costs are to be accumulated through the general accounting system and then transferred to the cost of funds cost center. Noninterest cost of funds is to be accumulated through the general accounting system to which will be allocated costs of benefit-providing units using the step method.

Total cost of funds is to be determined as described above and allocated to the profit areas on the basis of dollars invested using the single pool method of allocation.

People and facility costs are to be allocated directly to the profit areas through the general accounting system.

Benefit-providing units are to have their own costs allocated directly to each through the general accounting system. These costs are then to be allocated to the profit areas using the step method of allocation.

Step 5. Calculate the Cost

See Figure 12.3 for cost calculation.

Figure 12.1 (Continued)

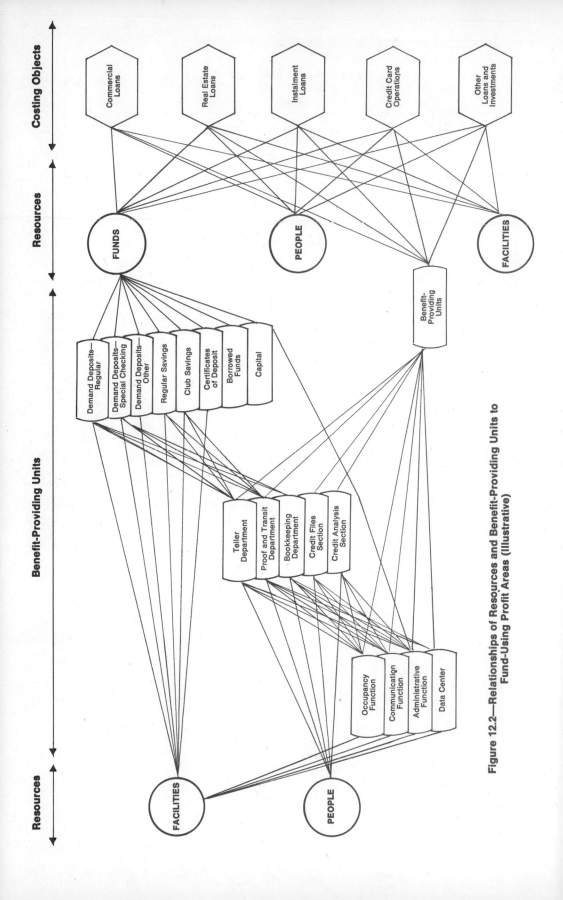

Costing Objects

Commercial Loans

Real Estate Loans

Instalment Loans

Credit Card Operations

Other Loans and Investments

Resources

FUNDS

PEOPLE

FACILITIES

Benefit-Providing Units

Demand Deposits—Regular

Demand Deposits—Special Checking

Demand Deposits—Other

Regular Savings

Club Savings

Certificates of Deposit

Borrowed Funds

Capital

Benefit-Providing Units

Teller Department

Proof and Transit Department

Bookkeeping Department

Credit Files Section

Credit Analysis Section

Occupancy Function

Communication Function

Administrative Function

Data Center

Resources

FACILITIES

PEOPLE

Figure 12.2—Relationships of Resources and Benefit-Providing Units to Fund-Using Profit Areas (Illustrative)

	Commercial Loans	Real Estate Loans	Instalment Loans	Credit Card	Other Loans and Investments
Cost of funds, 2.98% of funds invested, as listed in Step Two[1]	$1,065,000	$348,000	$575,000	$ 30,000	$587,000
Annual cost of people and facilities allocated directly to fund-using departments through general accounting system (Figure 10.5)	105,600	50,000	110,000	38,400	34,000
Allocated portion of costs of benefit-providing units (Figure 10.5)					
Occupancy cost center	6,800	5,000	6,000	2,000	
Communication function	2,600	3,000	2,000	3,000	600
Administrative function	100,000	60,000	76,600	3,900	10,000
Data center	4,800	3,000	3,000	6,000	1,500
Tellers department	8,000	12,000	13,000		
Proof and transit department	4,000	5,000	4,000		
Credit files section	58,000	20,000	50,000	20,000	
Credit analysis section	110,000	20,000	36,000	20,000	
Total costs of fund-using profit areas[2]	$1,464,800	$526,000	$875,600	$123,300	$633,100

[1]2.98% is the single pool average rate for cost of funds calculated in Figure 11.4.
[2]General overhead is not included because it cannot be allocated on other than an arbitrary basis and therefore management does not believe it would improve the usefulness of the cost information derived.

Figure 12.3—Costs of Fund-Using Profit Areas

step method of cost allocation and the single pool method of allocating cost of funds were used. Further, general overhead costs were not allocated. The costs used in the illustration build upon costs developed for illustrative purposes in Chapters 10 and 11. Finally, profitability of each profit area is determined in Figure 12.4 both in terms of amount and as a percent of invested funds. The following points should be noted as these figures are reviewed.

First, the methods used in allocating costs could make a significant difference in the results of the calculation. For example, the cost of funds allocation amounts to about 70% of the total costs of the profit areas. The single pool rate used is 2.98%. If a multiple pool method had been used (using the illustration shown in Figure 11.6), the rates for each profit area could have ranged from 2.10% to as high as 3.47%.

Further, the use of the step method rather than the direct method for allocating costs from benefit-providing units to the profit area can result in differences (again using our illustrations here) that range to over ten percent of the profit amount (see real estate loans, below) .

	Costs Before Allocation of Cost of Funds				
	Step Method	**Direct Method**	**Difference From Step Method**	**Profit (Loss) Amount (From Fig. 12.3)**	**Difference as a percent of Profit or Loss (Rounded)**
Commercial loans	$399,800	$391,150	$(8,650)	$385,200	2%
Real estate loans	178,000	185,650	7,650	54,000	14
Instalment loans	300,600	306,050	5,450	214,400	3
Credit card	93,300	93,060	(240)	(37,300)	1
Other loans and investments	46,100	45,700	(400)	100,900	0

It should be remembered that the step method more closely approximates the actual flow of costs than the direct method. Where the costing purpose requires a more precise calculation, the step method should be used.

When management uses the profit data calculated in Figure 12.4 in drawing conclusions concerning the emphasis to be given, it is important to keep in mind alternative costing that could be carried

	Interest Income	Fees	Revenue from All Sources	Cost	Profit (Loss) Amount	Rank
Commercial loans	$1,850,000		$1,850,000	$1,464,800	$385,200	1
Real estate loans	550,000	$30,000	580,000	526,000	54,000	4
Instalment loans	1,050,000	40,000	1,090,000	875,600	214,400	2
Credit card	78,000	8,000	86,000	123,300	(37,300)	5
Other loans and investments	724,000	10,000	734,000	633,100	100,900	3
Total	$4,252,000	$88,000	$4,340,000	$3,622,800	$717,200	

Profitability as Percent of Invested Funds

	Invested Funds	Interest Income	Revenue from All Sources	Cost	Profit (Loss) Percent	Rank
Commercial loans	$35,935,000	5.15%	5.15%	4.08%	1.07%	2
Real estate loans	11,681,000	4.71	4.96	4.50	.46	4
Instalment loans	19,299,000	5.44	5.65	4.54	1.11	1
Credit card	1,022,000	7.63	8.41	12.06	(3.65)	5
Other loans and investments	19,603,000	3.69	3.74	3.23	.51	3
Total	$87,540,000	4.86	4.96	4.14	.82	

Figure 12.4—Summary of Profitability of Fund-Using Profit Areas

out if the course of action to be taken is not clear. An additional alternative, of course, would be to allocate the general overhead costs to the profit areas. Other alternatives such as special promotions, etc. could be costed as well. Although a certain required amount of estimating and judgment is inherent in the costing process for fund-using profit areas (as with other profit areas), these costs can be effective in assisting with management decisions.

Fund-Providing Profit Areas

Profitability for planning encompasses the fund-providing functions as well as the fund-using functions. Banking efforts are directed to obtaining funds as well as to making loans. Sometimes, because of changes in the money market, the emphasis fluctuates between providing and using. Therefore, it is useful to have a technique to ascribe a profit to the deposit and other fund-providing areas. It is particularly useful when planning with respect to branches and customers, which are fund-providing as well as fund-using areas.

The approach used is called "200% allocation." This approach assigns loan and investment revenue to the deposit function, just as cost of funds is allocated to the lending function. Since loan and investment revenues are also assigned to the fund-using functions, the assignment to deposit functions results in assigning revenue twice, hence the term "200% allocation." This is no problem because we are interested in the profitability of a function at this point, and not the total bank. The doubling up of revenue assignment (or "allocation" if preferred) is similar to intercompany profit and would be eliminated in a bank-wide consolidated operating statement.

In computing the profitability of a fund-providing function, the cost problems are similar to the calculation of profitability for fund-using functions, except that revenues are allocated instead of costs. The expenses that have been considered up to this point as being a part of the cost of funds are now the costs of the fund-providing functions. Although there is service charge revenue earned directly by the deposit function, the greater part of bank revenue (interest) is derived from lending. This revenue is "imputed," or allocated, to the fund-providing functions in the same manner as the cost of funds was allocated to the fund-using functions. Service charges may be considered negative expense. The example used to illustrate the calculation of profitability for the fund-providing functions uses the same data as the fund-using example (Figures 12.1 through 12.4). The calculation of the cost is illustrated in Figures 12.5 through 12.7, and profit is calculated in Figure 12.8.

Step 1. Define the Purpose

- Management wants to know what fund-providing functions should be given priority in management effort.
- The criteria is their comparative profitability.

Step 2. Define the Costing Object

- The costing objects are the eight fund-providing functions: regular demand deposits, special demand deposits, other demand deposits, regular savings deposits, club saving deposits, certificates of deposit, borrowed funds, capital.
- They are composed of the following resources:
  - • Funds (obtained by the payment of interest for savings deposits, certificates of deposit and borrowed funds and by services to demand deposit customers).
  - • People and facilities directly associated with the fund-providing functions.
  - • The resources of the following benefit-providing units to the extent they provide services to depositors:
    - Occupancy cost center
    - Communication function
    - Administrative function
    - Data center
    - Teller department
    - Proof and transit department
    - Bookkeeping department

    The relationships of the resources and benefit-providing units to the fund-providing functions are shown in Figure 12.6.

Step 3. Specify Cost Data

Funds

Interest cost

People and Facilities

Costs of employees, space, equipment, etc. used directly by the fund-providing profit areas.

Total Allocated Costs from Benefit-Providing Units:

- Administrative function
- Data center
- Teller department
- Proof and transit department
- Bookkeeping department

Step 4. Specify the Allocation Process

Interest cost is to be accumulated through the general accounting system and segregated by analysis to savings deposits, certificates of deposit, and purchased funds.

People and facility costs are to be accumulated through the general accounting system by fund-providing profit area.

Costs from benefit-providing units are to be allocated to fund-providing profit areas using the step method of allocation.

Step 5. Calculate the Cost

See Figure 12.7 for calculation of cost for the fund-providing profit areas.

Figure 12.5—Calculating the Costs for Fund-Providing Profit Areas

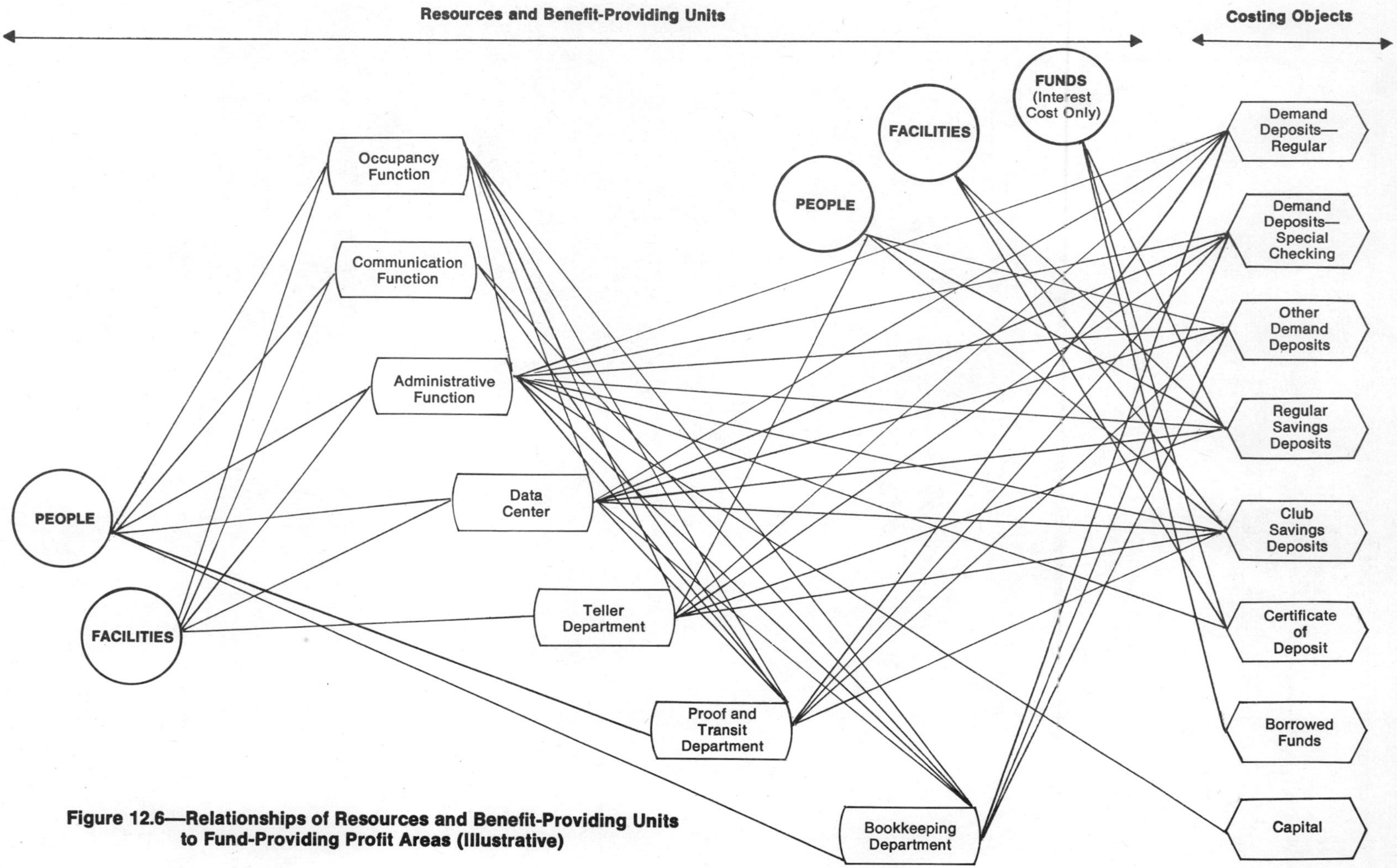

Figure 12.6—Relationships of Resources and Benefit-Providing Units to Fund-Providing Profit Areas (Illustrative)

	Demand Deposits Regular Checking	Demand Deposits Special Checking	Other Demand Deposits	Regular Savings Deposits	Club Savings Deposits	Certificates of Deposit	Borrowed Funds	Capital	Total
Interest				$1,291,400		$350,000	$371,000		$2,012,400
Cost of people and facilities allocated directly to fund-providing function through general accounting system (see Figure 10.5)	$ 32,400	$ 7,000	$3,000	25,000	$1,000	4,000			72,400
Allocated portion of costs of benefit-providing units (Figure 10.5):									
Administration function	51,400		1,000	10,000		500		$8,000	70,900
Data center	99,000	36,700		19,200					154,900
Tellers department	115,300	10,000		29,400	600				155,300
Proof and transit department	124,800	17,900		14,800	200				157,700
Bookkeeping department	60,000	23,400							83,400
Total Cost	482,900	95,000	4,000	1,389,800	1,800	354,500	371,000	8,000	2,707,000
Less: service charge revenue	72,000	30,000							102,000
Net cost of fund-providing profit areas	$410,900	$65,000	$4,000	$1,389,800	$1,800	$354,500	$371,000	$8,000	$2,605,000

Figure 12.7—Costs of Fund-Providing Profit Areas

| | Imputed Revenue | | | | | | Profit (Loss) as Percent of Average Balance |
	Investable Funds (Figure 11.4)	Revenue at 3.8925%[1]	Cost (Figure 12.7)	Profit (Loss) Amount	Rank	Average Deposit Balance (Figure 11.4)	
Demand deposits—regular checking	$25,952,000	$1,010,200	$ 410,900	$ 599,300	1	$ 33,826,000	1.77%
Demand deposits—special checking	2,968,000	115,500	65,000	50,500	4	3,869,000	1.31
Other demand deposits	400,000	15,600	4,000	11,600	6	521,000	2.23
Regular savings deposits	37,523,000	1,460,600	1,389,800	70,800	3	38,684,000	.18
Club savings deposits	800,000	31,100	1,800	29,300	5	825,000	3.55
Certificates of deposit	6,897,000	268,500	354,500	(86,000)	7	7,337,000	(1.17)
Borrowed funds	5,000,000	194,600	371,000	(176,400)	8	5,000,000	(3.53)
Capital	8,000,000	311,400	8,000	303,400	2	11,061,000	2.74
Totals	$87,540,000	$3,407,500	$2,605,000	$ 802,500		$101,123,000	.79%

[1]Calculation of rate of imputed revenue

	Amount	Percent of Investable Funds
Interest revenue, Figure 12.4	$ 4,252,000	4.8572%
Less: Cost of lending (amounts from Figure 12.3, excluding cost of funds and credit card costs):		
Commercial loans	399,800	
Real estate loans	178,000	
Instalment loans	300,600	
Other loans and investments	46,100	
Total	924,500	
Less fees (excluding credit card) (Figure 12.4)	80,000	
Net cost of lending	844,500	.9647
Net revenue	$ 3,407,500	3.8925%
Investable funds (Figure 11.4)	$87,540,000	
Net revenue as percent of investable funds	3.8925%	

Reconciliation

Net cost of lending	$ 844,500
Credit card cost	123,300
Fees (excluding credit card)	80,000
Cost of funds (excluding credit card)	2,575,000
Total (Figure 12.4)	$3,622,800

Figure 12.8—Summary of Profitability of Fund-Providing Profit Areas

It should be noted that profit as a percent of average balance (not percent of investable funds) varies significantly, because the level of investable funds for each fund-providing category varies significantly. For example, demand deposits, with their higher reserve requirements and significant portion of uncollected funds, receive a lower profitability rate per dollar of deposits than do savings deposits. For this reason, it is important when computing the profitability of a fund-providing function (or even of a customer) to first determine the investable funds for each category of funds provided.

In calculating the net revenue to be imputed in Figure 12.8 ($3,407,500), the cost of lending was deducted from the interest income, and the resulting net revenue was allocated to the fund-providing functions on the basis of investable funds.

In arriving at the net cost of lending, the cost of the credit card operation was omitted, on the grounds that such costs relate to the cost of providing the credit card service rather than to lending costs. The omission of the credit costs and fees from the calculation of the profit contribution of the fund-providing functions accounts for the difference in profit shown in Figures 12.4 and 12.8:

Total profit of fund-using functions (Fig. 12.4)	$717,200
Add cost of credit card operation (credit card costs from Fig. 10.5, $93,300 less $8,000 fees)	85,300
Total profit of fund-providing functions (Fig. 12.8)	$802,500

If credit card costs had been considered to be a lending cost, they would not have had a material effect on profit rankings.

The calculation of profit on the fund-providing functions uses a single pool average revenue. A "market-oriented" (incremental) method of allocating revenue could have been used. The amount and rate per dollar of deposits would have been different, but the rankings would be the same. In theory, a multiple pool allocation of revenue also could have been used. Both amounts and rankings would change, depending on the mix of liquidity pools among fund-providing profit areas.

Branch Profitability

Branches are providers and users of funds. Therefore, the profitability measurement of a branch requires an analysis of three cost factors: the directly related costs incurred at the branch; the costs incurred by the home office in providing centralized services to the branch (e.g., data processing, accounting, etc.); and the cost of funds (if the branch is a net user of funds) or a credit for funds calculation (if the branch is a net provider of funds).

The directly related costs incurred by a branch are normally accumulated by the general accounting system. The allocation of service costs from the home office to the branch follows the allocation process discussed in Chapter 10. The cost or credit for funds involves allocating the cost of funds or imputing a credit for funds. Both were discussed in the fund user and provider sections above, but there are some additional complications.

The branch seldom is able to match all investable funds it provides with its own loan requirements, since it will either have greater loan requirements than the investable funds it generates, or vice versa. Investable funds required to meet the loan demand of a branch in excess of its own ability to provide investable funds must be provided by the home office. Conversely, funds in excess of the branch's loan demand will flow into the home office. Consequently, most branches are either net users or net providers of funds. This concept is illustrated in Figure 12.9.

For purposes of determining branch profitability, two methods will be used: single pool and net pool.

In the single pool concept all funds flow in and out of a single pool for the entire bank. A single bankwide credit for fund providers and a single bankwide cost of funds for fund users is applied to the deposit and loan functions of all branches.

In the net pool concept it is assumed that the branch first applies its funds against its own loans. Any excess of funds would flow to the home office, and the branch would receive credit at the bankwide credit rate. Similarly, any deficiency of funds would flow from the home office to the branch, which would be similarly charged at the bankwide cost rate.

The cost rates involved would be determined by top management and could either be the average cost of all funds or be based on market-oriented rates. Both approaches were discussed in Chapter 11.

The credit rates for funds provided could be based on one of several approaches:

- An average return on all excess investable funds received by the home office.
- A rate based on the external market rates.

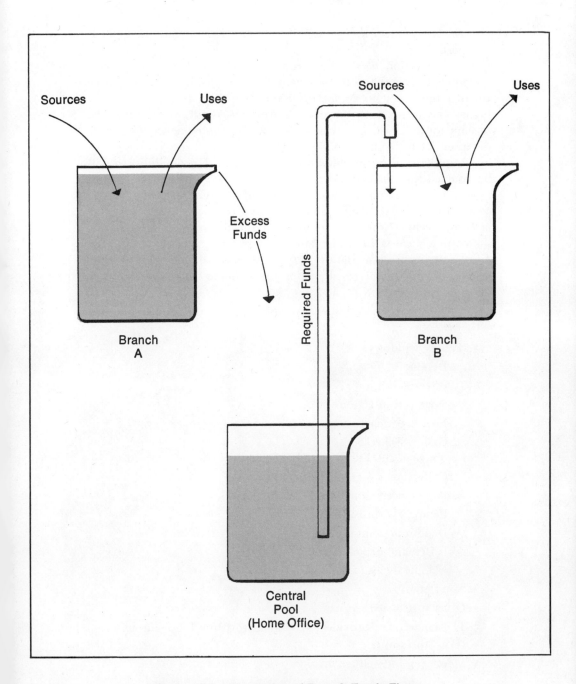

Figure 12.9—Illustration of Branch Funds Flow

- An average return on the bank's entire loan and investment portfolio.

The selection of the rate would depend on top management's preferences. One of top management's major considerations would be whether they want to emphasize branch acquisition of deposits. The higher the credit rate for excess investable funds, the greater the revenue for a branch supplying the funds and consequently the greater the incentive to acquire deposits.

In order to illustrate the calculation of branch profitability, it will be assumed that profitability is being determined with the thought of expanding the branch. The branch is a net fund provider and is credited for the excess investable funds at a bankwide single pool rate of five percent (Note: for simplicity of illustration only Step Five is shown in Figure 12.10). The costs of operating a branch are (1) the direct costs incurred at the site, (2) the allocated home office costs for services provided, and (3) a portion of the home office administrative costs.

The salary, rent, and other expenses relate to the following on-site activities:

- Tellers' windows
  - . . Deposits
  - . . Check cashing
  - . . Savings transactions
  - . . Loan payments
  - . . Cashiers' checks
  - . . Traveler checks
  - . . Collections
- Banking officers' functions
  - . . Lending within authority limits
  - . . Deposit account openings and closings
    - Demand deposit accounts
    - Time deposit accounts
- Safe Deposit
- Other specialized services

The home office provides the branch with the following services:

- Data processing
- Messenger and mail
- Purchasing
- Advertising and promotion

Step 5. Calculate the Cost

Directly related branch costs:

Salaries and fringe benefits	$150,000
Interest on savings deposits	90,000
Rent	20,000
Other	10,000
Total directly related costs	$270,000

Allocated costs of home office benefit-providing units:

Data center	$ 68,000
Proof and transit department	45,000
Bookkeeping department	15,000
Purchasing department	12,000
Other	60,000
Total allocated costs of home office benefit-providing units	200,000
Allocated home office administrative costs	50,000
Total allocated home office costs	$250,000

**Figure 12.10—Illustration of Calculating the
Cost for a Branch (Step Five Only)**

- Personnel administration
- Bookkeeping
- Proof and transit
- Accounting
- Administration

The home office administrative costs include those required to supervise the lending functions and general operations of the branch.

In Figure 12.10, those costs directly related to the branch's operations amount to $270,000, while allocated home office costs amount to $250,000, which includes $50,000 of administrative costs.

In Figure 12.11 the profitability of the branch is calculated. A major consideration in determining profitability is the branch's ability or inability to provide funds, and in this case it has been assumed that the branch can generate $12,000,000 in deposits, resulting in $10,000,000 of investable funds. The branch costs of $270,000 and the allocated home office costs of $200,000 represent the cost of providing $10,000,000 investable funds and using $6,000,000 in loans. The branch receives a credit for the unused $4,000,000 of investable funds at a rate (five percent) that recognizes the lending costs associated with the use of those funds elsewhere. The credit rate is calculated in the same manner as that described in calculating a rate for imputing revenue to fund-providing functions.

Customer Profitability

Customers, individually or collectively, are considered as profit areas. In analyzing the profitability of customers, it is necessary to determine the revenue arising from the use of the resource (funds) that they have made available to the bank as deposits as well as the revenue derived from the funds they have borrowed. In addition, the cost of acquiring and servicing deposits and of making loans must be calculated. Thus, the calculation of customer profitability involves essentially the same procedures as branch profitability, which has already been described.

The approaches to calculating customer profitability involve three questions:

- At what rate is a customer charged for cost of the funds that he borrows?
- At what rate is a customer credited for the funds he leaves on deposit?
- Whose funds does a customer borrow?

The first question relates to considering the customer as a fund user. As pointed out earlier, the cost of the funds can be computed by using the single pool method, the multiple pool method, or the market-oriented method.

The second question relates to considering the customer as a fund

Flow of Funds

Funds provided:	
Gross deposits	$12,000,000
Less, uncollected balances and reserves	2,000,000
Investable funds provided	10,000,000

Funds used:	
Loans	6,000,000
Excess of funds provided over funds used	$ 4,000,000

Branch Profitability

Revenue:	
Interest income received by the branch on $6,000,000 loans	$ 360,000
Home office credit for $4,000,000 provided at 5%	200,000
Total branch revenue	560,000

Costs (Figure 12.10):	
Directly related branch costs	270,000
Profit after directly related branch costs	290,000
Allocated home office costs	200,000
Profit after directly related and allocated home office costs	90,000
Allocated home office administrative costs	50,000
Profit after deducting directly related and all allocated home office costs	$ 40,000

Figure 12.11—Determination of Branch Profitability

provider. The same considerations apply as in the first question, except that the rate to be used provides a credit for funds provided.

The third question considers the source of funds borrowed by the customer. For the borrower who, over the course of a year, also provides deposits (the usual situation), there is a choice as to how the flow of funds used can be viewed. One way (the net method) considers the funds loaned to the customer as his own, and in this case the investable funds provided by him over a year's time are applied to his loan first. Excess funds provided, for which the customer is given credit, flow to a common pool. Conversely, if the funds borrowed exceed the average balances on deposit over a year's time, then funds flow to the customer from a pool, and he is charged accordingly. An alternative approach (the gross method) gives the customer credit for all funds provided in the form of deposits and charges him for all funds used in the form of loans.

The two methods are illustrated in Figure 12.12 for both a net borrower and a net depositor. The basic assumptions in the profitability calculation are:

	Customer 1 Net Borrower	Customer 2 Net Depositor
Average daily balance of demand deposits	$75,000	$75,000
Less uncollected funds and reserves	15,000	15,000
Average investable funds	60,000	60,000
Average loan outstanding	90,000	50,000
Requirement for funds from bank pool	$30,000	
Excess of investable funds available to bank pool		$10,000

The costs required to carry out the costing portion of the calculation are show in Figure 12.13. An added concept introduced here is a provision for loan loss, a recognition of the risk factor involved in lending. In the preceding example, it was considered as a cost. Some may wish, however, to consider the risk factor not as cost but as a factor to be taken into account when setting the effective interest rate and determining the return on the capital assigned.

In Figure 12.12 the gross method indicates higher profits for both customers. Since the total profits of the bank have not increased, there is an element of "intercompany" profit that would be eliminated in

	Net Method		Gross Method	
	Net Borrower	Net Depositor	Net Borrower	Net Depositor
Interest income from money borrowed (at 6%)	$5,400	$3,000	$5,400	$3,000
Earnings credit for excess of average investable funds over borrowing ($10,000 at 5%)		500		
Earnings credit for average investable fund balances (at 5%)			3,000	3,000
Total revenue	5,400	3,500	8,400	6,000
Less costs (Figure 12.13—Step 5)				
Cost of funds borrowed in excess of average investable funds ($30,000 at 2.98%)	894			
Cost of funds for money borrowed (at 2.98%)			2,680	1,490
Handling costs[1]	1,047	1,047	1,047	1,047
Loan loss provision	225	125	225	125
Total costs	2,166	1,172	3,952	2,662
Customer profitability	$3,234	$2,328	$4,448	$3,338

Figure 12.12—Illustration of the Net and Gross Methods for Calculating Customer Profitability

[1] Allocation of tellers, proof and transit, etc. costs.

Step 1. Define the Purpose

- Management wants to review its relationship with its major customers in order to plan for the coming year. The possible alternative courses of action resulting from this review are:
  - • Change compensating balance requirements
  - • Change service fee structure
  - • Change promotional emphasis
  - • Make no changes

- The criterion is customer profitability.

Step 2. Define the Costing Object

- The costing objects are the resources that provide services to a customer.
- They are composed of the benefit-providing units that service the fund-providing and fund-using functions.

Step 3. Specify the Cost Data

- Cost of departments that provide services to customers
- Cost of funds
- Loan loss provision
- Cost of lending departments

Step 4. Specify the Allocation Process

- Costs to be accumulated through the general accounting system, to which the costs of the benefit-providing departments are to be allocated as shown in Figure 10.5. Average unit transfer costs for the following items using time weighted transaction counts:
  - • Tellers department
    Average deposit (Figure 10.8)
  - • Proof and transit department:
    Deposit items
    On-us checks
  - • Bookkeeping department:
    Deposits filed
    Checks filed
    Statements mailed
    Additional postage
  - • Data center:
    Deposits and checks posted
    Statements mailed

- Interest and costs of fund-providing units are to be accumulated through the general accounting system to which the costs of the benefit-providing units are to be allocated as shown in Figure 10.5. The average unit transfer cost (a dollar of investable funds) using the single pool method as shown in Figure 11.4 is to be calculated and expressed as a percent of investable funds.

Figure 12.13—Illustration of Calculating the Costs for a Customer

- A loan loss provision is to be developed outside the general accounting system and allocated to loans on the basis of risk classification and average amount of loan, expressed as a percent of the amount loaned.
- Lending costs to be accumulated through the general accounting system to which are to be added the costs of the benefit-providing units allocated as shown in Figure 10.5.

Step 5. Calculate the Cost

- Calculation of average unit transfer cost.

	Deposit Item	Deposits	Checks	Statement
Tellers		$.055		
Proof and transit	$.021		$.005	
Bookkeeping		.012	.012	$.430
Postage				.250
Data center		.014	.010	.070
Totals	$.021	$.081	$.027	$.750

- Calculation of cost of funds (Figure 11.4)

Annual cost of funds	$ 2,605,000
Average balance of investable funds	$87,540,000
Cost as a percent of investable funds	2.98%

- Loan loss provision (determined by historical record)   0.25%

- Calculation of the cost of lending departments

Total cost of lending departments (Figure 12.8)	$ 924,500
Less fees earned (Figure 12.4)	80,000
Net cost of lending departments	$ 844,500
Divided by invested funds	$87,540,000
Cost of lending as a percentage of invested funds	1%

	Customer 1 Net Borrower	Customer 2 Net Depositor
Customer Activity Costs:		
200 deposits at $.081 each	$ 16.20	$ 16.20
22,000 checks deposited at $.021 each	462.00	462.00
20,000 checks entered at $.027 each	540.00	540.00
26 payroll account statments at $0.75 each	19.50	19.50
12 regular statements at $0.75 each	9.00	9.00
	$1,046.70	$1,046.70
Loan loss provision: 0.25%	$ 225.00	$ 125.00
Cost of funds: 2.98%	$ 894.00	$ —

Figure 12.13 (Continued)

consolidation. Because of this factor, calculations of customer profitability are of more use when they are studied in terms of their relationship to each other. No attempt is made to consider them as precise results.

The profit amount that is shown does not include all related costs. From this profit amount the estimated cost of officers' time spent on an account could be deducted if it can be determined in a reasonably reliable way. Time spent in negotiation of loans, international banking assistance, and conferences are examples of specific activities, the cost of which could be included in the calculation of profit for a customer.

Trust and Other Nonfund Activities

Revenue producing nonfund activities include travel services, safe-deposit accommodations, data center services, and the trust division. The calculation of costs of nonfund activities does not involve the cost of funds and the accumulation of costs of deposit and other fund-providing functions. Since there are many variations of nonfund activities that do require costing techniques that have not already been discussed, they will be covered here only in general terms.

The variety of types and complexity of nonfund activities is great—from the relatively simple travel service department to the complex trust operations. The trust division, although it does provide funds incidental to administering trust accounts, is included among nonfund activities. The range of trust services includes administration of trusts created by wills, which themselves may range from simple to complex estates; administration of pension and profit sharing trusts; corporate trusts including such activities as transfer agent, dividend paying agent, etc. Each of these call for a varied degree of talent ranging from highly skilled money managers to clerical operators.

From a profit standpoint, each of these nonfund activities may be considered to have varying degrees of profit emphasis. Some exist in order to produce a profit in their own right—a major trust division for example. Some activities are basically promotional, with profit being incidental—a travel service for example. Some activities exist principally to reduce fixed costs—sale of data center services for example. The profit contribution emphasis is an important consideration for costing in these instances. For example, management may be content with revenues that only cover variable costs and contribute toward fixed costs. Defining the purpose is therefore especially important when costing nonfund profit areas.

QUALITY OF PROFIT

Thus far this chapter has been concerned with the quantity of profit generated by a profit area, but quantity by itself often does not indicate whether or not the profit performance is adequate. Therefore, management must assess its quality in addition to measuring quantity of profit. In order to do this, it is necessary to compare the profit to some bench mark. The role of costing in making these measurements in some cases lies in determining profit and in others in establishing the bench mark itself.

Measures Based on Profit

Profit comparisons are varied; for example, in the more commonly used bench marks profit is compared with:

- Itself over comparable periods of time.
- Itself in terms of a plan or a potential.
- Other profit areas within the bank.
- Its associated revenues.
- The funds employed.
- The nonfund resources employed.
- The capital employed.

Each of these comparisons has its advantages and disadvantages.

A comparison of profit with profits in comparable periods is useful in assessing the quality of profit, but it is not as effective a tool for managing as a comparison of profit to plan. The plan takes into account those factors that affect profits of prior periods, and it provides a superior bench mark for comparison because it represents a well-thought-out management goal.

Although comparisons with other profit areas indicate the relative importance of profit areas to overall bank profitability, they do not indicate which areas should be contributing the most in terms of quantity of profit. Those factors that give rise to profits must be considered in order to assess quality of profit.

A comparison of profit with revenue can be useful in determining whether a reasonable amount of revenue remains as profit. Due to the marked differences among types of revenues, however, assessments using these comparisons must take into consideration the type of revenue involved.

A comparison of profit with resources employed is another effective method for assessing profit quality. Since resources are employed to generate profit, this comparison has strong merit for management purposes, but special caution must be exercised in costing the facility resources. Since these resources are obtained over a long period of time and are recorded typically at historical cost, it may be necessary to use economic value, replacement value, or some type of valuation other than the one available in the general accounting system to provide a comparable basis for measurement of resources employed.

The final comparison noted above would be a good measure to use, except for the problem of determining the capital employed by a particular profit area. There are a number of approaches to assigning capital, but each must make certain assumptions (risk, for example), with the result that the comparison can become quite abstract and can depend heavily on the assumptions made.

Figure 12.14 shows a ranking of quality of profits as contrasted to quantity for various fund-using bank functions. Comparing the quantity of profits serves to highlight the big profit makers. When profit is expressed as a percent of total revenues earned (a measure of the effectiveness of the various managers in generating revenues and controlling current costs), the performance picture changes somewhat. And when profit is expressed as a percent of the funds employed (a measure of the efficiency with which a resource is employed), the picture changes even more. Thus, with the data shown in Figure 12.14 management may be able to draw some tentative conclusions about the fund-using activities of the bank:

- Commercial loans are the major profit makers for the bank, but
- Instalment loans are the best investment (best yield rate).
- Therefore, instalment loans should have priority on the use of any available funds and promotional efforts.
- Real estate, other loans and investments, and credit cards should either be de-emphasized or reviewed for possible changes in operations.

Figure 12.15 illustrates additional measures of profit quality, again in bank fund-using activities dealing with resources employed other than funds. The personnel resource valuation is most easily approximated by the salary and fringe benefits of the people assigned to each activity. This valuation is valid if the people are compensated in direct proportion to their value to the bank. Facilities resource valuation is the value of all space, fixtures, and equipment directly employed within a profit area. Personnel and facilities are examined together because they are frequently interchangeable. The capital valuation is made on the basis of 100% of all building, land, equipment, and fixtures and the remaining sum is allocated to the various

| | Quantity of Profit | | Profit on Revenue | | | Profit on Invested Funds | | |
| | | | | | | | | |
Profit Area	Profit (Loss) Contribution[1]	Ranking[1]	Revenue from All Sources[1]	Profit (Loss) as a Percent of Revenue	Ranking	Fund Resource Valuation[2]	Return of Invested Funds (Yield)	Ranking
Commercial loans	$385,200	1	$1,850,000	20.82%	1	$35,935,000	1.07%	2
Real estate loans	54,000	4	580,000	9.31	4	11,681,000	.46	4
Instalment loans	214,400	2	1,090,000	19.67	2	19,299,000	1.11	1
Credit card	(37,300)	5	86,000	(43.37)	5	1,022,000	(3.65)	5
Other loans and investments	100,900	3	734,000	13.75	3	19,603,000	.51	3
Total	$717,200		$4,340,000	16.53 % Avg.		$87,540,000	.82% Avg.	

[1]Data obtained from Figure 12.4
[2]Data obtained from Figure B.8

Figure 12.14—Ranking of Quantity of Profits Contrasted to Rankings of Quality of Profits of Fund-Using Profit Areas

	Profit (Loss) Contribution	Personnel Resource[1]	Facilities Resource[2]	Total Nonfund Resources	Return on Nonfund Resources Employed	Rank	Invested Capital[3]	Return on Invested Capital	Rank
Commercial loans	$385,200	$ 83,000	$264,000	$347,000	111.0%	2	$2,920,000	13.2%	1
Real estate loans	54,000	41,000	181,500	222,500	24.3	4	949,000	5.7	4
Instalment loans	214,400	75,000	231,000	306,000	70.1	3	1,631,000	13.1	3
Credit card	(37,300)	28,000	66,000	94,000	(39.7)	5	86,000	(43.4)	5
Other loans and investments	100,900	29,000		29,000	347.9	1	764,000	13.2	1
Total	$717,200	$256,000	$742,500	$998,500	71.8%		$6,350,000	11.3%	

[1]Personnel earning 18.8% of bank's total annual payroll (Figures B.7 & B.9)
[2]Building and equipment book value allocated on basis of floor space
[3]Stockholders' equity has been allocated to fund-using profit areas in accordance with the capital adequacy ratios suggested by Federal Reserve Bank of New York

Figure 12.15—Return on Resources Employed for the Various Fund-Using Profit Areas

uses of funds in the same proportion as the capital adequacy ratio suggested by Federal Reserve Bank of New York.[1] Possible conclusions that can be drawn from Figure 12.15 are:

- The real estate loans profit area is not an efficient user of nonfund resources. There are too many people and/or the people are overvalued (overpaid), and too much space and equipment is utilized.
- Commercial loans and other loans and investments provide the highest return on invested capital.
- Real estate loans provide a poor return on invested capital primarily because of higher capital requirements.

Other Measures

In addition to the more commonly used measures of profit quality just discussed, there are other less commonly used measures, some of which concentrate more on cash flow than on profit. They have been chosen to illustrate the other approaches (there are many variants) to measurement of profit quality. The methods are:

- Payback method.
- Average rate of return.
- Net present value.
- Residual income.

The first method (payback) measures the time required to recover an initial investment from the standpoint of cash flow, while the second measures the average profit return on investment. The next method (net present value) is included here to illustrate another approach to measuring the quality of profitability using only cash flow but discounting the cash flows to be received in the future to a present value. The last method (residual income) is a variant of the comparison of profit to capital employed discussed above.

Payback Method. In the payback method, a payback period for an investment is determined. The payback period indicates the number of periods of operation required to recover the initial investment. The payback period is compared to some required maximum and/or payback periods of alternative investments. The major shortcoming of the method is that it does not consider the cash flows occurring after the payback period and, consequently, cannot be regarded as a true

[1] Bank Management Committee, The American Bankers Association, "The Role of Investments in Bank Asset Management Study 4: Objectives and Principles," p. 30.

measure of profitability. Also, it does not take into account the timing of cash flows occurring during the payback period; it only considers the recovery period as a whole. It does, however, provide management limited insight into the risk and liquidity of an alternative course of action.

Average Rate of Return. The average rate of return is the ratio of the average annual profits after taxes to the average investment or, occasionally, to the initial investment. It is a relatively simple method to use and makes use of readily available accounting information. Once the average rate of return of the alternative investment has been calculated, it may be compared with a required minimum and/or rates of return of alternative investments. The principal shortcomings are that it is based on accounting income rather than cash flow and that it fails to take account of the timing of the cash inflows and outflows. The time value of money is ignored; benefits in the last period are valued the same as benefits in the first year.

Net Present Value. The present value method is a discounted cash flow approach to selecting alternative investments. With the present value method, all cash flows are discounted to present value, using a required rate of return or a rate for the cost of capital. Any alternative having a positive value for its net discounted cash flow is considered acceptable. The alternatives can then be ranked in accordance with their net discounted cash flows. The present value method, like all discounted cash flow methods, is highly dependent upon the propriety of the rate used to compute the discount. The method does, however, recognize that cash currently held has a greater value than cash to be received in the future.

Residual Income. Residual income is an extension of the theory of return on capital employed. Instead of determining a rate of return measure for capital, a "cost of capital" is developed. Residual income is the amount of profit remaining after a predetermined charge has been made for the use of capital. The cost of capital can be the opportunity rate of the best alternate investment, a target rate of return, or a historical rate of return on capital. This method is preferred by some over the rate of return on capital employed measure, because instead of emphasizing a rate of profit it emphasizes the dollar amount of profit available after covering the cost of capital. The analyst, however, is still faced with developing assumptions with which to determine the amount of capital invested in the various profit areas of the bank.

SPECIAL PROFITABILITY DECISIONS

The preceding sections of this chapter have discussed costing to determine profitability for a profit area in terms of both quantity and quality. The use of that profit information will in some cases lead to a decision to consider reducing or eliminating, or conversely, adding or enlarging a profit area. Since the principles relating to eliminating or adding are the same as for reducing or enlarging, the discussion will be confined to the elimination or addition of a profit area.

Eliminating a Profit Area

In evaluating a decision to eliminate a profit area, the revenue that will be lost as well as the costs that will be eliminated must be considered. A profit area is a collection of resources operating in concert under management control to generate revenues and to provide a profit contribution. The effect of a change in a profit area and the chaining effect on other bank areas add complications but do not change the basic approach to profitability analysis—that is, to consider all relevant eliminations of revenues and costs, and then to determine the effects on overall bank profits.

When a bank considers eliminating a profit area, the costing required will vary with each situation. There are a few points, however, that can be generalized. The revenue affected as a direct result of an action taken is, of course, involved. So, too, are the directly related costs that would be eliminated. The allocated costs of the services must be carefully identified and reviewed individually to determine the effect of the contemplated action. If a benefit-providing unit is already operating far below capacity, then one of the effects of eliminating a profit area may be to permit elimination of these under-utilized units.

In order to illustrate the costing principles involved, Figure 12.16 shows the changes in net loss for the trust function using different assumptions as to certain expenses of the trust division. Column I contains the present revenues and costs for the trust division. The present loss for the division is $3,000.

The fee income, salaries, fringe benefits, and supplies would be avoided if the trust service were eliminated. Analysis of the phone bill shows that the avoidable portion of the allocated cost for the instruments and long-distance tolls amounts to $400. Analysis of data processing shows that the cost of operating the facility would not be affected materially by eliminating the trust service; the costs therefore remain. Further, it is assumed that space occupied by the trust division is rented under a long-term lease. The figure depicts the

	Present Revenue and Costs I	Costs Remaining After Eliminating the Service		
		A Vacated Space Not Utilized II	B Vacated Space Used for Other Purpose III	C Vacated Space Sublet for $5,000 IV
Net income	$ 13,000	$ 0	$ 0	$ 0
Department salaries, fringe benefits and supplies	8,000	0	0	0
Rent	3,000	3,000	3,000	3,000
Rent saved elsewhere			(2,000)	
Revenue from sublease				(5,000)
Telephone	1,000	600	600	600
Data processing	4,000	4,000	4,000	4,000
Total cost	16,000	7,600	5,600	2,600
Net Loss	$ (3,000)	$ (7,600)	$ (5,600)	$ (2,600)

Figure 12.16—Effect on Profit of Eliminating a Profit Area

result of eliminating trust services under the following three assumptions concerning the disposition of the rented space:

Column II—Vacated space not utilized.

Column III—Vacated space used for another purpose (thereby avoiding $2,000 rental elsewhere).

Column IV—Space sublet for $5,000.

Under these circumstances, the net effect for the period of dropping the service shown in Columns II, III, and IV depends on the utilization of the vacated space. In this illustration, overall bank profit would suffer unless the space were sublet (Column IV).

To extend this example further, the $1,000 telephone expense, comprised of a $400 direct cost element and $600 traceable cost, represents an allocation of a centralized facility, switchboard, WATS line, etc., for which the bank pays $3,000 a month. The utilization of the telephone facility is only 60%, and if the trust service were dropped, this utilization would be reduced to 40%. At this point a less expensive facility, costing only $2,000 a month, can easily handle the load. If this conversion could be made at a minimal cost, an additional cost reduction of $1,000 could be attributed to eliminating trust services.

As illustrated in the example, the costs allocated to a profit area for purposes of determining profitability must be reanalyzed if consideration is to be given to eliminating the area. Some allocated costs will not be reduced—even if they were initially incurred specifically for the profit area involved—if the profit area is eliminated. The "sticky" nature of costs is a common phenomenon. Because of this characteristic of some costs and because a profit area will usually help other profit areas "absorb" some bank-wide expenses, it is possible that a particular profit area showing a loss could, in fact, result in further loss to the bank if it were eliminated.

Adding a Profit Area

The same principles apply to the addition of a profit area, but conversely. Using an illustration similar to that in the preceding section, the following shows the effect (simplified, of course) of adding a profit area:

Projected Operations—Added Service

	Additional Revenue and Added Cost I	Utilization of Present Resources (Allocated Costs) II	Total Projected Operations III
Expected revenue	$20,000		$20,000
Department salaries, fringe benefits, etc.	12,000		12,000
Occupancy		$3,000	3,000
Telephone	400	600	1,000
Data processing		4,000	4 000
Total cost	12,400	$7,600	20,000
Net profit (loss)	$ 7,600		$ —0—

Under these circumstances the added service is expected eventually to increase the bank's total net profit by $7,600 a month (Column I), although the monthly profit calculation for the profit center would show only a breakeven operation (Column III). The key factor in this case is that the added operation would be able to utilize resource capacity, the total fixed expenses of which ($7,600 in Column II) would otherwise be absorbed by fewer profit areas.

SUMMARY

Profitability is the major criterion of performance used by management. It is a complex determination not only because the resources used to generate revenue are usually complex in nature, but because considerable judgment goes into determining the revenues to be associated with a profit area and the specific costs to be allocated to that profit area. Further, after the profit has been determined, the manager still must view the results in the context of the bank as a whole and with a view to short- and long-term objectives in both a quantitative and qualitative sense.

An understanding of the costing process and the characteristics of costs is necessary for making intelligent decisions about profit areas. Because of the complexities involved and the sometimes deluding effect of precise-looking numerical results, a particular course of action that appears logical may all too often prove detrimental if carried out.

13

CONTROLLING COST PERFORMANCE—PROFIT CENTER ACCOUNTING

The profitability of organizational units and bank functions was discussed in Chapter 12 from the standpoint of analyzing alternative courses of action to be taken by the bank. The importance of considering only those costs that bear on the purpose of the analysis was stressed. In the control phase of the planning and control cycle, however, it is necessary to recognize that the purposes of the costing are now to communicate the plan and measure results. As pointed out in Chapter 8, bank organization is a most effective mechanism for both planning and controlling cost. It is also an effective mechanism for planning and controlling revenue and therefore can be effective for control of the net of cost and revenue—profit.

If profit measurement is to be used for control purposes, management should:

1. Establish a plan that relates planned revenues and costs to specified organizational units within the bank.
2. Assign responsibility to a manager in each organizational unit and entrust him with sufficient authority so that he can fulfill his responsibilities.
3. Provide itself with the means to measure results against the plan.

This chapter will examine how bank management may approach profit measurement for control, which involves establishing a plan, assigning responsibility, and measuring results.

THE PROFIT PLAN

Planning, as discussed in the previous chapter, involves examining profitability by analyzing costs as a basis for making a decision concerning a course of action to be taken. This requires an analysis of alternatives: adding or eliminating a function, department, or activity, changing the level of activities or the committed resources of a department, function, or activity, etc. After one course of action has been selected, based on the profitability analysis, the plan must be developed and presented in order to translate the decisions made into action steps.

The form taken by the profit plan depends upon management's views as to how the bank is to be managed. The profit plan for the bank, operating as one unit, would show total revenues from loans and investments, credit card operations, trust and other revenue functions, while total costs could be shown by natural expense categories for the whole bank. This reflects a bank-wide approach to revenue and expenses, where top management is responsible for profit (Figure 13.1).

An alternative to the bank-wide approach in developing the profit plan is to reflect revenues and expenses by the responsible organizational unit (Figure 13.2). This approach assumes that management has assigned responsibility for control over revenues and over costs, but not profit. Chapter 8 spelled out this approach in some detail as it relates to costs, indicating that responsibility center accounting was considered to be a minimum level of control necessary for most banks. An organizational unit controls revenue by establishing planned levels for meeting targets such as return on loans, new business, return on investments, etc. A disadvantage of attempting to control revenues and to control costs as separate items is the strong inclination by managers to net costs against revenue. This tends to obscure the organizational unit's separate responsibility for certain expenses and revenues and improperly assumes responsibility for a profit result. A third alternative for control, profit centers, allows the bank to control revenues and costs through organizational units in terms of profit.

MANAGEMENT BY PROFIT CENTER

Definition of Profit Center

A profit center is similar to a venture in that the profit center concept regards organizational units of the bank as business entities. Therefore, the profit center's activities should include those normally thought of in a business entity as necessary to the development of

Profit Plan

Revenues

Loan interest	$3,528,000
Investment interest	724,000
Credit card service charge fees	180,000
Trust department fees	150,000
Safe deposit vault fees	5,000
Other income	5,000
Total Revenues	4,592,000

Expenses

Salaries and fringe benefits	1,362,000
Interest expense	2,012,000
Rent, utility, taxes, etc.	150,000
Equipment rental	161,000
Other operating expenses	302,000
Provision for loan loss	75,000
Total Expenses	4,062,000
Profit	$ 530,000

Note: The profit plan submitted to the president would normally include comparable amounts for the previous year. Such amounts have been omitted here for simplicity.

Figure 13.1—Bank-Wide Profit Plan Showing Revenues by Source and Costs by Natural Expense Categories

	Revenues	(000's Omitted) Direct Expenses
Commercial loans	$1,850	$ 207
Real estate loans	580	111
Instalment loans	1,090	187
Credit card	86	42
Other loans and investments	734	44
Demand deposits	102	94
Savings		42
Tellers (universal)		137
Proof and transit		132
Bookkeeping		64
Data center		192
Credit files		125
Credit analysis		147
Trust	150	154
Communications		58
Bank-Wide Costs:		
Occupancy		150
General overhead		164
Interest on time deposits		2,012
Total Revenue and Expenses	$4,592	$4,062
	4,062	
Profit	$ 530	

Figure 13.2—Profit Plan by Organizational Unit

profit. In banking, such "business entity" activities would encompass obtaining and loaning funds, obtaining and servicing trust accounts, etc.

The profit center concept further assumes that each venture is under the control of some one individual. It is, therefore, a management concept more than an accounting concept. Costs and revenues can be matched to determine profitability in a number of profit areas for analytical purposes. These profit areas, however, do not represent profit centers unless management has, in fact, assigned the profit responsibility to an individual in the organization.

In addition to the requirement that a profit center represent an organizational responsibility, there is implicit in the concept the spirit of entrepreneurship, which allows a manager to operate with relative freedom to make day-to-day decisions without undue influence from higher management. The concept of management by profit center can be rendered ineffective, perhaps even made harmful to the bank, if there has not been a realistic delegation of decision-making authority required for effective profit center control.

In a profit center the manager operates to a significant degree as an independent businessman responsible for the results of his operations. His responsibility is not just for control of revenues and costs as separate items; he is responsible to see that decisions made to incur cost yield a profitable result. In summary, a profit center is a bank department or division that is responsible for its own profit. Such responsibility extends beyond that for revenue and expenses to responsibility for the outcome of his decisions made in the interest of the profit center under his control.

The Use of Profit Centers

The major advantages associated with the use of profit centers are:

- They provide workable units of control when the size or complexity of the bank makes it desirable, perhaps even necessary, to delegate profit decision-making authority to lower levels of the organization.

- They provide strong motivation to a manager to meet profit targets by encouraging him to view his responsibility as he would if he were managing a separate business entity.

These advantages are principally applicable to a bank that has developed a reasonably formalized organization structure.

However, in certain situations, the development of a strong profit motive in individual managers can cause them to make decisions that might enhance the profits of their units, but it may prove detrimental to the operations or profits of the bank as a whole. It is the responsibility of senior management to see that the objectives of each profit center are in concert with overall bank objectives.

Further, costing for profit centers must be carried out with the purpose of helping each manager understand his objectives and his progress toward those objectives. The costing must (1) represent costs that the profit center manager can understand, and (2) clearly define those resource costs that he should properly be concerned with. Improper costing procedures can make it difficult for him to see the management action he should take and the results of that action.

Bank Profit Centers

There is a perceptible trend toward organizing around profit centers. An example of the common organization structure of today is included in the Appendix, Figure A.1. Figure 13.3 presents an organization structure that recognizes the profit center concept more fully. It seems reasonable to classify the following as profit centers because they have attributes similar to a venture and are often assigned as the responsibility of some one person in the bank:

- Banking (defined as combined fund-providing and fund-using functions)
- Branches
- Trust

There are other units for which profit analyses are frequently prepared for planning purposes that might be considered by management to be profit centers:

1. Banking functions
   a. Commercial loans
   b. Instalment loans
   c. Savings
   d. Demand deposits
2. Customers
   a. Individual customers
   b. Market groupings of customers (for example, retail, wholesale)

        c. Geographic groupings of customers

        d. Industry groupings of customers

    3. Trust by various types of trusts

Of the above classifications, market groupings of customers (2b) seems to represent the most natural extension of the profit center concept because this classification has attributes similar to a venture— obtaining and using funds.

On the other hand, to consider individual banking functions as profit centers begins to stretch the concept to the point where a manager might have difficulty viewing his area of responsibility as a venture. For example, in the fund-using functions (commercial loans, for example) the manager usually lacks control over the funds available and there also may be rather severe constraints on the latitude allowed a fund-using function manager because of the bank's established loan policy. These factors limit the range of action available to the manager of the commercial loan function to the point where it becomes impractical to assume that the manager has a profit center responsibility.

When the profit center concept includes profit areas that do not have the attributes of a venture, the responsibility for costs to be assigned to the profit center becomes obscure. For example, if a loan function is considered as a profit center, it is necessary to allocate the cost of funds, or in the case of a fund-providing function, it is necessary to allocate an assumed amount of revenue (imputed revenue). The responsibility for planning and for control of cost of funds and imputed revenue cannot reasonably be assigned to managers of such individual functions, and yet they are significant elements in determining profitability of the functions.

PROFIT CENTER MEASUREMENTS

In considering the specific costs to be allocated to the profit center, it must be remembered that the profit center manager, as well as those to whom he is responsible, will be expected to use these costs in making decisions and that such decisions will affect profits. The costs allocated therefore serve two purposes: (1) they provide cost information to the profit center manager for making day-to-day decisions, and (2) they are part of the measure of his performance.

There are several levels of profit contribution that can be measured for a profit center. Each results in a different quantitative measure of profit. To avoid erroneous conclusions when comparisons of profit center performance are made, the same levels of profit con-

Notes

[1]Each responsibility center tabbed with a ◢ in the upper left-hand corner is also a profit center.

[2]Managers of trust and banking, and the latter's subordinate managers for wholesale banking, retail banking, and correspondent banks, are each responsible for their own
- Customer group sales
- Administrative and operating functions

[3]Each account group manager and branch group manager has responsibility for

- Fund-using functions
  - Customer loans
  - Instalment loans
  - Real estate loans
  - Other
- Fund-providing functions
  - Demand deposit
  - Savings deposits
  - Certificates of deposit
  - Other

[4]The new divisions of the traditional banking function are defined as
- **Wholesale Banking:** Those banking (fund-providing and fund-using) activities conducted with customers, who, for either reasons or their account size or transaction activity, are able to negotiate the terms and/or conditions of loans and are able to extract special services or considerations for their deposits and continued banking activities. The customers may be individuals, institutions, governmental units, or corporations.
- **Retail Banking:** Those banking (fund-providing and fund-using) activities conducted with customers who are *not able* to negotiate the terms and/or conditions of loans or able to extract special services or considerations for their deposits and continued banking activities.
- **Correspondent Banks:** (Unchanged).

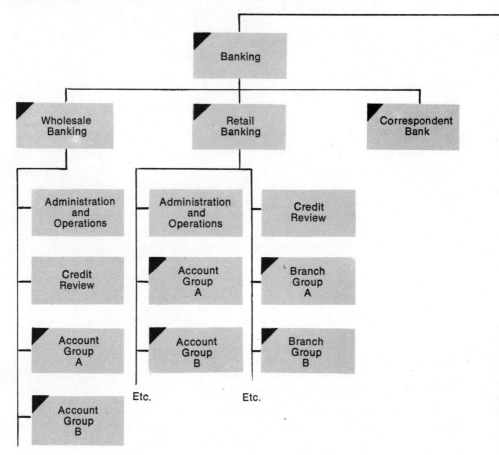

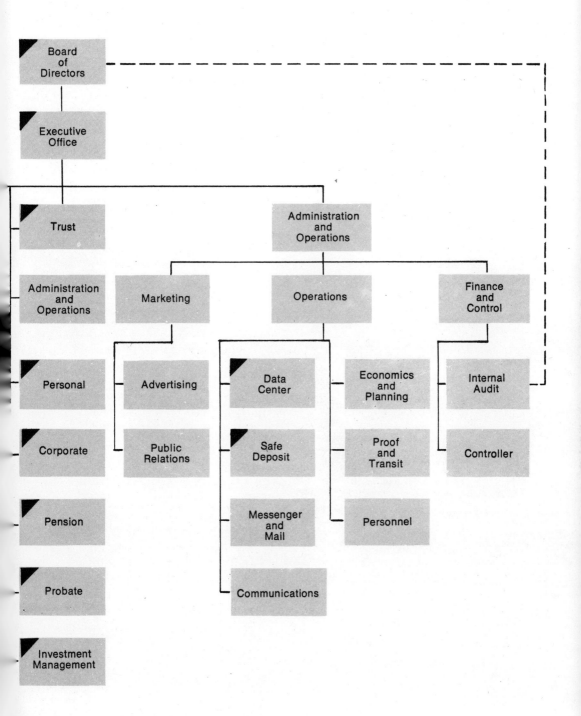

Figure 13.3—Organization by Profit Center

tribution must be used. For purposes of this discussion, four levels of profit contribution will be used:

Level I Profit Contribution—Revenue After Direct Controllable Costs

Direct controllable costs are those costs that are directly incurred by the profit center and for which the profit center manager has direct administrative responsibility.

Level II Profit Contribution—Revenue After Direct and Allocated Controllable Costs

Allocated controllable costs are those costs that are incurred outside the profit center but for which the profit center manager has a degree of responsibility because his decisions can affect the amount of resources used by another bank unit.

Level III Profit Contribution—Revenue After Controllable and Allocated Noncontrollable Costs

Allocated noncontrollable costs are those costs that can reasonably be assumed to be incurred on behalf of the profit center but for which a direct, measurable cause-and-effect relationship cannot be determined. These costs are not under the direct control of the profit center manager.

Level IV Profit—Revenue After Controllable, Noncontrollable, and Arbitrarily Allocated Costs

Arbitrarily allocated costs are those costs (some administrative costs, for example) that are required in order for all profit centers to function, but they cannot be clearly identified with any one profit center. These costs are allocated in order to calculate profits in all profit centers the sum of which equals the profit of the bank as a whole.

These levels of ability to control costs provide a means of segregating costs in a manner similar to that used in analyzing a profit area (Figures 12.10 and 12.11—Chapter 12). Figure 13.4 illustrates the use of the four levels of profit contribution applied to a branch as a profit center. In addition, the Figure includes a comparison of costing for control to the costing used for analysis purposes as discussed in Chapter 12 where the characteristics of cost and their relatability to a profit area were emphasized. Note that the Level III profit amount corresponds to the profit calculated for analytical purposes before allocation of indirect costs.

The essential difference in levels is the degree of responsibility assigned to the profit center manager, and the levels are used to segregate cost so as to emphasize control responsibility. The profit

BRANCH A
(000's Omitted)

Illustrative Costing for Profit Analysis and Planning Purposes

Revenue
Interest income	$360	
Home office credit	200	
Total revenue		$560

Costs
Salaries and fringe benefits	150	
Interest on savings deposits	90	
Rent	20	
Other	10	
Data center	68	
Proof and transit department	45	
Bookkeeping department	15	
Other allocated costs	72	
Branch administration	20	
Total Costs		490

Profit contribution before allocation of indirect costs		70
Allocation of indirect costs		
Home office administration		30
Profit		$ 40

Illustrative Costing for Profit Center Control Purposes

Revenue
Interest income	$360	
Home office credit	200	
Total revenue		$560

Direct Controllable Costs
Salaries and fringe benefits	150	
Interest on savings deposits	90	
Rent	20	
Other	10	
Total Direct Controllable Costs		270
Level I Profit contribution		290

Allocated Controllable Costs
Data Center	68	
Proof and Transit Department	45	
Bookkeeping Department	15	
Other allocated costs	72	
Total Allocated Controllable Costs		200
Level II Profit Contribution		90

Allocated Noncontrollable costs
Branch administration		20
Level III profit contribution		70

Arbitrarily Allocated Cost
Home office administration		30
Level IV profit		$ 40

Figure 13.4—Profit Center Costs for Control Compared with Revenue Center Costs for Profit Analysis—Branch A

center manager must have an understanding of the characteristics of all costs that are related to his profit center as he makes decisions, but his performance will be measured with emphasis on the "controllable" items of cost rather than on "noncontrollable" items. An even greater performance emphasis may be put upon those costs for which he has direct administrative responsibility (direct controllable costs).

In deciding what level of profit contribution should be related to a profit center, it is essential to decide what costs are relevant in making day-to-day profit decisions. There are two factors that must be considered in determining the level of cost to be allocated to the profit center

- The degree to which the profit center manager's decisions are likely to affect the costs being considered.
- Materiality of the costs being considered.

The degree to which profit center decisions will directly affect costs declines generally with each succeeding profit contribution level as defined above. In making day-to-day decisions, the profit center manager should be concerned, at a minimum, with those costs through Level II, since they are a direct result of profit center activity. In many situations it will be important to include Level III costs because the relationships are traceable even though they are less determinable.

In fact, as the time span and the sphere of control increase, the alternatives available to the profit center manager broaden. For example, he can influence the type of physical facilities provided or the manner in which other departments perform. As a result, costs related to Level III profit contribution tend to become controllable.

In making a decision as to Level III, the nature of the particular costs is an important factor. If, for example, the costs here represent a portion of administrative costs that are clearly incurred on behalf of the profit center, they should be included. If, on the other hand, the types of decisions made by the profit center manager are not likely to affect the level of such administrative costs in any significant way, then they should not be included.

Materiality should also be considered in determining the level of costs to be used. If the costs are directly relatable and yet are immaterial, it is questionable whether the information provided the profit center manager is worth the cost of accounting for it. In this case, the costs should not be included in the evaluation.

Level IV profit is used to convey to the profit center manager the concept that the profit contribution must be sufficient to cover *all* costs and to provide a profit. The allocation of all costs, even if done on an arbitrary basis, serves to emphasize this point to the profit center manager.

A further cost consideration is that a bank's management philosophy affects the types of costs allocated to the profit center. If management wants to specify how certain profit decisions are to be made, these specifications can be used in the calculation of costs to assist the profit center manager in making his decisions.

A good example of this is the way in which fund costs are calculated for the profit center. As discussed in Chapter 11, there are various methods for calculating these costs, each with a different result. If the bank wishes to emphasize, say a tight money market, it might charge a branch that is a net user of funds using the market-oriented method rather than a pool average cost. For the branch to maintain its profit targets, the lending rates must then reflect the higher money market rates.

Similarly, the data center costs per unit of activity can vary depending upon the way the bank wishes to manage the data center. For example, it is likely that under some circumstances the adding of a substantial group of new demand deposit customers may not result in increased EDP costs for processing the added volume of checks. If sufficient data center capacity were available, the result could be a decrease in the *unit cost* of processing a check because of the higher volume of checks. In this situation the profit center manager would find the unit costs decreasing. On the other hand, the added volume may necessitate substantial incremental cost to the data center. In this situation, the bank's management might decide to pass the incremental cost on to the profit center that caused the increase.

The manner in which the specific costs are calculated is also important from the standpoint of credibility. It is important that the costs allocated to the profit center are believable and understandable to the profit center manager. Otherwise, the cost information may not be used in making profit decisions. If a cost is allocated on a highly generalized. or obscure basis, the credibility of the cost information could impair its usefulness for control. One of the most important points is that the transfer unit must be stated in terms that are easily understood.

SUMMARY

The use of profit centers can be an effective management technique when top level bank managers wish to assign profit responsibility to lower levels in the organization. However, when attributes similar to those of a venture do not exist, the use of profit centers results in assigning profit responsibility to a manager who has little effective control over profit results.

The somewhat complex nature of profit centers and the desire of management to provide motivation in a particular way introduces sophisticated costing techniques into the information system of the bank. Before the profit center technique is implemented in the bank, it must be recognized that a more complex and costly accounting and reporting system will be required and that profit center managers must have a relatively high level knowledge of accounting.

14

COSTS FOR PRICING

Pricing is one of the more important reasons for seeking cost information. Although historically pricing for banks has been concerned primarily with the lending function, other important bank services also require careful attention in developing price strategies. These include money depositories (demand and time), charge cards, check payment services, safe-deposit facilities, travel services, data processing, and other services.

The purposes of this chapter are (1) to discuss various approaches that can be taken to pricing, (2) to explain the relationship of cost to price, and (3) to describe the costing appropriate for establishing or evaluating prices of certain selected services.

APPROACHES TO PRICING

Pricing bank services can be a very complicated process because there are many intangible factors to be evaluated and weighed, such as the effect a price change might have on customers and the community, on long- and short-range plans, and on competition. A judicious approach to pricing would weigh all available information factors carefully and logically to arrive at the pricing policy and structure that best meets the bank's objectives, taking into consideration, of course, the realities of the market place.

In comparison to this more judicious approach, the banker has several fairly simple pricing approaches available to him: arbitrary pricing, market-dependent pricing, and cost-plus pricing.

If he uses arbitrary pricing, the banker arbitrarily sets his price on the basis of his judgment as to the value of the service to his customers. When he does this without knowledge of costs, he will not know whether the price is such that the service will contribute to bank profit. Market-dependent pricing simply uses the current published market price established by competition, and cost-plus pricing is merely the addition of a percentage of cost to establish a price, the percentage usually being based on desired profit margin.

If the banker wishes to take a more creative approach to pricing, he will find it necessary to study costs closely in relationship to his pricing objectives. This approach may be called "cost-visible pricing."

COST-VISIBLE PRICING

Cost-visible pricing can be complex, and the difficulties it presents will not be minimized here. For purposes of this book, however, pricing will be discussed in a somewhat simplistic fashion in order to illustrate the general ways in which cost can be helpful in establishing prices.

Relationship of Cost to Pricing

With a few exceptions, such as revenue from investments, most bank revenue results from an established price structure for all services rendered. For the bank as a whole to profit from all the services it renders, its overall price structure must produce revenues in excess of the total costs of rendering those services. If the total costs of the bank (all costs incurred including all general overhead costs) are divided up among all services and thus can be said to have been "fully absorbed" by those services, the bank has a bench mark against which to measure the price structure for each of the services.

This does not mean that it is necessary for each service to produce the same percentage of profit. Moreover, because of the interdependence of services, it is not necessary that the price of each service results in a profit on a fully absorbed basis. It is, therefore, possible to vary prices among the services so long as the bank as a whole achieves the greatest potential profit.

When prices are being set to cover the total costs of a particular service, it is important to understand how much capacity is available to provide that service. Thus, a bank may have additional capacity in an area of service for which the established prices are now providing an overall profit. If opportunities arise to sell the additional service capacity, the bank has an option as to how to cost the service in setting its price for this additional utilization. The fixed costs incurred by the bank for the service have already been "absorbed." Prices have proven adequate not only to pay for these fixed costs but for the variable costs as well, and they are also providing a profit.

When making a pricing decision, therefore, it is important to know:

- The available capacity of the service, expressed as volume.
- How much of that capacity can be sold (i.e., what volume) and when.
- The fully absorbed costs of the service (the bench mark) at the assumed volume level.
- What will happen to those costs under varying volume assumptions.
- What will happen to volume under varying price assumptions.
- What will happen to profit under varying cost and volume assumptions.
- What effect demand (expressed as volume) will have on capacity.
- What would be the effect on cost if it were necessary to augment capacity in order to meet demand (thus incurring an incremental cost).

In short, the complex relationships among cost, volume, and price must be explored fully under differing assumptions to ascertain the effects of different pricing strategies. This necessitates an analysis of cost-volume-profit relationships, which will be explored here only in simplistic form.

For discussion purposes, it is assumed initially that capacity is always available (and so therefore incremental costs are not a factor) and that the costs are the "fully absorbed" costs referred to earlier. The effect of changes in capacity and consideration of costs other than "fully absorbed" will be discussed following the review of cost-volume-profit relationships.

Cost-Volume-Profit Relationships

The relationship between cost, volume, and profit is shown in Figures 14.1, 14.2, and 14.3.

Figure 14.1 shows the basic cost-volume-profit relationships. Line R represents total revenues at varying volume levels (O through O_1) at a specific price per unit. Line C represents the total costs at the same volume levels. Total costs are separated into their fixed and variable components. The following cost-volume-profit relationships are shown:

- Fixed costs remain constant as volume increases.
- Variable costs increase as volume increases (the slope of the total cost line being caused by the variable cost component).

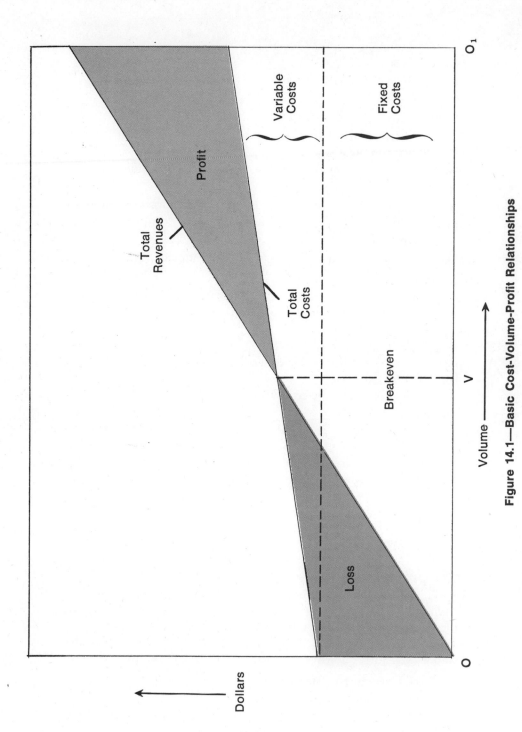

Figure 14.1—Basic Cost-Volume-Profit Relationships

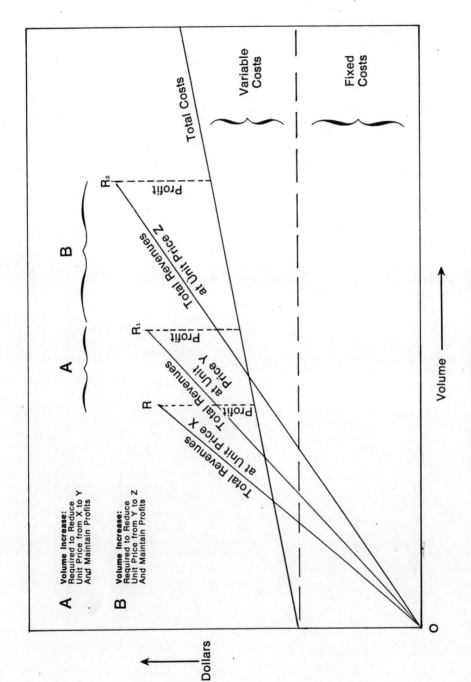

Figure 14.2—Cost-Volume-Profit Analysis

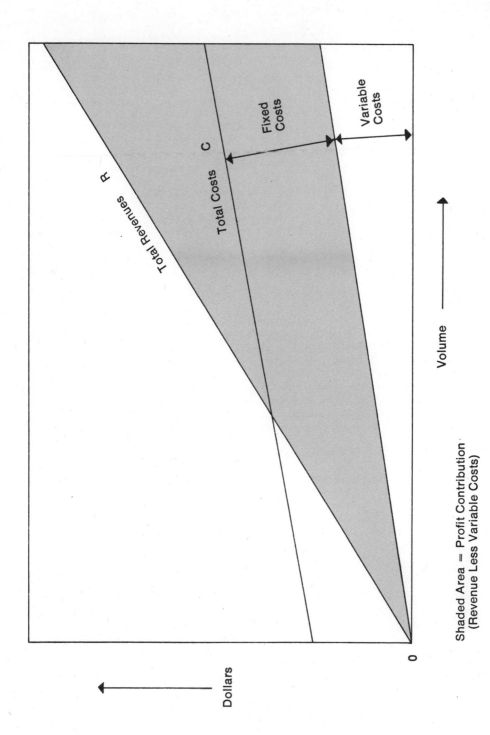

Shaded Area = Profit Contribution
(Revenue Less Variable Costs)

Figure 14.3—Profit Contribution

- Break-even volume (V) is reached when total revenue equals total cost.
- Total profit is measured by a vertical line drawn at actual volume; total profit is equal to total revenue (R) less total cost (C).

It is important to recognize that cost-volume-profit charts do not assume an overall average cost per unit. They assume that the fixed costs are present before the first unit of service is sold and that only variable costs are incurred as each additional unit of service is sold.

Figure 14.2 is similar to Figure 14.1 except that two additional revenue lines have been added $(R_1$ and $R_2)$. These lines have different slopes, indicating that R_1 has a smaller unit price (price Y) than R (price X), while R_2 has a smaller unit price (price Z) than R_1. In addition, each revenue line has been extended only to the volume level at which each unit price results in the same amount of dollar profit as the profits achieved by the other two unit prices at their volume levels. This Figure shows that:

- If the price is decreased from R to R_1, the volume must increase to maintain the same profit level.

- If the price is decreased from R_1 to R_2 (and by the same amount as the price decrease from R to R_1), a much larger volume increase is required to reach the same profit level than that which was required when the price changed to R_1. The reason for this is that the same fixed costs must be covered under both increases.

In short, if higher volume levels are obtained through price decreases, the change must take into account the fixed costs to be met. Volume must, therefore, grow at an increasing rate if profit levels achieved at previous prices are to be maintained.

Other Cost-Price Relationships

Although the price of a service should theoretically generate sufficient revenue to cover the fully absorbed costs of that service, there are other costs that can be considered when pricing. The use of these "other" costs (directly related costs, variable costs, or incremental costs) indicates that in special situations overall profit of the bank may be increased by pricing at less than fully absorbed cost. Thus, in a given situation, pricing strategy to achieve overall bank objectives may indicate that a service should be priced in one of the following three ways:

- A price sufficient to cover *directly related costs*. In this case, it is assumed that it is adequate to cover only all those costs that can reasonably be associated with the service rendered. Of course, it is still necessary for some other service or services to cover the overhead costs that cannot be directly associated with the service being priced.

- A price sufficient to cover at least the *variable costs* of providing the service. In this case, it is assumed that the fixed costs will be present in any event. Any revenue generated from the use of capacity still available that exceeds the variable costs incurred from using that additional capacity will contribute directly to providing a profit (profit contribution). See Figure 14.3.

- A price sufficient to cover the *incremental costs* that are created as a direct result of providing the service. It is assumed that the majority of these incremental costs are the variable costs, which by definition are caused by the service. However, under special circumstances, other additional costs may be incurred when added capacity of some kind is required to provide the service. Thus, if a new, sizable customer is to be served, it may be necessary to increase staff, expand space, obtain a larger computer, etc. In situations of this kind, management often will assume that these incremental costs (normal variable costs plus increased capacity costs) result from many past actions or relate to anticipated increased service volume in the future. These costs are not, therefore, attributable to the current situation that gives rise to the increment in cost. Nonetheless, depending on the circumstances involved, management may wish to include some or all of the incremental costs in the price. For example, if a larger customer asks for a special service for which it is necessary to add special EDP devices, it may well be proper to include the full price for the devices in the price charged to that customer.

PRICING BANK SERVICES

To focus properly on cost-visible pricing, costs for pricing will be discussed for several important types of bank services:

- Demand deposit services.
- Loans.
- Trust services.
- Miscellaneous services.

For demand deposit services, a rather detailed costing will be illustrated, using the five costing steps. The other types of bank services will be discussed in more general terms.

Demand Deposit Services

Pricing of services related to demand deposits is a problem most banks must deal with. It also provides a good example of the role of costing in developing a pricing strategy.

The costs of providing demand deposit services can be divided into three types. The first type of costs are those incurred because of demand deposit account activities (activity costs). They are:

- Teller costs
  - . . Check cashing
  - . . Receiving checking account deposits
    - Counter
    - Mail
- Bookkeeping costs—posting transactions to accounts
- Proof and transit costs, which involve processing
  - . . "On us" checks
  - . . "On others" checks
  - . . Checking account deposits
  - . . Stop payments
  - . . Return items

The second type of costs are those associated with maintaining accounts (maintenance costs), which involves:

- Opening and closing accounts.
- Preparing account statements.
- Mailing or distributing statements.

The third type depends on the average deposit balance and consists of FDIC insurance and other similar insurance on demand accounts.

There are many ways of pricing demand deposit services, depending upon management's policies and objectives and the bank's competitive situation. Some of the alternatives are:

- Service charge based upon an average daily deposit balance.
- A fixed service charge plus a charge for each check.
- A fixed service charge only.

In each of these situations, the bank can allow a credit for earnings (imputed revenue) of an account's balances. This recognizes the fact that deposits held by the bank can be used by the bank for loans and investments. The credit for earnings would normally be based upon only that portion of the account balance that is investable by the bank (investable funds).

Step 1. Define the Purpose

- Management is concerned about the lack of a service charge and minimum balance policy for personal demand deposit accounts and wants to analyze the current situation with a view to either establishing a minimum balance and transaction charge schedule, or making no change.

- The criterion for decision will be the minimum balance, by stratum of account, which through loans and investments earns sufficient revenues to offset the monthly costs required to process transaction activity, maintain, and insure the account. This amount can then be compared with the actual average daily balances of each stratum of accounts.

Note: The cost purpose requires two costings: the calculation of cost related to a personal demand deposit account and the calculation of cost of the lending function, the latter to be netted against gross loan and investment earnings. The cost of the lending function has already been determined to be .9647% of investable funds (Figure 12. 8) and the calculation need not be repeated here. Furthermore, for purposes of illustration, costing will be limited to calculating the transaction and maintenance costs required for a personal demand deposit account with the same number of transactions as the average account in the $0-800 range of average daily deposit balance.

Step 2. Define the Costing Object

- The costing object is a personal demand deposit account included in the regular demand deposits; one account that represents the average activity for each stratum has been chosen.

- The costing object consists of the services required to process deposits and checks and to maintain and process customers' statements and insurance.

- These services are supplied by the teller, proof and transit, statement and data center departments. These departments in turn consist of services received from other benefit-providing departments and functions (occupancy, administration, communication, etc.).

Step 3. Specify the Cost

- With respect to the resources listed in the definition of the costing object:

  - - People
    Salaries and fringe benefits

  - - Facilities
    Space rental
    Equipment depreciation
    Supplies

  - - Services received
    Occupancy, communication, administration, etc.

Note: FDIC premium has been screened out due to the immateriality of amount for this costing purpose.

Figure 14.4—Illustration of Costing To Assist in Establishing a Pricing Policy for Personal Demand Deposits

Step 4. Specify the Allocation Process

- Allocate people and facility costs directly to cost centers for the demand deposit function from the general accounting records. The cost centers are teller, proof and transit, statement, and data center.

- Allocate the costs of the benefit-providing departments (occupancy, communication, administration, etc.) to the cost centers identified on various bases, using the step method.

- Calculate the average unit transfer costs for
  - • • Processing a deposit (proving, posting, etc.)
  - • • Processing a check (clearing, posting, etc.)
  - • • Maintaining an account (preparing statements and mailing, etc.)

- Allocate costs to the costing object based on activity (deposits, checks and statements).

Step 5. Calculate the Costs

- The average unit transfer costs of deposits, checks, and statements are calculated as follows:

Cost Centers	Total Cost per Figure 10.5	Reference to Detail Calculation	Average Unit Transfer Costs Deposits	Checks	Statements
Teller	$188,300	Figure 10.8	$.088[1]	$	$
Proof and transit	170,700	Not shown ·	.021[2]	.005[5]	
Statement	83,400	Not shown	.012[3]	.012[3]	.430[6]
Data center	219,200	Not shown	.014[4]	.010[4]	.070[7]
Average Unit Transfer Costs			$.135	$.027	$.500

The costs represent the work done, referenced as follows:
[1] Receiving at window and through mail
[2] Proving
[3] Filing
[4] Posting
[5] Clearing
[6] Verifying and mailing statements
[7] Printing statement

- The cost of the lending function as computed in Figure 12.8 is .9647% of investable funds.

Figure 14.4 (Continued)

An example of costing to assist in establishing a pricing policy for personal demand deposits is shown in Figure 14.4. For purposes of illustration, it has been assumed that the bank does not presently charge for demand deposit services and that the bank does not require that a depositor maintain a minimum balance. At the present time, demand deposit customers are paying for the service they receive only by leaving their money on deposit. Management has decided therefore that it is important to know whether the present demand deposit customers maintain balances adequate to offset the cost of handling their accounts, as a basis for considering further action.

In order to make this determination, the cost of handling an average account (defined as an average amount of transaction activity) will first be calculated for accounts in various ranges of size. Next the average daily deposit balance required to offset the costs will be calculated, assuming approximately a four percent earnings credit for investable funds (Figure 14.5).

After having calculated the average daily deposit balance required to cover the cost of handling the accounts in each stratum (a range of $0-800 having been used in Figure 14.4), the actual daily average deposit balance for each such account would be determined. These actual balances would then be compared to the minimum balance required. The characteristics of those accounts that are below the minimum balance requirement could be further examined in terms of type of customer, location, likely effect of a service charge, etc., to provide further information for use in making a pricing decision.

Once a tentative pricing decision has been made, further calculations can be carried out to test the assumptions as to effects on customers, balances, etc.

Loans

Pricing of loans involves many factors:
- Market conditions.
- Legal restraints, such as state usury laws.
- Management's desired profit margins.
- Risk.
- Availability of funds.
- Value of the customer.
- Cost of funds.

In the area of lending, the opportunity open to banks for pricing action is limited. While interest rates, compensating balances, and commitment fees may be custom tailored to the individual borrower, these decisions depend heavily on economic conditions.

The cost of funds can have an influence on the price a bank charges for loans. As described in Chapter 11, the cost of funds can be specifically allocated, or pool averages (single or multiple) or a market-oriented cost based on current market rates can be used. When the

- Sampling of personal demand deposit accounts with balances up to $800 shows
  - • Monthly average number of deposits—2
  - • Monthly average number of checks paid—20
- The activity and maintenance cost of a personal demand deposit account up to $800 is calculated as follows:

Deposits handled	2 at $.135	$ .27
Checks processed	20 at .027	.54
Maintenance	1 at .50	.50
	Total cost per month	$1.31

The remainder of the calculation relates the monthly cost for the average account to the balance required to offset those costs, assuming a gross earnings rate on investable funds of 4.8572% per year.

- The credit rate for investable funds is calculated as follows:

Gross earnings rate per year	4.8572%
Less computed cost of the lending function	.9647
Net earnings rate per year	3.8925%
Earnings rate per month (3.8925% ÷ 12)	.3244%

- Amount of investable funds required to offset $1.31 monthly cost:

$$\frac{\$1.31}{.003244} = \$404$$

- Amount of average daily deposit balance required to offset the monthly cost of handling the account:

  It is necessary to convert investable funds to an average daily deposit balance by applying a factor to represent legal reserve requirements and float. For illustration, the factor used here is 20% of the average daily deposit balance:

$$\frac{\$404}{(1-.20)} = \$505$$

Figure 14.5—Illustration of the Calculation of the Required Minimum Balance To Assist in Establishing a Pricing Policy for Personal Demand Deposits

market-oriented approach based on current market rates is employed, the cost would likely have a more direct relationship to the price charged customers for loans.

With respect to retail loans, such as personal, auto, home improvement, etc., there may be a greater degree of pricing flexibility. These types of loans are characterized by low dollar amounts, many borrowers, and a large volume of service transactions in the form of instalment payments. While the interest rates are primarily influenced by outside factors, the effective rate of charge for the service (including interest) may vary due to discount policy, service fees, etc.

The costing problems are very similar to those discussed in Chapter 12 in connection with fund user profitability, except that the cost is reduced to a unit cost per loan and a unit cost per loan payment.

Trust Services

The trust area is noted for being highly competitive, with all of the problems that this implies in setting prices. Moreover, pricing options are limited when fee rates for the administration of estates and certain other trusts come under court jurisdiction or when these rates are set by state law.

The costs associated with trust activity are primarily salary costs, of which a large portion may be officer administration time. To determine accurately the amount of time spent on a particular trust, or type of trust, this time must be recorded. This may be done by having officers maintain a time report for each trust account handled.

A frequently used technique for pricing has been to set fees based on the total value of the assets held in the trust. The main advantage of this method is its simplicity, since the asset values are readily available. The valuation of trust assets may be determined in one of three ways: current market value, original cost, or par value (for bonds). The major disadvantage in using asset valuation is that different accounts with the same assets incur different costs because of different activity levels (buying and selling of securities, for example) and differing administrative problems.

Assuming that the activity costs for trust accounts have been determined and that each account has been ranked according to total activity costs allocable to it, the accounts can be further ranked for purposes of evaluating a fee schedule, according to these factors:

- Size of the trust.
- Type of trust.

- The asset mix of the trust (e.g., bond, real estate, etc.).
- Amount of responsibility (e.g., custodial, investment, fiduciary, etc.).

These factors may give rise to special pricing considerations due to other factors as, for example, an unusually high amount of top management time that is not reflected in time records; pricing may be based on judgment as to fairness and market factors.

After a fee schedule has been established for a trust, the costs and revenues generated by the service should be reviewed at regular intervals. If a trust account is not generating enough revenues to create a profit, it should be analyzed to determine the advisability of a fee increase.

The key to trust pricing is a knowledge of costs. To determine these costs, an accurate account of officer and employee time must be kept through the use of time reports.

Miscellaneous Services

There are many other services offered by banks, and their number has been increasing as customers demand more help from their banks. Some examples of these services are:

- Safe-deposit boxes
- Travel services
- Travelers' checks
- Cashiers' checks
- Tax assistance
- Investment services
- Data processing services
- Letters of credit

When a new service is being considered, an analysis should be made of the current market demand, the expected volume, and the projected costs and revenues associated with that volume.

Moreover, the costs of a new service during its development phase should be carefully considered. These costs are incurred and recorded before the start-up of the service, and they can be incorporated in the total projected costs of the service by spreading them over a future period as specified by management.

A price can then be established on the basis of this analysis and the anticipated activity volume. A detailed discussion of the cost factors involved in establishing a new service is contained in Chapter 12.

SUMMARY

Since banks operate in a competitive marketplace, there are many factors that affect what they may charge for their services. A fundamental role of cost in pricing is to furnish management with a bench mark (fully absorbed cost) indicating the lowest price that can be charged by each service without incurring a loss for the bank as a whole.

The key to understanding the role of costing in pricing services is a knowledge of cost-volume-profit relationships. Although these relationships can become complex, they are conceptually simple to understand.

A major factor affecting cost-volume-profit relationships is the capacity to render the service involved. The availability of additional capacity gives rise to special cost considerations in analyzing such a pricing approach as that involved in pricing to obtain a profit contribution (excess of revenue over variable cost). If additional capacity must be obtained to accommodate a new service, incremental costs may occur (over and above the variable costs) that should be taken into consideration in setting a price for that service. Since each service has a different revenue-generating capability, cost also helps to determine when the bank can cost below the cost bench mark and still contribute to a greater total profit.

Part VI

SPECIAL COST CONSIDERATIONS

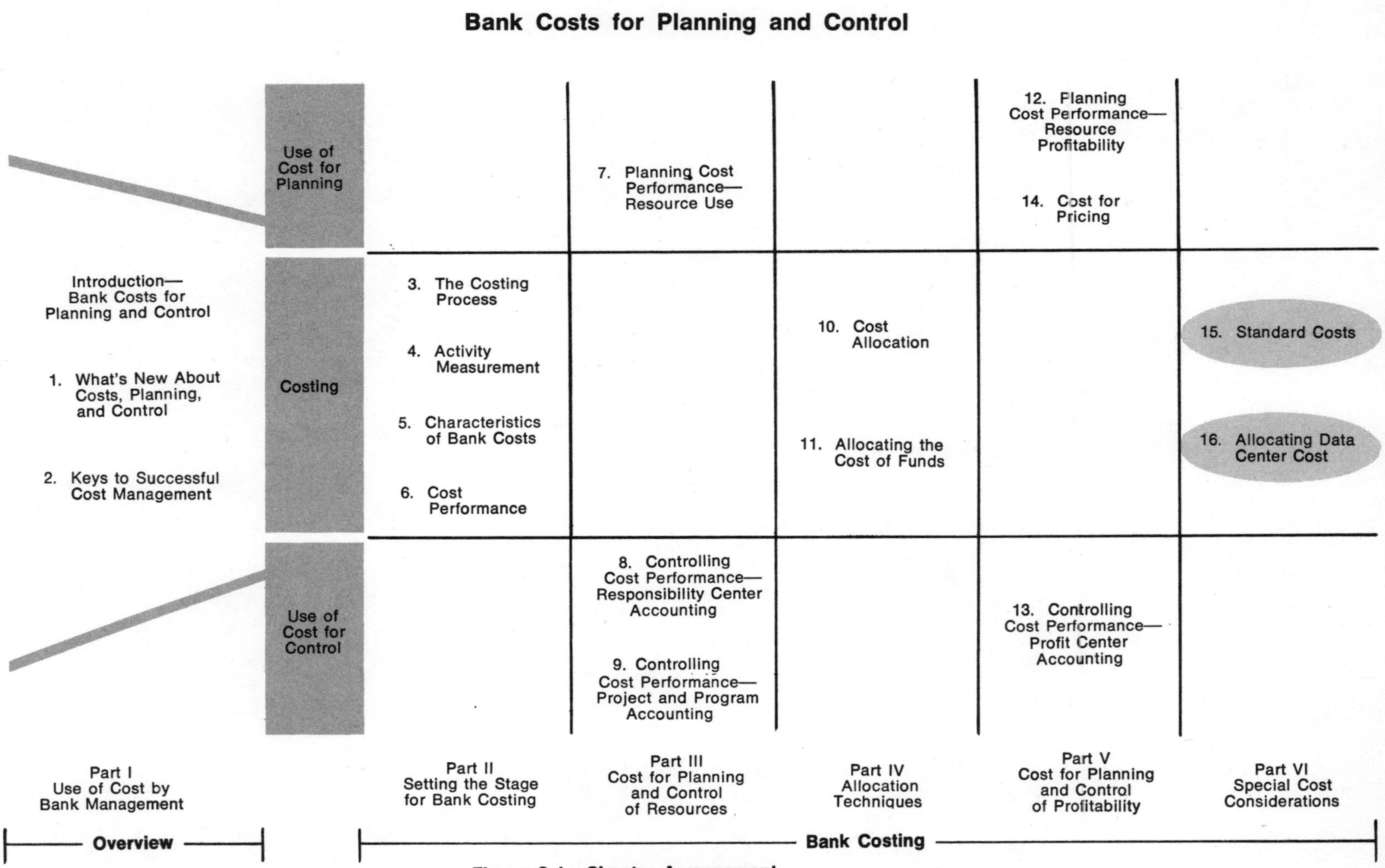

Bank Costs for Planning and Control

Figure O.1—Chapter Arrangement

Part VI

SPECIAL COST
CONSIDERATIONS

The concluding section of this book discusses standard costs and flexible budgets (Chapter 15) and allocating data center costs (Chapter 16). These topics currently are receiving much attention. Each requires explicit definition and great skill to apply. It is not within the scope of this book to present the detail design of a standard cost or a flexible budgeting system. Rather, the discussion is limited to the positioning of standard costs and flexible budgets within the framework of the previous discussions relating to planning and control and costing.

Data processing costs have proven difficult to allocate for many accountants. Chapter 16 shows the applicability of the costing principles set forth in preceding chapters to the allocation of such costs. At the same time a specific approach to allocating EDP costs is shown by a detailed example for those who must deal with the problem. As more banks utilize EDP, the problem of allocating such costs will confront many bankers.

15

STANDARD COSTS

S tandard costs are not too difficult to understand—especially with the costing background developed up to this point. On the other hand, the variety of ways that standard costs can be used and the handling of differences between actual and standard is a very complex subject. The purpose of this chapter then is not to discuss standard costs in all their complexity but to give the reader a better understanding of standard costs and how they fit into the planning and control and costing frameworks that have been established.

As a bank improves its planning and control of costs, it may reach a point where the use of standard costs should be considered if further significant improvement is desired. Standard costs may offer this additional improvement opportunity for those resources that have measurable productive activity by providing a disciplined approach to predetermining the activity and attendant costs that should occur in given circumstances. It should be recognized, however, that work measurement, an important technique in developing standard costs, can also be used without costs to provide a level of control that may be adequate for many banks.

Standard costs can be defined as "carefully predetermined target costs that should be attained under efficient operations."[1] "Carefully predetermined" can be thought of as referring to exercising care in developing the standard cost so that

- The measurements and estimates used are documented to facilitate analysis of differences between actual and standard (variance analysis), and
- The resulting cost is reasonably accurate.

[1] Horngren, *op. cit.*, p. 854.

"Target costs" refer to those costs that *should* occur under given circumstances. The phrase "attained under efficient operations" implies that the resources whose costs are included in the standard are used efficiently. Further, standard costs are usually expressed in the form of a unit cost.

In manufacturing, standards are generally developed separately for variable and fixed costs. For example, a cost such as material is usually considered to be variable (vary directly with volume) and a standard is developed specifically for material. For each unit of production, a unit of standard material cost is applied. As to fixed costs, the standard cost per unit must be determined based upon an assumption concerning the number of units to be produced (a utilization level). A standard overhead cost is then applied to each unit of production based upon the assumed level of utilization.

In a bank, however, a large portion of noninterest costs are fixed (see Chapter 5). As a result, unit costs are highly influenced by resource utilization levels. Although there may be certain situations where a standard cost can be developed for the variable portion of the cost of producing a unit of activity, there seem to be few costs that can be considered clearly variable as material cost usually is in a manufacturing environment. Therefore, this chapter will discuss standard cost from the standpoint of fixed costs and the importance of determining utilization levels in developing the standard costs.

Standard costs are used primarily

- To facilitate planning by providing carefully predetermined target costs for use in analyzing alternatives.
- As an index for measuring the operating efficiency of a unit, function, or activity (or in some cases, a specific resource such as a piece of equipment, etc.).

In order to explain the nature and use of standard costs, their role in the allocation process will be discussed first since that process is fundamental to the use of such standards for planning and control. This will be followed by a more specific discussion concerning the uses of standard costs for planning and for control.

ALLOCATION USING STANDARD COSTS

In Chapters 3 and 10, the use of average unit transfer cost in allocation was discussed. It was pointed out in Chapter 10 that when the allocation of costs must await determination of the transfer unit activity or volume, the average unit transfer cost is, in a sense, held in suspension pending that determination. This occurs, for example, when the cost allocation is being accomplished on a routine basis, as is the case when periodic planning is being accomplished or when monthly reports of results are being prepared. For report results, activity volume (of transactions, for example) is determined at the end of the month and costs associated with that volume are allocated, using the average unit transfer cost. If actual costs are used, it is necessary to calculate these costs each time an allocation is to be made in order to reflect actual cost. This is a time-consuming requirement, especially in larger banks.

Furthermore, the use of actual average unit transfer costs can be unsatisfactory when allocating costs between organizational units if the costs in the benefit-providing units reflect unusual levels of efficiency or inefficiency. In these situations, the unit or function to which the cost is being transferred displays costs that reflect levels of unusual efficiency or inefficiency of another unit.

The use of a standard cost (or, in this case, any predetermined cost) eliminates the need to recalculate costs frequently in order to reflect actual costs. Furthermore, if the predetermined cost represents a reasonable level of efficiency and has been carefully predetermined (a standard cost), then the benefit-receiving unit to which the cost is being allocated is not unduly penalized or rewarded.

STANDARD COSTS FOR PLANNING AND FOR CONTROL

Standard costs are planned unit costs based on efficient operation. They simplify planning by making a carefully predetermined cost available for a particular resource whenever an alternative being analyzed requires the use of that particular resource (or combination of resources). Otherwise, it would be necessary to calculate these costs each time an alternative was analyzed.

Standard costs also increase the level of confidence that management has in the analyses of alternatives. Since the costs are "carefully predetermined target costs," this tends to reduce the degree of error frequently associated with cost projections.

Standard costs provide an opportunity for improving cost control because the makeup of the standard is known, making it possible to analyze the reasons for differences between standard and actual costs. A standard cost can be considered to be composed of three elements: (1) resource cost, (2) an assumed level of resource efficiency (an effective pace), and (3) an assumed level of activity volume. If these three elements of the standard are known, and the corresponding elements in the actual cost are determined, the variances (differences) between the standard elements and actual elements can be shown as follows:

Elements of Standard Costs	Compared to →	Elements of Actual Costs		Variances (Differences)
Planned resource cost		Actual resource cost	=	Spending variance
Planned efficiency		Actual efficiency	=	Efficiency variance
Planned volume		Actual volume	=	Volume variance

A simplified example will be used to illustrate this concept, in which it is assumed that the encoding section of the proof and transit department has developed a standard cost for encoding magnetic ink characters on checks

- Based on observation of encoding operators and applying work measurement standards that take into account operator fatigue and personal time allowances, and by adding an allowance for balancing and transporting activities, a standard of 800 checks encoded per man-hour was established.

- The proof and transit department planned for the ensuing period on the basis of an expected average check volume of 280,000 per month. They further planned for two full-time clerks.

- The standard cost of encoding one check is $.0034, calculated as follows:

Expected average number of checks per month	280,000
Standard number of checks encoded per man-hour	800
Man-hours required monthly for encoding (280,000 ÷ 800)	350

Planned staff complement:	
2 full-time clerks—8 hours a day, 22 days a month, or 350 man-hours at an actual rate of $2.72 per hour	$ 952
Cost for each item ($952 ÷ 280,000)	$.0034

For illustration, it is assumed that the encoding section processed 200,000 items during a month and that the following information was reported by the finance and control division to the supervisor of the encoding section:

Actual cost of encoding section (salaries and fringe benefits of two full-time clerks)	$ 952
Standard cost allowance (200,000 items at $.0034 each)	680
Unfavorable variance	$ 272

In this example, the unfavorable variance is apparently due to volume. 200,000 items encoded at the standard rate of 800 an hour require only 250 man-hours, but 350 man-hours were paid for. There could be a number of causes for the cost variance—for example:

- Inefficient clerical work or machine functioning.
- Efficient clerical work, but only 200,000 available checks for processing.
- An unusually large number of items requiring special encoding.
- A combination of the preceding factors.

To some extent, the encoding supervisor should have some understanding of the reason for the unfavorable variance, especially since this variance is so substantial. On the other hand, if a number of factors were causing the variance, the reasons might not be so apparent.

The preceding example is a very simple one, since the only "standard data" incorporated in the standard cost is the time required to process an average item using efficient methods. Other elements of the cost could also be brought under standards control as well and incorporated in the standard cost in order to make more detailed analysis as to the nature of the variances, for example:

- Clerical salary rates.
- Efficiency of operation.
- Mix of special encoding.
- Batch size.

Each month the actual dollars or statistics for these items would be determined and compared to standard to determine the variance between actual and standard for the month. The list of items mentioned above is only partial, and as more standards are introduced into the calculation of costs, more analysis can be done for management. Recording, reporting, and analysis, however, become increasingly more complex.

To illustrate a more detailed analysis of the variance, assume that the encoders recorded the actual time spent encoding to permit comparison with the 250 man-hours of standard time allowed. It would then be possible to state the variance in terms of the amount caused by the difference between standard and actual volume (volume variance) and the amount caused by inefficient operations (efficiency variance). Management would then be led to inquire about the causes of the differences between planned volume and actual volume and between planned efficiency and actual efficiency. Note that a spending variance did not occur in the preceding example because the actual clerical costs were the same as those used in developing the standard cost.

DEVELOPING STANDARD COSTS

Developing a standard cost involves the following actions:

- Determining a target cost for the resource or resources whose cost or costs are included in the standard.
- Determining the level of utilization at which it is to be assumed the resources will be used. This consists of two factors:

    . . The efficiency with which it is assumed the resources should be used (how fast can the resources produce).

    . . The volume of activity that should occur assuming the above level of efficiency and also assuming the volume of input work to be done (checks, for example) is available.

- Using the utilization level of the resource or resources to calculate standard cost per unit of activity volume.

Target or "reasonable" resource costs can be set for clerical salaries, for example, by class of employee, whereas for supplies they can be set by using established vendor price lists. Once a target cost for a resource has been established, it is then necessary to determine the number of units of activity that should be produced by the resource, that is, its utilization level. Activity measurement, as discussed in Chapter 4, again plays an important role both in quantifying activity volumes and in determining efficiency, the two factors that together determine utilization.

First it is necessary to determine how many units *can* be produced by a given resource. Work measurement standards as well as capacity ratings for equipment are helpful. Second, it is necessary to determine the levels of activity volume to be assumed in calculating the standard cost. It was pointed out in Chapter 7 that costs per unit will vary, depending upon the level of resource utilization. In addition, the cost of unused capacity diminishes as use rises. Therefore, the level of utilization used in calculating the standard will directly affect the standard unit cost. In a bank, with its relatively high proportion of fixed costs, the level of utilization is particularly important in determining standard unit costs.

Generally, it is assumed that the use of ideal or full-rated capacity as a level of utilization for any resource probably results in a standard so difficult to meet that it tends to discourage rather than to encourage higher achievement. On the other hand, the use of too low a level of utilization may result in a standard that does not provide incentive or a good basis against which to measure results.

There are three concepts of utilization that will serve adequately for purpose of illustration:

- Ideal or full-rated capacity.
- Expected utilization.
- Practical capacity.

Ideal or full-rated capacity refers to a utilization level that is the maximum productivity possible. The use of standards for this purpose results in a variance from actual that reflects the remainder of unused capacity. For some purposes, such as keeping management aware of remaining unused capacity, this utilization level may be appropriate, but mostly it tends to create an unreasonable standard.

Expected utilization is the anticipated level of utilization for a given period. As usage forecasts change (yearly, for example), the expected utilization would be likely to change.

Practical capacity refers to an attainable level of utilization assuming efficient operations. Practical capacity will frequently be greater than actual utilization.

If expected utilization is used to set the standard cost, variances will reflect the differences in volumes and levels of efficiency at actual and at expected utilization. If practical capacity is used, the nature of the variances is similar except that the volume variance reflects additional attainable capacity.

For planning purposes the use of practical capacity in setting standards might result in unrealistic costs being used to analyze alternatives. Expected utilization could, in this case, provide more useful cost data since it would likely approximate actual results more closely.

If the standards are to be used to judge performance of a responsibility center manager, practical capacity has the advantage of keeping management aware of the unused capacity. The use of practical capacity to set the standard may, therefore, result in better information for managerial purposes. If, however, the standards are to be used to transfer costs between responsibility or profit centers, larger volume variances would likely result from using practical capacity and could raise serious questions as to which unit should absorb the variance. A possible solution for selective units would be to charge such variances to a special "top management" account on the theory that under-utilization is more a result of their decisions than the decisions of the unit managers. A second possible solution is to use expected utilization for calculating the standard in such cases.

Since the actual utilization level and the level used to set the standard costs will usually be different, a volume variance generally will occur. An approach that, to a great extent, eliminates volume variances, but retains the advantages of using "carefully predetermined" costs, is flexible budgeting.

FLEXIBLE BUDGETS

A responsibility center or profit center budget contains expense plans for a specified time period. The plan should be well thought out and based on a level of utilization. After the specified period is over, actual results can be compared to the budget as a basis for evaluating each manager's performance. This type of budgeting is sometimes called "static" budgeting, and it assumes one (or a "static") level of utilization.

Though management exercises care in determining the utilization level to be used in preparing the budget, actual volume will be different in most cases. One way of showing this difference is through the volume variance discussed in the previous section on developing standard costs. Another approach is to use the flexible budgeting technique. Using this technique, expenses are planned at varying levels of utilization. At the end of a period (a month, for example) actual expenses are compared to expenses that should have occurred at the actual utilization level. The result of this approach is to eliminate the effect of differences in volume on the analysis of results.

Some costs are fixed over wide ranges of volume. As mentioned before, a large portion of bank costs fits this category. Other costs vary in proportion to volume, such as deposit tickets used. Not all costs fit neatly into these two categories; some increase in steps while others have both a fixed and a variable portion. Flexible budgets reflect these characteristics by providing cost data related to varying utilization levels. The costs are used both in developing the budget and later for

Encoding Section

Flexible Budget

For the Month Beginning ─────────────────

Check volume	Utilization levels		
	240,000	280,000	320,000
(1) Supervision	$ 900	$ 900	$ 900
(2) Encoder labor	825	955	1,115
(3) Maintenance	120	140	160
(4) Supplies	60	70	80
(5) Equipment depreciation	1,200	1,200	1,200
Total expense	$3,105	$3,265	$3,455

Assumptions for each expense are as follows:

(1) Supervision costs will not vary within the volume ranges shown here (240,000-320,000).

(2) Encoder labor includes a full-time staff of two encoding clerks. Work measurement standards have been developed and a reasonably efficient and well-trained encoding clerk should process 800 checks per hour. The two clerks are required full time at a utilization level of 280,000 checks. At a level of 320,000 checks, part-time encoders will be required. It is assumed that part-time clerks can only process 600 checks per hour, thus requiring an additional 67 hours or $160. At 240,000, the encoders have 50 hours of available time. Arrangements have been made for the encoding clerks to work in another unit during slack hours. The applicable portion of their salaries will be charged to the other unit.

(3)-(4) Based on experience, these costs vary with volume—approximately $.50 and $.25 per 1,000 checks, respectively.

(5) Equipment depreciation expense does not vary within the volume ranges shown here.

Figure 15.1—Illustration of a Flexible Budget

Encoding Section

Flexible Budget Report

For the Month Ending _____

Actual volume—300,000 checks

	Budget	Actual	Favorable (Unfavorable) Variance
(1) Supervision	$ 900	$ 900	$ —
(2) Encoder labor	1,035	1,200	(165)
(3) Maintenance	150	370	(220)
(4) Supplies	75	70	5
(5) Equipment	1,200	1,200	—
Total expenses	$3,360	$3,740	($380)

Explanation of variances

(1), (4), (5)—no significant variances.

(2) Part-time clerks inefficient—usual part-time help from another section not available.

(3) Machine breakdown.

Figure 15.2—Flexible Budget Report

adjusting planned expense levels to reflect the actual utilization that occurred.

There are a number of approaches to the preparation of flexible budgets: using charts showing expenses at various levels of utilization; having tables with values shown for calculating expenses at various levels of utilization; using graphs showing curves for each expense. Figure 15.1 illustrates a flexible budget prepared for the encoding section based on three levels of utilization. The characteristics assumed for each expense at the various levels of utilization are discussed in the Figure. Figure 15.2 illustrates a report prepared at the end of the month. Actual utilization was 300,000 checks processed.

In the approach to flexible budgeting shown in Figure 15.1, the encoding section supervisor monitors the expenses of the section according to the actual level of utilization experienced. At the end of the month, the expenses shown in the budget are adjusted to the actual utilization for comparison with actual expense.

Flexible budgets can be kept simple and yet they provide a measure of control (through recognizing the fixed and variable aspects of costs) not available in static budgets. A disadvantage of flexible budgeting is the tendency to provide a moving target for organizational unit managers. A separate plan might be necessary to provide a basis for assessing overall progress toward bank goals.

STANDARD COST SYSTEMS

The use of standard costs to develop budget amounts against which to measure and analyze results on a routine basis constitutes a standard cost system.

A standard cost system must encompass the means not only to report results but also to establish and maintain the standards themselves. There must be some way to develop good standard data and then periodically to test the adequacy of the data and the need for change. A time-consuming part of this task is the measurement of activity required to establish standards for productivity.

Another requirement for an effective standard cost system is a sound definition of either responsibility centers, profit centers, or both. Standards provide both incentives to management by establishing goals or targets and a means for measuring and analyzing results. The results measurements must therefore be identified with organizational responsibilities if the information is to be used effectively in controlling costs.

Finally, it should be evident from the discussion in this chapter that a standard cost system can be complex. It requires expertise in setting and maintaining the standards and it requires expertise on the part of management in understanding and using the results of analyses. Furthermore, a standard cost system can require a significant commitment to systems discipline and a substantial capability to process data.

SUMMARY

Standard costs can be helpful for planning and controlling costs of resources with measurable productivity. Due to the nature of bank costs, however, care should be exercised in developing and using such standards to assure their usefulness to management in making decisions.

Some banks may find that limiting the use of standard costs to but a few vital areas is sufficient. Others may find that the principal value of the standard cost approach lies in measuring and setting standards for productivity, and they will not want to attach costs to those standards. Still others may find that the flexible budgeting technique may provide a sufficient degree of cost control.

The use of a standard cost system requires a systematic approach to setting and maintaining standards and it provides a means for reporting results and analyzing variances. Each bank should give careful consideration to the value of such a system, because the requisite management and systems commitments can be substantial.

16

ALLOCATING DATA CENTER COSTS

An electronic data processing capability will be referred to here as a "data center." The expense of operating such a center is relatively high; moreover, a great many segments of a bank use these expensive services. Therefore, the allocation of data center costs has far-reaching ramifications and can be important for many management planning and control purposes, including profitability analysis and profit center management. Also, since many bank data centers provide services to other companies, it is important to understand data center costs as they relate to prices for these services.

A data center has cost characteristics similar to those of the bank as a whole. Therefore, consideration of data center costs also serves to review and further illustrate some of the bank's overall costing problems.

As pointed out in Chapter 5, banks experience fluctuating transaction volumes, the cost of which contains a high proportion of fixed expenses. This pattern is followed by the data center, which also has a high proportion of fixed expenses. As with the bank as a whole, costs to be allocated must be expressed as averages that, to the extent possible, bear a reasonable relationship to the normal range of operating conditions likely to occur.

The major costs of the data center are salaries and fringe benefits of personnel (computer operators, programmers, and keypunch operators), supplies, rent of the computer and peripheral devices, and depreciation of purchased equipment.

Allocation procedures for data center costs are similar in many respects to the procedures required for other benefit-providing activities of the bank (e.g., bookkeeping). The specific problems of allocating data center costs relate directly to the difficulty of measuring its activities under certain special circumstances, such as "multiprogramming" or "on-line processing." This chapter will, therefore, emphasize the allocation of the costs normally associated with the operations of the computers (i.e., processing of data as opposed to systems development). It also will describe how some of the more difficult costing problems can be handled.

The dollar amounts used in the examples in this chapter are purely illustrative and intended solely to show the costing approach used. They are not intended as guides for the operations of any data center. They are of a general magnitude that might correspond to the operations of a medium-sized bank.

NATURE OF DATA CENTER COSTS

As noted above, the characteristics of data center costs generally resemble those of bank costs as a whole. Although they are predominantly fixed, some costs vary with changes in volume. In Figure 16.1 data center costs are broken down organizationally within the data center. The total costs shown are the same as the data processing costs used in Chapter 10 through 13.

The costs shown in Figure 16.1 relate both to the day-to-day operation of the center and to specific systems projects. For example, costs of data preparation, computer operations, a portion of data center administration costs, and a portion of programming costs (related to updating existing programs) are related to day-to-day operations. The remainder of programming costs (frequently a major part) and a portion of data center administration costs are allocated directly to specific systems projects.

Costs of the data preparation and programming sections include a high proportion of variable costs. It is in these sections, therefore, that the greatest opportunities lie for achieving efficiency, which can be done by improved scheduling of full-time personnel and selective use of part-time employees.

The high proportion of fixed costs in a data center makes it important to bear in mind two points that have been made previously:

- Maximization of resource utilization and minimization of cost are the principal strategies available to management to increase bank profitability (see Chapter 7).

Annual Expenses Distributed Directly Through The General Accounting System

	Total Data Center	Data Center Administration	Data Preparation Section	Programming Section[1]	Operations Section
Fixed Expenses:					
Salaries and fringe benefits	$ 60,750	$10,000	$ 8,367	$27,750	$ 14,633
Machine rental	81,700		1,800		79,900
Machine depreciation	9,500		1,500	600	7,400
Machine maintenance	6,300		300		6,000
Miscellaneous	1,200		150	150	900
Total fixed expenses	159,450	10,000	12,117	28,500	108,833
Variable Expenses:					
Salaries and fringe benefits, arising from part-time employees and overtime	20,250		4,133	9,250	6,867
Supplies	11,500		3,000	2,000	6,500
Miscellaneous	1,200		150	150	900
Total variable expenses	32,950		7,283	11,400	14,267
Total Expenses	$192,400	$10,000	$19,400	$39,900	$123,100
Percent fixed	83%	100%	62%	71%	89%
Percent variable	17		38	29	11
Total percent	100%	100%	100%	100%	100%

[1] For purposes of this illustration, it has been assumed that systems design work is accomplished by an organizational unit separate from the data center.

Figure 16.1—Illustrative Data Center Expense Characteristics

- Knowledge of the level of resource utilization is important when allocating costs.

Utilization is basic to each of these points. The following section will review the measurement of data center activity, a key factor in determining the level of utilization. It will concentrate on the computer operation activities carried out in the operations section of the data center.

ACTIVITY MEASUREMENT IN A DATA CENTER

Data center equipment is made up of manually operated machines (such as key punches and encoders), mechanically operated equipment (such as printers and sorters), and electronically operated units (such as a central processor).

The capacity of data center equipment is rated in terms of the number of transactions that can be handled during a short interval of time, usually a second. For example, magnetic tape transports are rated by the number of bytes or characters they can read or write per second, optical character readers by the number of documents they read per second. Similarly, the central processor is rated by the number of instructions processed per second. Figure 16.2 shows a representative list of units used to measure activity and rated capacity of data processing equipment of a type that is frequently found in banks.

Each piece of equipment represents a different amount of cost. The greater the cost, the more important it becomes to achieve a high degree of utilization so that the size of the cost can be justified. Thus, it would make little difference if a low-cost key punch machine were idle most of the time, but it would be of serious consequence if a high-cost central processing unit did not show a correspondingly high level of utilization.

Both operating mode and computer application influence the measurement of activity and utilization of a data center. The term "operating mode" refers to how the computer operates, e.g., a single-program computer system or a computer system capable of storing in its memory several programs on which it will operate.

Single-Program Computer System

A single-program computer system is sometimes referred to as a "batch processing" system because it is necessary to gather input for any program into a batch of sufficient size to warrant setting up the computer to run that program. When the computer is in operation (processing a computer run), only one program and its associated

Computer System Component	Units Commonly Used for Measuring Activity and Rated Capacity of Equipment
Central processor	Instructions per metered second or programs (many instructions) per metered hour
Input and output devices	
Card reader and punches	Cards per minute
Paper tape readers and punches	Characters per second
Magnetic tape transport	Bytes or characters per second
Optical character reader	Documents per second
Typewriter	Characters per second
Disk file	Average seek time and character transfer rate
Line printers	Lines per minute
Visual display	Characters per second

Figure 16.2—Bases of Measuring Computer System Component Activity and Rated Capacity

input and output data are processed. When the processing run has been completed, it is necessary to load a new program and place the new input data in the card or tape reader before processing can begin again.

As a result, the activity of a single program computer system is measured by the time required to process the program from the time the computer is being readied for processing until processing is completed. Even though each program being processed through the computer may require differing amounts of time for processing input and output, and for internal (central processor) processing, the entire computer system is dedicated to handling only the one program during a processing run. Thus, its entire cost during the time devoted to a particular run would be properly allocated to that program.

Multiprogramming Computer System

Multiprogramming refers to a sectioning of computer memory to accommodate more than one program in memory and to permit switching from one program to another whenever a particular program does not require central processor operation (as, for example, when the program causes the central processor to wait for input or output devices to function). Because of the central processor's high internal operating speed and the relative slowness of such electro-mechanical input and output devices as card readers and line printers, the central processor can find itself obliged to spend a large portion of its time waiting for such devices to complete their functions. Multiprogramming interleaves other program processing into this waiting time. Although this mode of operation substantially increases central processor utilization and data center productivity, it also creates some unusual cost allocation problems. To facilitate understanding of these problems, Figure 16.3 compares a single program system with a multiprogram system.

In the single program computer system the amount of time required to process input data, accomplish internal processing (processing calculations, updating computer files, etc.), and process output was not of concern, since the entire computer system was dedicated to processing only the one program. When using multiprogramming computers, however, several programs (and several inputs and outputs) are being processed at varying times during a processing run. Since it is necessary to measure the time required to process each program in order to establish a basis for allocating costs to the user associated with a program, some way of measuring the time for each program is required.

In establishing procedures for measuring the time required for processing, it is important to recognize the highly individual characteristics of various computer applications, which may vary greatly as to the proportionate amount of time spent on input, internal processing, and output. Demand deposit account bookkeeping, for example, creates a high daily input volume (processing checks and deposits), with a high output volume (listings, statements, etc.) but only a moderate amount of daily internal processing (posting to customers'

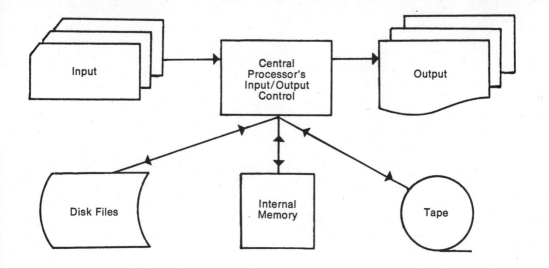

Single Program System

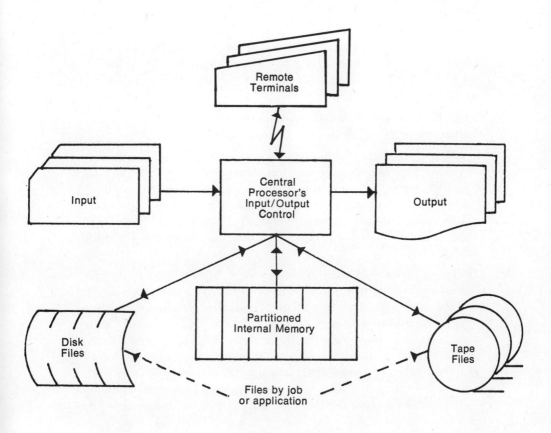

Multiprogram System

Figure 16.3—Structures of Single Program and Multiprogram Systems

statement computer files). Salary payroll, on the other hand, calls for a relatively low input (payroll changes), heavy internal processing (calculation of pay, deductions, and updating earnings records), and a high output (payroll checks). Therefore, in a data center that operates in a multiprogramming mode, handling a number of applications at once, it is necessary to determine the input, output, and processing time for each application separately in order to allocate cost to a particular application with accuracy.

If all input and output activity were directly handled by each program being processed within the central processor (when multiprogramming), measurement of the time to process each program would be a reasonable basis for allocating all operations section costs, since the cost of the central processor is a major part of operations cost. Many multiprogramming computers, however, have special programs (not associated with any particular application) that handle input data and output data. In these cases, the time required to process input and output is not directly associated with the application program and therefore must be calculated separately. (This procedure will be illustrated later as part of an example showing the calculation of average unit transfer costs for allocating data center costs—Figures 16.5-16.9.)

Central Processor Time Measurement in the Multiprogramming Mode

Because equipment manufacturers have recognized that measuring central processor time presents problems, many computers capable of multiprogramming are equipped with interval timers. In addition, if there is sufficient memory capacity, the manufacturers and many software houses furnish software packages (job accounting programs) for use in recording central processor utilization by program identification.

The diagram in Figure 16.4 shows some basic activities that take place in a computer if it is operating in a multiprogramming mode. It indicates how time may be utilized by various activities, beginning with the execution of certain steps of Program A, through the execution of certain steps of Program B, then returning to Program A. An operating system supervisor program functions as a supervisor for all program handling within the computer. With the job accounting program measuring the time duration of all such activities (including its own), elapsed time information is available for compilation by program.

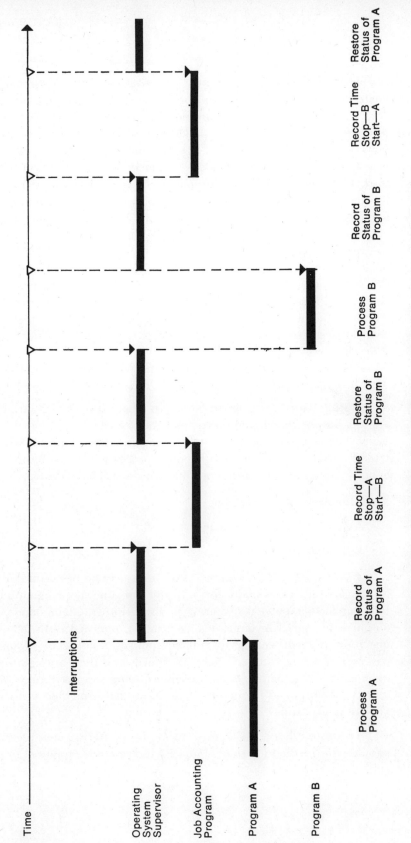

Figure 16.4—Recording Central Processor Time by Program—Multiprogramming Mode

The manager of a data center operating in a multiprogramming mode should consider using an appropriate software package of this type to develop adequate utilization records. Before using the information developed by such a package as the basis for cost allocation, however, he should recognize that some currently available programs may have been written for older equipment and therefore may not work efficiently with newer equipment. It often happens that after replacing its old computer equipment, a bank will continue to use some programs for certain bank applications that were designed for its older equipment. By doing so, it may realize a certain saving in cost, but the older programs may not work efficiently with the new equipment. At the same time, the bank may have developed new programs for certain other applications. The bank unit using the older programs is penalized if costs are allocated on the basis of central processor time. Although the processing service to the user may be the same, the time-charges have become relatively higher.

Alternatives to Central Processor Time Measurement in the Multiprogramming Mode

Costing bases, as pointed out throughout this book, must be appropriate for the circumstances, and the degree of precision that is being obtained must be warranted. In certain circumstances there are several alternatives to the use of central processor time that could be appropriate for allocating the costs of a processor. These include:

- Allocation based on output.

- Allocation based on value to the users.

- Estimated allocation.

Allocation Based on Output. Allocation may be based on output if there are only a few major users. In this case, one simply ignores the fact that the computer is operating in a multiprogramming mode. Its output is measured in terms of lines printed, punched cards, elapsed operation time of key peripheral equipment, number of inquiries passing through remote terminals, etc. However, if there are significant differences in the nature of the programs being processed (e.g., high input—low output vs low input—high output), this method has some obvious shortcomings.

Allocation Based on Value to the Users. While not precisely parallel, this method has some similarity to procedures followed in the oil industry and the meat packing industry, where numerous products are derived from a single resource and cost is allocated on the basis of the relative market values of the products produced. For example, the cost of crude oil is frequently allocated to the various products of the cracking process in proportion to their market worth.

There is obviously no external market value for the work of a data center that is dedicated exclusively to providing service for other departments within a bank. The value to internal users of its output, however, can be reasonably estimated, in one of two ways:

- Clerical cost savings realized.
- Estimated clerical work to be done.

Originally most banks justified installing their data centers on the basis of the clerical cost savings they would realize, and many still devote a major portion of their computer capacity for this purpose. It is appropriate in such cases, therefore, to allocate EDP costs in proportion to the cost savings experienced by user departments when the clerical work was first taken over by the computer. This method is equitable when the current computer applications were those developed to replace clerical operations.

It would not be appropriate, however, to allocate in this fashion if computer applications have changed to include new operations that were developed after the computer was acquired. For example, if a computer replaced a bookkeeping operation for trust and demand deposits, and no other major uses were added, the clerical cost saved by each activity would provide an equitable basis of allocation. On the other hand, if a credit card operation that had not previously existed was subsequently added, this allocation approach would no longer be valid. In such cases, a reasonable basis of allocation would be the estimated clerical work required for both the bookkeeping and credit card operations, as determined by the use of work measurement standards. This method does not take into account the relative efficiencies obtained by replacement of clerical activities with data processing systems.

Estimated Allocation. If the number of users is small, central processor time measurement may not be necessary. For instance, if one user accounts for 85% or more of the activity of the data center, a reasonable estimate of the cost could be an adequate method of allocation.

Step 1. Define the Purpose

1. Management is reviewing several profit areas as a basis for deciding on possible changes in emphasis on the various services it provides.
2. The criterion is profitability.

Step 2. Define the Costing Object

- The costing objects are several profit areas, most of which require services of the data center.
- The costing object consists of:
  - • Funds
  - • People (directly engaged in providing the service)
  - • Facilities (space, equipment, and supplies used directly by the service)
  - • Services received—from, among others, the data center, which in turn consists of:

    People (supervisors, keypunch operators, programmers, etc.)

    Facilities (computer and related equipment and supplies)

    Services received (space, communications, and administration)

Note: This example is concerned only with the data center, which is comprised of four organizational units: administration, data preparation, programming, and operations. For convenience of costing the resources of the operations section are grouped around three cost centers: internal processing, card reader, and line printer.

Step 3. Specify the Cost Data

- Salaries and fringe benefits of employees directly assigned to the data center.
- Computer rental, depreciation of equipment, and supplies cost for the data center.
- Costs of space, communications, and administration related to the data center.
- Average unit transfer costs of the operating section are to be calculated for the following cost centers: card input, internal processing, and line printer.

Note: For purposes of illustration, only the calculation of the average unit transfer costs of data preparation, card input, and internal processing (magnetic tape transports, disk devices, and central processor) will be shown here, although the allocation to a specific profit area would also have to include the costs of the line printer.

Step 4. Specify the Allocation Process

- Costs for the data preparation and operations sections are to be determined by compiling the costs distributed directly to these sections within the data center by the general accounting system, plus allocations for bank-wide occupancy, communications, and administrative costs.

Figure 16.5—Computation of Data Center Costs

- Average unit transfer cost of data preparation are to be calculated using the costs for data preparation section. Average unit transfer costs for card input and for internal processing time are to be calculated using costs allocated to the card reader cost center and the internal processing cost center, respectively, in the operations section.

- Data preparation, punched card input, and internal processor cost center costs are to be allocated to the profit area based on the number of punched cards prepared, the number of cards fed into the computer, and the meter time required, respectively.
Note: Same as for Step 3, above.

Step 5. Calculate the Cost

Costs are calculated in the manner shown in Figure 16.6 to the lowest level cost center required.

Average unit transfer cost calculations and an illustration of cost allocation are shown in separate figures:

- Data preparation in Figure 16.7.

- Internal processing in Figure 16.8.

- Punched card input in Figure 16.9.

- Illustration of data center cost allocation in Figure 16.10.

Figure 16.5 (Continued)

ALLOCATING DATA CENTER COSTS (MULTIPROGRAMMING MODE)—AN EXAMPLE

One reason for allocating data center costs is that such an allocation can be helpful to management in analyzing such alternatives as whether or not to add a certain new lending service that will require EDP support. Another reason for allocating these costs can be to communicate plans and measure results. This would apply, for example, if management wished to show data center costs expected to be incurred by profit centers, or by responsibility centers, and to measure actual allocated costs against the anticipated costs. In both circumstances the five costing steps would be used.

To illustrate the concepts regarding data center costs discussed in this chapter, average unit transfer costs will be calculated for three types of data center costs, assuming that the computer is being operated in the multiprogramming mode. This will be done to allocate costs to profit areas. Illustrative average unit transfer costs will be calculated for:

- Data preparation.
- Internal processing.
- Punched card input.

Annual Expenses

	Total	Organizational Units Recognized by the General Accounting System				Allocation of Operations Section Expenses to Cost Centers		
		Data Center Administration	Data Preparation Section	Programming Section	Operations Section	Internal Processing	Card Reader	Line Printer
Expenses distributed directly through accounting system:								
Salaries and fringe benefits	$ 81,000	$ 10,000	$12,500	$ 37,000	$ 21,500[1]	$ 7,167	$ 7,167	$ 7,166
Machine rental	81,700		1,800		79,900	74,900	2,000	3,000
Machine depreciation	9,500		1,500	600	7,400	7,400		
Machine maintenance	6,300		300		6,000	5,400	300	300
Supplies	11,500		3,000	2,000	6,500	1,500	300	5,000
Miscellaneous	2,400		300	300	1,800	1,200	300	300
Total expenses from accounting system	192,400	10,000	19,400	39,900	123,100			
Allocated expenses:								
Occupancy	7,700		2,600	1,500	3,600	2,700	300	600
Communications	5,200		1,300	1,300	2,600	2,600		
Administration	13,900	13,900						
Total expenses	219,200	23,900	23,300	42,700	129,300			
Allocation of data center administration expense (Allocated on basis of salaries)		(23,900) (100%)	4,300 (18%)	12,400 (52%)	7,200 (30%)	2,400 (33%)	2,400 (33%)	2,400 (33%)
Total before allocation of program maintenance expense	219,200	—	27,600	55,100	136,500	13,775		
Allocations of program maintenance (25% of programming section expenses)[2]				(13,775)	13,775	13,775		
Total Expenses	$219,200	$ —	$27,600	$41,325	$150,275	$119,042	$12,467	$18,766

[1] It has been assumed that the data center operators tend all three groups of equipment simultaneously; therefore the salary cost has been divided equally between each cost center.

[2] As noted the unallocated portion of programming section costs (after receiving an allocation of data center administration costs) relates to specific projects and is therefore not included in the day-to-day operating costs of the data center for which average unit transfer costs are to be computed.

Figure 16.6—Allocation of Expenses Within the Data Center

Annual expense of the data preparation section of data center (Figure 16.6)	$27,600
Number of cards to be keypunched (average of 22 strokes per card)[1]	1,000,000
Average unit transfer cost per 1,000 cards $\dfrac{\$27,600}{1,000,000} \times 1,000 = \$27.60$	

[1] For simplicity of illustration, it has been assumed that at least 85% of the cards punched require 19 to 25 key strokes each, thus permitting the use of cards as transfer units. If there were a significant variance from this range, however, new average unit transfer costs based on the new range of strokes should be calculated. As an alternative the average unit transfer cost could be calcuated per 1,000 key strokes in the event it were not practical to use card count.

Figure 16.7—Average Unit Transfer Cost—Data Preparation

Internal processing annual expenses to be allocated on basis of metered hours (Figure 16.6):		$119,042
Metered hours of internal processing available 2 shifts (assumes third shift not practical)		4224 hours
Less maintenance down-time	528 hours	
Other unavoidable nonproductive time	528	
Total nonproductive hours		1056
Practical capacity		3168
Expected utilization		50%
Expected utilization in metered hours		1584 hours
Average unit transfer cost per metered hour $\dfrac{\$119,042}{1584}$		$75.15

Figure 16.8—Average Unit Transfer Cost—Internal Processing

Annual expense of card reader (Figure 16.6) $12,467

Allocated cost of internal processing
time necessary to read a card:

- Processing time to read card, edit and write to
  magnetic storage—4/1000th second[2]

- Estimated volume of cards to be read—1,500,000 cards

- Allocated cost of internal processing using the average
  unit transfer cost calculated in Figure 16.8

$$\frac{\$75.15}{3600 \text{ seconds}} \quad x \quad \frac{4}{1,000} \quad x \ 1,500,000$$

                                                                        125

Total cost of reading cards $12,592

Average unit transfer cost per 1000 cards

$$\text{read } \frac{\$12,592}{1,500,000} \quad x \ 1,000 \qquad \qquad \$ \ 8.395$$

[1] Average unit costs for output would be computed using a similar approach.
[2] Assumes input/output being handled by a special nonapplication program. Does not include application program processing time.

Figure 16.9—Average Unit Transfer Cost—Punched Card Input[1]

These costs, along with others, will be used to determine the profitability of those areas. The average unit transfer cost for punched card input will be calculated due to the assumption that a special program is handling the entire mix of input cards and that central processor time by application program does not include input processing time. A further assumption is made that costs calculated for current profit area operation will provide adequate information concerning decisions about future profit area emphasis. The detailed steps required to carry out the costing process are shown in Figures 16.5 through 16.10.

The example also illustrates the use of cost centers as convenient parts of organizational units. As shown in the column headings of Figure 16.6 the operations section is divided into three cost centers: internal processing, card reader, and line printer. The internal processing cost center is comprised of the central processor, the magnetic tape transports, and the disk devices.

Assumptions

The specific profit area to which data center costs are to be allocated has the following data processing activity volume for the year:

- Cards keypunched and verified (22 keystroke average)   30,000

- Estimated meter hours required per period to process all programs (includes time for three major programs run only at the end of the year and one run quarterly)   185

- Lines of output printed by line printer   100,000

Cost allocation for data preparation, card input, internal processing and line printer cost centers is as follows:

- Data preparation
  30,000 cards x $27.60 per thousand = $ 828.00

- Card input
  30,000 cards x $8.395 per thousand =   251.85

- Internal processing 185 meter hours x $75.15 =   13,902.75

- Line printer
  100,000 lines x $.010[1] =   1,000.00

Total cost allocated $15,982.60

[1] Detailed calculation not shown

Figure 16.10—Illustration of Data Center Cost Allocation

The magnetic tape transports and disk devices are combined with the central processor because, as a practical matter, they are used simultaneously. Although theoretically they are separate, the costs of the magnetic tape transports, disk devices, and central processor can be combined without sacrificing the degree of precision needed.

AVERAGE UNIT TRANSFER COSTS—
SPECIAL SITUATIONS

There are situations in which it is necessary to use more than one average unit transfer cost in order to allocate data center costs. For example:

- If additional or special equipment is required to handle a particular application, an average unit transfer cost related to the added costs for such equipment would be calculated to permit allocation of a premium cost to that application (over and above the normally applicable data center costs). See the calculation below.

- If the data center has idle time available that could be sold to an outside user, the average unit transfer cost might be calculated using only the added (incremental) costs created by the service rendered to that user. Costs would be allocated to original users by employing the average unit transfer costs that represent total costs excluding incremental costs of the data center.

In each of these cases, it becomes necessary to determine the incremental costs and metered hours that apply to the situation. To illustrate this point, it will be assumed that the memory of the central processing unit has been expanded because an application was added that requires immediate access to the computer through remote terminal devices whenever data input or output is available (i.e., an on-line application).

Total annual cost of internal processing	$119,042
Less an assumed cost for additional memory capacity required by the on-line application	(15,900)
Basic annual cost of operation	$103,142
Metered hours, regular applications	1,320
Metered hours, on-line application	264
Total metered hours	1,584

Basic average unit transfer cost per metered hour:
$$\frac{\$103,142}{1,584} = \qquad \$\ 65.115$$

Average unit transfer cost for additional on-line application expenses:
$$\frac{\$15,900}{264} = \qquad 60.227$$

Average unit transfer cost, on-line application, per metered hour $125.342

Illustrative allocation using the preceding
  average unit transfer costs:
    Off-line applications:
      1,320 metered hours at $65.115 $ 85,952
    On-line application:
      264 metered hours at $125.342   33,090
                                          $119,042

DATA CENTER STANDARD COSTING

The calculation of multiprogramming mode average unit transfer costs has taken practical capacity and expected utilization into account whenever necessary. If the efficiency factor were taken into account also, these average unit transfer costs would become standard costs ("carefully predetermined target costs that should be attained under efficient operations"—Chapter 15).

Developing standard costs for the preparatory function of the data center and for input and output devices presents no special difficulties. Developing standard costs for the central processor, however, can be difficult because it is necessary to determine what an efficient level of operation should be.

Central processor efficiency can be considered from two points of view:

- Hardware efficiency. (Does the equipment process instructions at its rated speed and does it operate without excessive downtime for maintenance?)

- Program efficiency. (How efficiently are the programs operating within the central processor?)

For some larger computer systems it may be difficult to separate hardware and program efficiency because of the unknown effects of combining sophisticated computer devices with highly sophisticated computer programs. For purposes of discussion, however, it will be assumed that central processor efficiency can be considered from these two viewpoints. Of the two factors mentioned, hardware efficiency is probably the easiest to determine. It would be possible to process a program through the computer with a known number of instructions and then calculate the time required to process them. Normally this is not done, since it is assumed that most manufacturers' rated speed specifications are reasonably accurate. The normal downtime to be experienced for maintenance can be determined from the manufacturer's preventive maintenance requirements, and it can be assumed that any downtime other than that for preventive maintenance is the result of hardware inefficiency. Maintenance downtime was taken into account in calculating the average unit transfer cost in Figure 16.8 by determining practical capacity. Thus, it is only necessary to determine program efficiency in order to calculate a standard cost.

The measurement of program efficiency can be a complex under-taking. Probably the most effective way to assess program efficiency would be to use a program simulator. This is a specialized computer program that, given input, output, volume, and equipment specifica-tions, can calculate the optimum metered hours required to process a program. The metered hours thus calculated can be measured against the actual processing time of an existing program, in order to de-termine efficiency.

To illustrate the use of the optimum metered hours determined through the use of the simulator, it will be assumed that all programs could be processed in, say, 1384 hours rather than the 1584 hours estimated as necessary in the example discussed earlier in this chapter. The 200 hour savings could be obtained by rewriting inefficient pro-grams to better utilize the central processor or to eliminate excessive program instructions. To rewrite the inefficient programs would re-quire employing two computer programmers for one year at an annual salary of $10,000 each. For this example the current estimated and optimum metered hours are chargeable to the following applications:

	Annual Metered Hours	
	Current Estimate	Optimum
Demand deposit accounting	500	400
Credit card	300	300
Trust	200	200
Payroll	84	84
Correspondents	500	400
Total metered hours	1584	1384

How should the annual internal processing costs of $119,042 be allocated to the applications? The procedures to be used will depend upon the action management wants to encourage:

- Rewrite the programs to reduce costs or to avoid costs that would otherwise occur as new applications are added, or

- Maintain programs as they are since rewriting does not produce a cost benefit.

If the potential 200 hour savings is desirable because total data center costs would be reduced or costs would be avoided due to time made available for new desirable applications, management should encourage rewriting the inefficient programs. This could be accomplished by charging the cost of inefficiency to the organizational unit that should incur the program rewriting costs. And this would be achieved by charging the user based on standard hours at $75.15 (Figure 16.8) and charging the organizational unit that incurs the program rewriting costs for the inefficiency, $15,030 (200 hours $\times$ $75.15). The organizational unit to be charged with the inefficiency, most likely either the user or the data center, is dependent upon the way management views this responsibility. This unfavorable efficiency variance is then a controllable cost of the organizational unit charged with those costs.

If the potential 200 hour savings would not affect total data center costs and processor time is not needed for new applications, i.e., utilization is 50% or less, management may not wish to incur the costs of rewriting the programs. However, if demand deposit accounting and correspondents are charged with 500 hours each at $75.15, their share of costs is unjustifiably high. This difficulty can be overcome by using optimum metered hours. However, a new standard unit transfer cost must be calculated if all internal processing costs are to be allocated. The standard unit transfer cost is calculated by modifying the average unit transfer cost by the expected program efficiency factor as follows:

- Expected program efficiency $\frac{1384}{1584} = 87.4\%$

- Standard unit transfer cost = $75.15 (Figure 16.8) $\div$ 87.4% = $85.98 per standard metered hour

Then internal processing costs would be allocated to the user using the rate of $85.98 times the standard metered hours (1384). This approach allocates costs as they would be in an efficient environment.

SUMMARY

Allocating data center costs can be a very complex costing problem. As a bank's use of data processing grows, its impact is felt more widely; and as EDP applications become more sophisticated, it becomes more difficult to understand cost relationships. Moreover, as the use of data processing grows, its costs become an increasingly important part of total bank costs. The result is that its costs cannot be dismissed by those receiving its services as being of immaterial significance to decision-making.

To these considerations must be added problems that arise from the technical complexity of a data center. If a single program computer system is involved, the costing is similar to that required for determining and allocating costs of other benefit-producing units of the bank. If multiprogramming is introduced, however, one is compelled to develop more sophisticated methods for measuring activity and for costing.

The establishment of standard costs for data centers has the merit of providing a precalculation of costs for use both in allocating costs and in measuring the efficiency of data center operations. Here again, as the data center becomes more complex technically, the methods used for measuring efficiency must become increasingly sophisticated.

APPENDIXES

APPENDIX A

ORGANIZATION AND FUNCTION REFERENCE CHARTS

Throughout this book numerous references are made to organizational units and to functions. Most readers will easily associate these references with their own bank, however, organization does vary from bank to bank. In order to clarify the references to organizational units and functions and to assist those readers not thoroughly knowledgeable in bank organization, Figure A.1 shows the prevailing organization structure used throughout this book. The reader can then position all references to divisions, departments, and sections.

Major activities or functions may be discerned from the name of the organization unit in some instances. In order that references to functions can be clearly understood, Figure A.2 lists functional activities grouped by banking (fund using, fund providing), nonfund, administrative and operation.

The charts presented here were devised to illustrate certain points in the book and to generally conform with present-day bank organization. They are not intended to be an ideal structure nor a guide to developing such a structure. Each bank must design its own organization and functional structure to best carry out its objectives and serve its customers. The number of departments and sections will depend largely on size of the bank.

The reader who refers to these charts frequently as he studies the various chapters will understand the material more readily and consequently, will be able to modify the examples to his own environment.

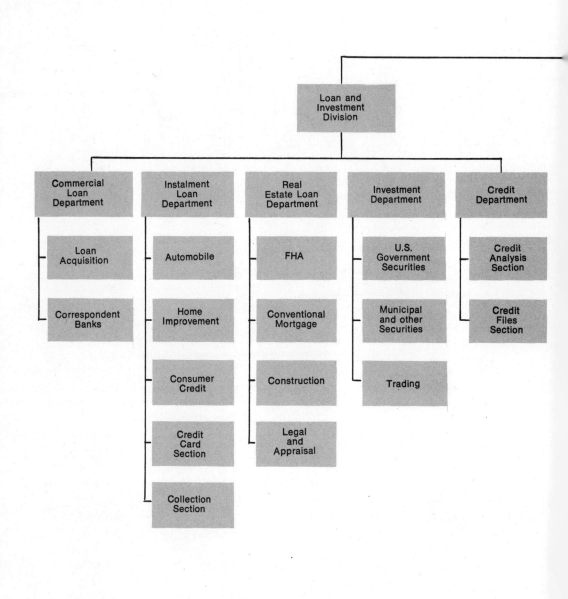

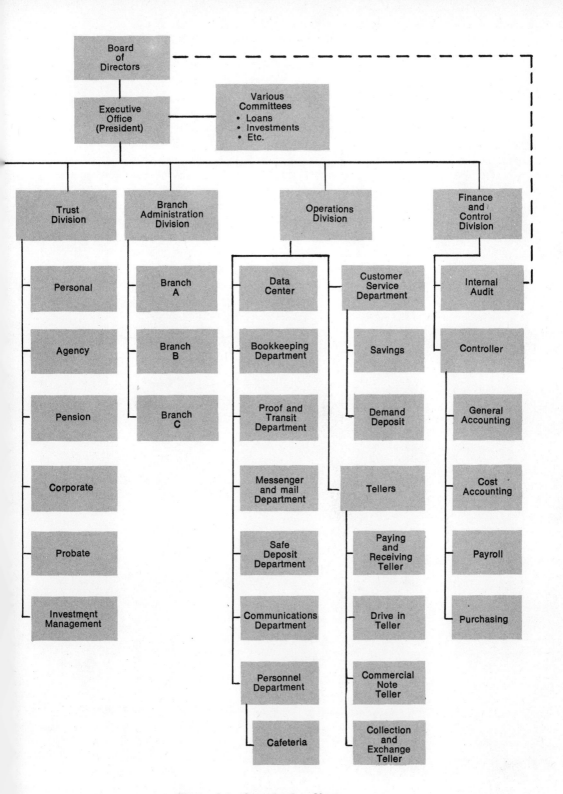

Figure A.1—Organization Chart

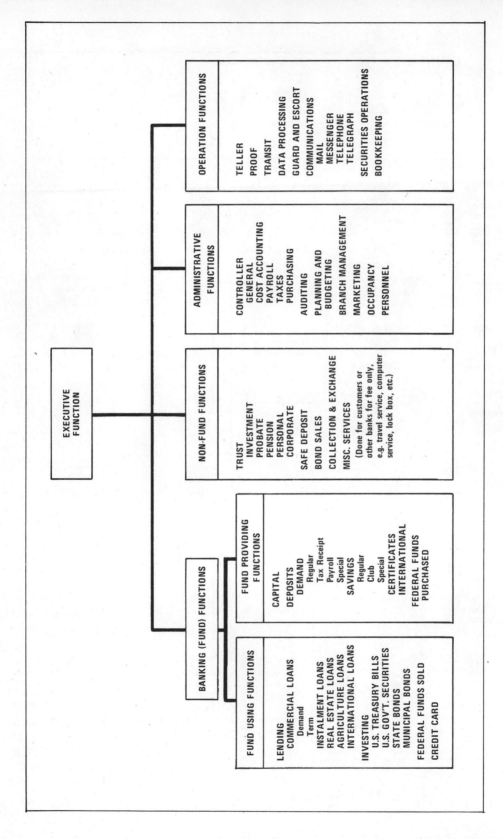

Figure A.2—Function Chart

- APPENDIX B

A BASIC PROCESSING
AND REPORTING SYSTEM

In Chapter 8 the concept of accounting by responsibility center was discussed. The purpose of this appendix is to incorporate responsibility center concepts in a basic information processing and reporting system that can be used as a basis for costing. In addition, requirements of management in implementing and operating such a system also will be discussed.

A decision to install the basic processing and reporting system described in this appendix should not be influenced by bank size, since this system can function in the smallest bank. The availability of data processing capability is also not a requirement. The system, as outlined, can be operated manually, or with accounting machines, tabulating equipment, or a computer, either within the bank or at an outside service bureau. The more advanced processing methods (tabulating equipment or computers) may reduce the time and effort required to arrive at the desired results, but they will not change the nature of the system.

DESIGNING A BASIC PROCESSING AND
REPORTING SYSTEM

Prerequisites

Before a bank can implement a system such as the one described here, bank management must become involved in the planning of this system and must make certain decisions in three very important areas: bank organizational structure, the bank's chart of accounts, and the reporting levels within the bank's organization.

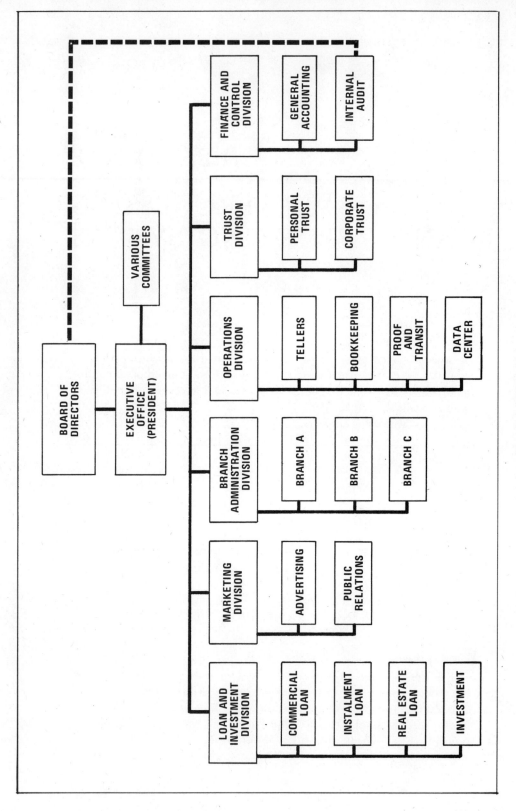

Figure B.1—Typical Organization

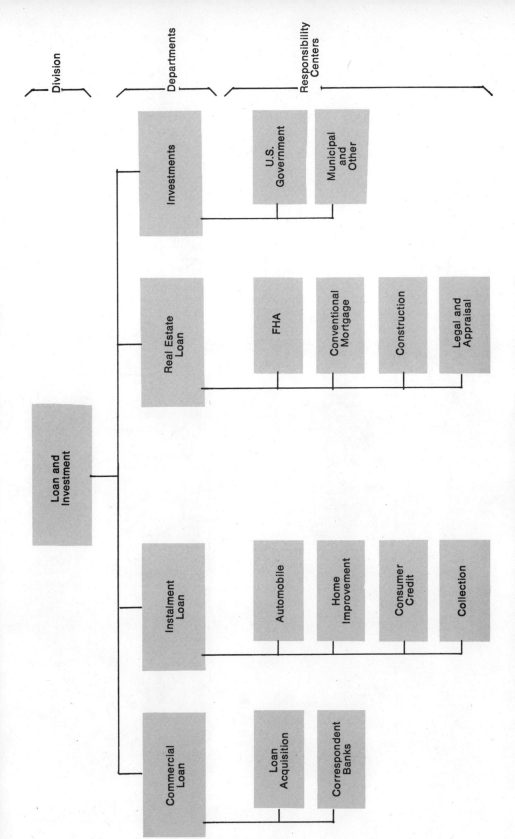

Figure B.2—Responsibility Center Organization—Loan and Investment Division

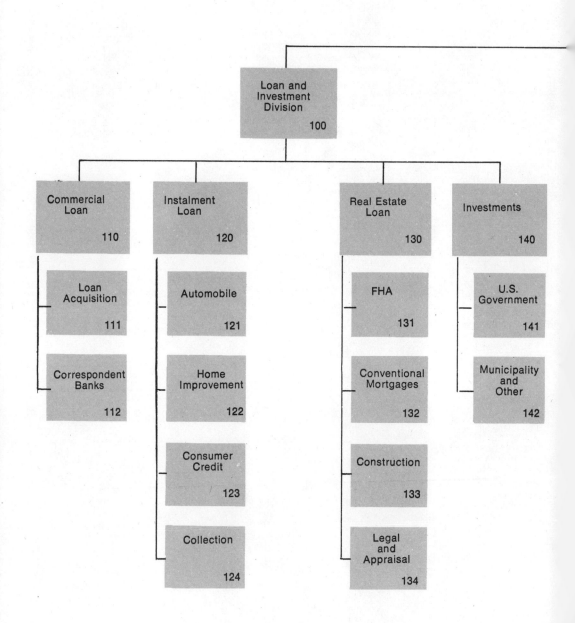

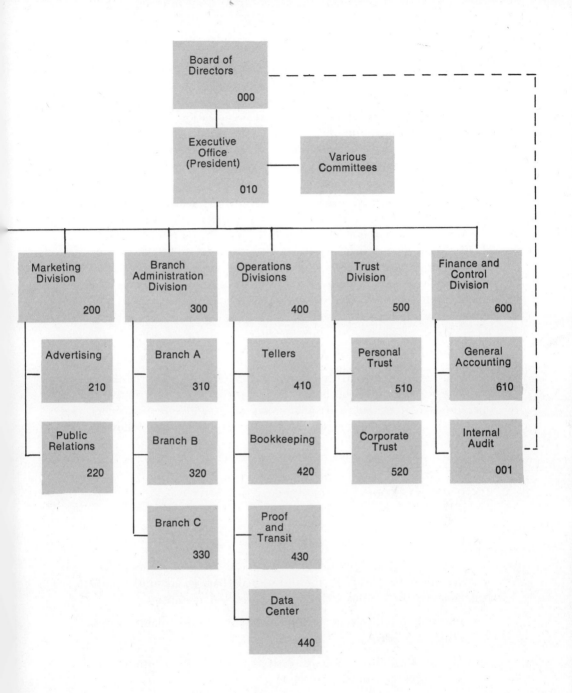

Figure B.3—Coding of Responsibility Center Organization

To function properly, the bank organization with which the system deals must be properly identified and defined. The basic processing and reporting system described in this appendix should report all revenues and costs to the lowest organizational units directly responsible for controlling these items. In describing the design of the system, a "divisional" organization is assumed (Figure B.1). Figure B.2 illustrates the responsibility center organization for the loan and investment division.

The basic system approach may be used with various organization structures. It is important, however, that the organization structure be carefully defined and documented because (1) this is fundamental to obtaining effective control over costs and revenues, and (2) a coding system must be designed for the accounting system to represent the organization structure. Figure B.3 illustrates a coding system for the organization structure and the individual responsibility centers previously shown in Figures B.1 and B.2.

Relation to the Chart of Accounts

The traditional chart of accounts utilized by most banks is adequate for reporting the bank's financial condition and results of operations to stockholders, regulatory agencies, and other outsiders. This chart usually classifies financial information into the following broad categories:

- Assets.

- Liabilities.

- Income by type.

- Expense by natural expense classification.

To make the data produced by the basic system more useful for analysis and control of costs, the traditional chart of accounts should be augmented by further coding to identify as far as practicable:

- The responsibility centers directly responsible for planning and controlling costs.

- The responsibility centers directly responsible for planning and controlling each source of revenue.

The overall coding structure developed for the chart of accounts and the organization chart should be formed so that these two charts may become directly associated within the basic system (Figure B.4).

Each item posted to an income or expense account in the general ledger should be coded to indicate the natural classification of revenue or expense and the responsibility for that item. For example

- Instalment, Automobile Loan Officers Salaries—#401-121
  - —401—Salaries expense
  - —121—Instalment, Automobile Loan responsibility center
- Pre-printed "Cash-In" tickets—#473-421
  - —473—Printing, stationery and supplies expense
  - —421—Paying and Receiving Tellers responsibility center
- Interest Income, U.S. Government Bonds—#321-141
  - —321—Interest Income
  - —141—U.S. Government Securities

Figure B.4—Examples of Coding of Revenues and Expenses

Reporting

The third area of decision facing management is the reporting of cost information within the bank. The number of reporting levels that can exist within the bank will depend directly upon the complexity of the organization of that bank. The lowest and highest levels of reporting described in this system are common to all banks:

- The lowest level report shows the details of revenues and of expenses by natural classification at the lowest organizational unit directly responsible for these items.
- The highest level report shows a summary of all income and expense by major classes and by "divisions."

As mentioned earlier, the number of intermediate reporting levels within a bank depends on the complexity of the organization of that bank. However, each of these intermediate level reports should show the details of the next lower level organizational units and the summary of the details to be reported to the next higher level.

INDICATORS AND MEASUREMENT OF ACTIVITY

In addition to the financial information generated by the basic processing and reporting system, certain other information is needed for decision-making and operational control, namely, transaction volumes, number of accounts, and statistical information concerning the operation of the bank. Most of this data can be gathered as a by-product of banking operations.

Useful volume or activity information includes the following:

- Number of customer accounts by type or classification. For example, the numbers of demand deposit accounts classified as commercial or business, individual, special, and public fund.

- Number of transactions by type and type of account. For example, the number of deposits to commercial checking accounts.

- Account activity or turnover. For example, new, closed, renewed, and opened accounts by type of classification.

Statistical data useful to management may take many forms, among which are:

- Distribution of accounts by various criteria such as balance levels, zip codes, industry types, etc.

- Distribution of transactions by various criteria.

- Staffing levels, both planned and actual, by position and classification.

Time measurement data also may be most helpful in improving the efficiency of bank operations and the utilization of bank employee time. The types of data that may be reported and used in this manner are:

- Arrivals of customers and customer demand, peak activity periods, and waiting times.

- External and internal deadlines such as transportation departures for transit items.

- Utilization of employee time, both productive and idle.

- Estimations or measurements of time requirements for each type of transaction.

The frequency of reporting nonfinancial or statistical data depends upon the uses that management makes of that data. Some information may be reported monthly, such as the numbers of accounts, staffing levels, and account activity. Other data, which may be used less frequently, should be recorded and accumulated regularly and be reported or used as needed for special reports, cost findings, or costing applications.

MECHANICS OF THE SYSTEM

This section describes in detail the procedures required for the operation of the basic processing and reporting system. These procedures are concerned with the (1) coding of the source media, (2) processing of data by one of several methods, and (3) preparation of the final output reports from the system.

Source Data

The data for the operation of this system is derived from many sources: expense check vouchers, cash disbursements vouchers, journal vouchers, payroll distribution reports, and various other journal entries. A six- to eight-digit distribution code is placed on each of these source documents formated as xxxx-xxxx. The first three- to four-digit number indicates the natural class of expense or the type or source of the revenue recorded on the document. The second three- to four-digit number indicates the responsibility center responsible for the particular item. Figure B.4 illustrated several examples of this coding and its use.

If the data is to be processed manually or on a mechanical accounting machine, the input media must be sorted before posting. These documents should be sorted into numeric sequence using the first or left three- to four-digit code indicating class or type of revenue or expense. These items may then be posted to the proper general ledger accounts as indicated by this code. A sample posting is shown below.

Date	Description	Code	DR	CR	Balance
2-10-xx	Credit Bureau Reports, January	459-112	$35		$35

At the end of the month, the entries to the general ledger can be analyzed and categorized by using the last or right-hand three- to four-digit code, which indicates the responsibility center. This analysis and distribution can be done manually by using spread analysis sheets, or it can be accomplished by using a multiple total accounting machine, or a proof machine. As an alternative to preparing this analysis and distribution within the bank, photocopies of the right-hand four columns of the ledgers shown above may be made and sent to a service bureau for keypunching and tabulating.

Processing Data

The use of a punched card tabulating system considerably simplifies the processing of responsibility center data and the preparation of necessary reports. Source media do not have to be presorted. Each source document is keypunched and verified as indicated below (numbers of digits are shown in parentheses):

- Card code (1).

- Class code (3, 4), type or classification of revenue or expense.

- Responsibility center (3, 4).

- Tracer or reference number for audit trail (optional).

- Debit or credit dollar amount (11).

- Description (30).

After punching and verification, the cards should be tabulated daily to establish and verify the necessary control totals, and to prepare various daily reports such as the statement of condition and the income statement.

At the end of the month the accumulated detail cards are sorted and tabulated as follows to prepare the indicated reports:

- Journal of entries (optional) by class, date, responsibility center.

- Revenue and expense by responsibility center by class and date.

- Lowest level detail reports and summary cards to be punched for higher level reports by responsibility center and class.

- Tabulate the summary card, changing control break keys to print intermediate and highest level reports.

The use of an electronic data processing system facilitates the accumulation, analysis, and distribution of responsibility center data and the preparation of the necessary reports. Again, the sources do not have to be presorted; each source document is converted to the appropriate input media and verified, using a content format similar to that described for the punched card tabulating system. Each day the input media should be read into the EDP system, recorded, and processed to verify and establish the necessary control totals, and to prepare the required daily reports.

At the end of the month the accumulated transactions for the month are sorted and summarized to prepare the reports listed above under the tabulating system.

Report Contents

The format and content of the reports created by this system are optional with the individual bank. However, these reports should contain at least "this month" and "year-to-date" information, and they may be expanded by adding the corresponding information from last year.

The lowest level reports should contain each natural classification of revenue and/or expense for each organizational responsibility center (for example, salaries, payroll taxes, insurance, etc., for paying and receiving tellers). The intermediate level reports should show the groups of natural income and expense classifications by responsibility centers for the next lower groups of such centers. The highest level reports should show the major groups or classifications of revenue and expenses by division.

Each of the above levels of reports may be expanded into control reports by adding budgeted or planned figures for each item, as follows:

This Month	Description	Year-to-Date
Actual Plan Variance		Variance Plan Actual

or

	Better (Worse)			Better (Worse)	
Actual	Than Plan			Than Plan	Actual

SAMPLE REPORTS

A set of sample reports prepared by this system is shown in the following figures. The data developed in these figures is used extensively in Chapters 10 through 14:

- Lowest level detail report (Figure B.5).

- Intermediate level summary report (Figure B.6).

- Intermediate and highest level summary report (Figure B.7).

- Statement of condition (Figure B.8).

- Income statement (Figure B.9).

Responsibility Center #124—Instalment Loan—Collection

	This Month		Year-to-Date	
	Actual	Better (Worse) Than Plan	Better (Worse) Than Plan	Actual
402—Salaries—Basic	$ 631	$ 76	$ 300	$11,390
403—Salaries—Overtime	588	(288)	(177)	2,777
411—FICA Tax	85	(15)	(157)	1,012
414—Group Insurance	49	(28)	(5)	215
418—Profit Sharing	48	(6)		480
Salaries and Benefits	1,401	(261)	(39)	15,874
441—Depreciation—F & F	16	(1)	(6)	186
443—Equipment Maintenance			(32)	32
444—Auto Maintenance	41	16	(149)	839
445—Depreciation Auto	27			330
Equipment	84	15	(187)	1,387
455—Fidelity Bond	11	1	4	146
459—Credit Service Fees			(11)	11
462—Dues, Memberships			(40)	40
467—Legal & Professional		50	(135)	735
473—Stationery & Supplies		60	716	4
476—Repossession Expense	85	(35)	(434)	1,034
480—Telephone & Telegraph	161	(4)	(713)	2,603
Operating	257	72	(613)	4,573
Responsibility Center Total	$1,742	$(174)	$(839)	$21,834

**Figure B.5—Sample Reports, Lowest Level Detail
Monthly Expense Comparison**

December 19

#120—Instalment Loan Department

	This Month		Year-to-Date	
	Actual	Better (Worse) Than Plan	Better (Worse) Than Plan	Actual
#121—Automobile				
Salaries and Benefits	$2,467	$ 411	$ 5,918	$ 31,621
Equipment	151	165	(281)	2,069
Operating	1,588	(723)	(4,232)	15,532
Total	4,206	(147)	1,405	49,222
#122—Home Improvement				
Salaries and Benefits	1,158	140	433	13,467
Equipment		24	927	
Operating	334	(188)	976	2,887
Total	1,492	(24)	2,336	16,354
#123—Consumer Credit				
Salaries and Benefits	1,237	73	343	14,969
Equipment	57	6	85	972
Operating	1,016	201	218	6,649
Total	2,310	280	646	22,590
#124—Collection				
Salaries and Benefits	1,401	(261)	(39)	15,874
Equipment	84	15	(187)	1,387
Operating	257	72	(613)	4,573
Total	1,742	(174)	(839)	21,834
#120—Instalment Loan Department				
Salaries and Benefits	6,263	363	6,655	75,931
Equipment	292	210	544	4,428
Operating	3,195	(638)	(3,651)	29,641
Department Total	$9,750	$ (65)	$ 3,548	$110,000

Figure B.6—Sample Reports, Intermediate Level Summary
Monthly Expense Summary

December 19

#100—Loan and Investment Division

	This Month		Year-to-Date	
	Actual	Better (Worse) Than Plan	Better (Worse) Than Plan	Actual
#110—Commercial Loan Department				
Salaries and Benefits	$ 7,264	$ 245	$ 4,432	$ 82,688
Equipment	397	240	785	3,190
Operating	2,407	(376)	671	19,682
Departmental Total	10,068	109	5,888	105,560
#120—Instalment Loan Department				
Salaries and Benefits	6,263	363	6,655	75,931
Equipment	292	210	544	4,428
Operating	3,195	(638)	(3,651)	29,641
Departmental Total	9,750	(65)	3,548	110,000
#130—Real Estate Loan Department				
Salaries and Benefits	3,741	317	2,171	40,281
Equipment	285	45	(68)	1,572
Operating	721	71	591	7,304
Departmental Total	4,747	433	2,694	49,157
#140—Investment Department				
Salaries and Benefits	2,422	115	2,231	28,938
Equipment	57	3	37	473
Operating	597	747	(385)	5,003
Departmental Total	3,076	865	1,883	34,414
#100—Loan and Investment Division				
Salaries and Benefits	19,690	1,040	15,489	227,838
Equipment	1,031	498	1,298	9,663
Operating	6,920	(196)	(2,774)	61,630
Division Total	$27,641	$1,342	$14,013	$299,131

**Figure B.7—Sample Reports, Intermediate and Highest Level Summary
Monthly Expense Summary**

(000 omitted)

December 31, 19____

Assets

100	Cash and Due from Banks	$10,282	
131	U.S. Government Securities	6,563	
137	Municipal and State Securities	11,833	
144	Other Securities	1,207	
	Total Cash and Securities		$ 29,885
151	Federal Funds Sold	—	
161	Commercial Loans	35,935	
162	Real Estate Loans	11,681	
164	Instalment Loans	19,299	
165	Credit Card	1,022	
169	Overdrafts	240	
	Total Loans		68,177
171	Bank Building	1,275	
175	Furniture and Fixtures	375	
184	Accrued Income Receivable	760	
199	Other Assets	651	
	Total Other Assets		3,061
	Total Assets		$101,123

Liabilities

201	Regular Demand Deposits	$33,826	
202	Special Demand Deposits	3,869	
208	Due to Banks	165	
209	U.S. Government	356	
230	Regular Savings	38,684	
231	Club Savings	825	
232	Certificates of Deposit	7,337	
233	Federal Funds Purchased	5,000	
	Total Deposits		$ 90,062
264	Unearned Discount	896	
267	Accrued Interest Payable	864	
270	Reserve for Income Taxes	214	
274	Accrued Expenses Payable	400	
278	Other Liabilities	408	
281	Reserve for Bad Debts	279	
	Total Other Liabilities		3,061
293	Capital Stock	5,445	
295	Undivided Profits	2,555	
	Total Capital		8,000
	Total Liabilities and Capital		$101,123

Figure B.8—Sample Reports
Statement of Condition

	December 19___	This Month	Year-to-Date
	Revenues		
300	Loan Income	$298,733	$3,528,134
320	Investment Income	50,626	724,000
330	Deposit Service Charge Income	9,572	101,711
340	Credit Card and Miscellaneous Service Charge Inc.	13,336	78,155
350	Trust Dept. Income	13,000	150,121
360	Safe Deposit Vault	386	5,100
370	Other Income (Collection & Exchange, etc.)	430	5,182
	Total Revenue	386,083	4,592,403
	Expenses		
400	Salaries and Benefits	107,300	1,362,238
420	Interest Expense	170,337	2,012,400
430	Rent, Utilities, Taxes, Etc.	12,700	149,901
440	Equipment Expense	12,500	160,718
450	Operating Expense	27,388	301,905
460	Provision for Loan Loss	6,250	75,000
	Total Expense	336,475	4,062,162
	Profit Before Taxes	$ 49,608	$ 530,241

Figure B.9—Sample Reports
Income Statement

IMPLEMENTING THE BASIC SYSTEM

Before authorizing the installation of a system such as the one described here, management must realize that the implementation of a basic processing and reporting system cannot be accomplished overnight. The elapsed time from the original management decision to install such a system until the complete operation of the system will depend upon many factors:

- The number of people assigned to the various steps in the project.
- The capabilities of these people.
- The size and complexity of the bank.
- The method of processing to be employed.
- And, most important, top management's emphasis, direction, cooperation, and participation in the project.

Figure B.10 shows the steps in the implementation project and a

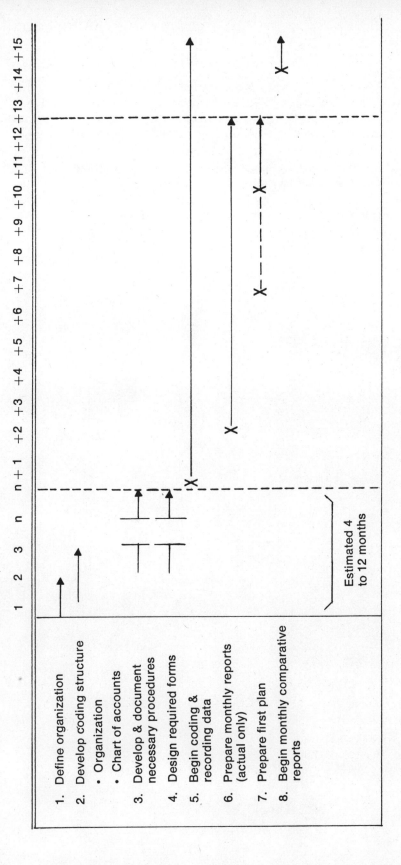

Figure B.10—System Implementation Schedule

general schedule for this implementation. The first four steps in this schedule may require as little as three months to accomplish, but they also may take as long as 12 months if computer programs are to be written and if general ledger accounting is to be integrated in this system. The remaining four steps (five through eight) are relatively fixed in time and should require approximately a year to complete.

In practice, the development of a reasonably accurate and functioning revenue and expense plan requires experience on the part of the entire bank staff. Reliance upon planned figures for control may have to wait until the second or even third planning cycle (third or fourth year of operation).

APPENDIX C

STANDARD TIME VALUES
FOR WEIGHTING

The following measures of times for various bank operations were determined by Bank Administration Institute to weight item counts in order to arrive at a basis of allocation. These times are for the purpose of facilitating the distribution of time only. They should not be considered standards of performance in this context. For uses other than weighting, the complete texts of related Bank Administration Institute publications should be used. The new BAI publication *Teller Staffing: A Guide to Improved Service and Lower Costs* may also be of interest.

Included in this appendix are: commercial and teller transaction standards[1]; proof and encoding standards[1]; check sorting standards summary[1]; instalment loan operations standard summary[1]; bookkeeping standards[2].

[1] Bank Administration Institute, *Performance Standards for Bank Operations*, 1967.
[2] Bank Administration Institute, *A Study of Dual-Posting Fully-Deferred Demand Deposit Accounting*, 1959.

Tables 1A and 1B
Commercial Teller Transaction Standards

A. Table of Standards (Stopwatch Data)

Transactions without Delay	Lobby No Machine	Lobby Burroughs Teller Machine	Lobby NCR Teller Machine	Lobby Validator Machine	Drive-in & Walk-up (All Systems Combined)
	Minutes Mode	Minutes Mode	Minutes Mode	Minutes Mode	Minutes Mode
Deposit—check(s) only	.28	.18	.17	.19	.31
Deposit—cash only	.41	.31	.30	.34	.48
Deposit—check(s) & cash	.62	.41	.37	.36	.75
Deposit—cash returned	.53	.59	.48	.55	.70
Cash check	.29	.37	.35	.29	.45

Transactions with or without Delay	All Systems Combined	
	Lobby Mode	Drive-in & Walk-up Median
Club or loan coupon payment	.51	.76
Certify check	.98	1.23
Sale of cashier's check	.81	1.06
Redeem "E" bonds	1.06	1.31
Sale of money order	.51	.76
Sale of traveler's checks	2.42	2.67
Sale of coin—currency	.33	.58
Non-bag mail deposit—open	.13	.38
Non-bag mail deposit—not open	.29	.54
Savings deposit[1]	.65*	.90
Savings withdrawals[1]	1.30*	1.55

*Median Value

[1] A more refined table of standards for savings transactions is presented in the Institute's report of "A Study of Time Deposit Accounting Methods and Systems," Volume 1

B. Table of Standards—Transactions with Delays (Stopwatch Data)

Transactions with Delay	Deposit— Check(s) Only Minutes (Median)		Deposit— Cash Only Minutes (Median)		Deposit— Check(s) & Cash Minutes (Median)		Deposit— Cash Returned Minutes (Median)		Cash Check Minutes (Median)	
	Lobby	Drive-in & Walk-up	Lobby	Drive-in & Walk-up	Lobby	Drive-in & Walk-up	Lobby	Drive-in & Walk-up	Lobby	Drive-in & Walk-up
Balance information from bookkeeping dept.	1.19	1.29	1.32	1.46	1.42	1.73	1.51	1.68	1.31	1.43
Signature verification	Not applicable		Not applicable				1.03	1.20	.83	.95
Require customer indentification					.99	1.30	.80	.97	.60	.72
Prepare deposit slip	.76	.86	.89	1.03	.76	1.07	1.08	1.25	Not applicable	
Prepare duplicate deposit slip	.53	.63	.66	.80	.86	1.17	.85	1.02		
Correct deposit slip	.63	.73	.76	.90			.95	1.12		
Prepare adding machine tape	.91	1.01	1.04	1.18	1.14	1.45	1.23	1.40	1.03	1.15
Require customer signature	.55	.65	Not applicable		.78	1.09	.87	1.04	.67	.79
Cash counting in deposit (Requiring more than one minute)	Not applicable		1.48	1.62	1.58	1.89	1.67	1.84	1.47	1.59

Tables 1A and 1B (continued)

Tables 2A and 2B

Commercial Teller Transaction Standards

A. Time Teller Serves Customers

Line Number	Transaction Workload	% of Time that Teller Serves Customer	Teller Windows Open to the Public				
			4 Hours (240 Min.)	5 Hours (300 Min.)	6 Hours (360 Min.)	7 Hours (420 Min.)	8 Hours (480 Min.)
			Number of Minutes Teller Serves Customers				
1	Low Volume	30 to 40	72 to 96	90 to 120	108 to 144	126 to 168	144 to 192
2	Average Volume	40 to 50	96 to 120	120 to 150	144 to 180	168 to 210	192 to 240
3	High Volume	50 to 70	120 to 168	150 to 210	180 to 252	210 to 294	240 to 336

B. Number of Commercial Transactions a Teller Should Handle

Line Number	Number of Minutes Waiting on Customer	Paying Receiving Teller*	Paying Only Teller* Transactions	Receiving Only Teller*
1	72	120	158	113
2	90	150	199	141
3	96	160	210	151
4	108	180	237	159
5	120	200	263	189
6	126	210	276	198
7	144	240	315	226
8	150	250	329	236
9	168	280	368	264
10	180	300	394	283
11	192	320	421	302
12	210	350	460	330
13	240	400	520	377
14	252	420	552	396
15	294	490	644	462
16	336	560	736	528

*For Drive-in or Walk-up, Reduce Transactions by 25%

Tables 2A and 2B (continued)

Table 3

Commercial Paying-Receiving and Savings Teller Combined

(For Drive-in or Walk-up Tellers Reduce Transactions by 25%)

Line Number	Number of Minutes Teller Waits on Customer	Number of Savings Transactions																				
		0	10	20	30	40	50	60	70	80	90	100	110	120	130	140	150	160	170	180	190	200
		Total Number of Transactions (including Savings) That a Teller Should Handle																				
1	72	120	117	114	111	107	104	101	98	95	92											
2	90	150	147	144	141	137	134	131	128	125	121	118	115									
3	96	160	157	154	151	147	144	141	138	135	131	128	125	121								
4	108	180	177	174	171	167	164	161	158	155	151	148	145	141	138							
5	120	200	197	194	191	187	184	181	178	175	171	168	165	162	159	155	152					
6	126	210	207	204	201	197	194	191	188	185	181	178	175	172	169	166	162	160				
7	144	240	237	234	231	227	224	221	218	215	211	208	205	202	199	196	193	188	185	182		
8	150	250	247	244	241	237	234	231	228	225	221	218	215	212	209	206	203	199	196	192	190	
9	168	280	277	274	271	267	264	261	258	255	251	248	245	242	239	236	233	229	226	223	220	216
10	180	300	297	294	291	287	284	281	278	275	271	268	265	262	259	256	253	249	246	243	240	237
11	192	320	317	314	311	307	304	301	298	295	291	288	285	282	279	276	273	269	266	263	260	257
12	210	350	347	344	341	337	334	331	328	325	321	318	315	312	309	306	303	299	296	293	290	287
13	240	400	397	394	391	387	384	381	378	375	371	368	365	362	359	356	353	349	346	343	340	337
14	252	420	417	414	411	407	404	401	398	395	391	388	385	382	379	376	373	369	366	363	360	357
15	294	490	487	484	481	477	474	471	468	465	461	458	455	452	449	446	443	439	436	433	430	427
16	336	560	557	554	551	547	544	541	538	535	531	528	525	522	519	516	513	509	506	503	500	497

Exceeds Standard Time

Table 4

Percentage of Distribution of Time Commercial Teller Transactions

Minutes in Tenths	Deposit—Check(s) Only					Deposit—Cash Only					Deposit Check(s) & Cash				
	No Mach. %	Burroughs %	NCR %	Validator %	Drive in %	No Mach. %	Burroughs %	NCR %	Validator %	Drive in %	No Mach. %	Burroughs %	NCR %	Validator %	Drive in %
0-.1	1.03	1.74	2.32	7.30	—	—	8.35	—	—	—	—	—	—	—	—
.1-.2	23.00	30.98	48.04	41.18	.52	.84	25.22	6.99	16.12	—	—	—	0.44	—	—
.2-.3	27.08	34.52	27.95	33.95	23.06	18.26	29.17	28.80	26.44	7.38	3.13	3.10	10.26	18.62	—
.3-.4	19.54	16.56	7.99	9.17	36.28	24.78	15.01	29.22	28.04	17.65	7.41	15.44	13.01	23.54	2.18
.4-.5	9.36	6.28	6.28	4.65	22.46	24.43	6.64	16.65	15.67	25.52	9.91	19.40	13.75	16.69	14.62
.5-.6	7.07	4.76	4.52	2.70	12.58	17.81	5.43	10.22	8.95	25.85	12.42	11.05	13.45	9.87	15.75
.6-.7	5.49	3.24	2.50	1.01	4.55	11.18	4.21	5.17	2.94	15.44	12.08	8.34	11.84	8.49	13.90
.7-.8	3.91	1.92	0.38	0.04	0.55	2.70	3.00	2.95	1.84	5.52	7.60	7.58	10.11	7.11	8.18
.8-.9	2.34	—	0.02	—	—	—	1.76	—	—	2.64	6.70	6.83	8.38	5.72	7.62
.9-1.0	1.18	—	—	—	—	—	0.65	—	—	—	6.21	6.08	6.66	4.34	7.61
1.0-1.1							0.19				5.72	5.33	4.93	2.95	6.77
1.1-1.2							0.37				5.23	4.58	3.20	2.67	6.35
1.2-1.3											4.75	3.83	1.47		5.92
1.3-1.4											4.25	3.05	2.50		5.49
1.4-1.5											3.77	2.20			4.03
1.5-1.6											3.28	1.83			2.00
1.6-1.7											2.83	0.70			
1.7-1.8											2.22	0.66			
1.8-1.9											1.68				
1.9-2.0											.81				
No. of Obsv.	814	1330	733	350		91	726	326	80		229	781	262	89	
Std. Minute	.28	.18	.17	.19	.31	.41	.31	.30	.34	.48	.62	.41	.37	.36	.75

Note:—Above figures are in hundredth minutes, not in seconds
To convert to seconds, multiply by 60—thus .30 minutes = 18 seconds.

Minutes in Tenths	Deposit—Cash Returned					Cash Check				
	No Mach. %	Bur-roughs %	NCR %	Vali-dator %	Drive in %	No Mach. %	Bur-roughs %	NCR %	Vali-dator %	Drive in %
0- .1	—	—	—	—	—	—	1.91	—	0.42	—
.1- .2	—	—	—	—	—	17.05	15.23	17.15	11.82	—
.2- .3	6.21	3.52	2.19	2.86	—	23.98	19.96	23.14	18.37	8.14
.3- .4	11.98	8.71	7.69	7.75	1.64	25.72	24.19	25.37	25.03	16.69
.4- .5	14.87	13.26	13.00	10.03	11.59	14.59	15.95	13.76	20.98	18.72
.5- .6	17.76	17.81	18.31	12.31	20.34	7.67	5.65	6.55	7.76	17.57
.6- .7	15.36	18.82	20.23	14.59	20.33	5.61	4.63	5.27	4.81	15.63
.7- .8	8.76	13.16	14.55	16.06	12.18	3.54	3.93	3.99	3.87	13.37
.8- .9	7.44	7.18	7.56	11.85	9.39	1.45	3.22	2.71	2.92	9.77
.9-1.0	6.08	4.64	5.91	8.54	7.73	0.15	2.52	1.49	1.98	0.11
1.0-1.1	4.77	3.93	4.49	6.63	6.07	0.24	2.81	0.38	1.03	
1.1-1.2	3.37	3.21	3.07	4.71	4.42			0.13	1.01	
1.2-1.3	2.00	2.50	1.64	2.80	2.76			0.06		
1.3-1.4	0.69	1.79	1.36	1.87	1.13					
1.4-1.5	0.71	0.56			2.42					
1.5-1.6		0.35								
1.6-1.7		0.30								
1.7-1.8		0.26								
1.8-1.9										
1.9-2.0										
No. of Obsv.	574	1100	500	171		1370	1293	1096	703	
Std. Minute	.53	.59	.48	.55	.70	.29	.37	.35	.29	.45

Table 4 (Continued)

Table 5

Proof and Encoding Standards

On-us items	Time in Seconds	Units per Hour
Machine type		
Burroughs—P703	2.57	1403
IBM—1201	2.46	1466
IBM—1203	2.10	1715
NCR—450	2.43	1482
NCR—481	2.69	1337
NCR—480	2.79	1290
Mixed item standards		
Machine type		
Burroughs—P703	2.91	1239
IBM—1201	3.79	949
IBM—1203	2.81	1281
NCR—481	3.03	1189
NCR—450	3.56	1011

Table 6

Check Sorting Standards Summary

	Time in Seconds	Units per Hour
Table top check sorting—two passes—numerical		
Rough sort by account number	1.69	2137
Fine sort by account number	3.96	910
Total for two pass table top check sorting	5.65	638
Table top check sorting—two passes—alphabetical		
Rough sort by account signature	1.95	1835
Fine sort by account signature	4.24	850
Total for two pass table top check sorting	6.19	581
Check rack sorting—two passes—numerical		
Rough sort by account number	2.20	1634
Fine sort by account number	3.17	1136
Total for two pass check rack sorting	5.37	670
Check rack sorting—two passes—alphabetical		
Rough sort by account signature	2.28	1585
Fine sort by account signature	3.46	1045
Total for two pass check rack sorting	5.74	630

Table 7

Check Sorting Standards Summary

Check rack sorting—one pass—numerical	Time in Seconds	Units per Hour
Rough and fine sort in one pass by account number	3.42	1052
Check rack sorting—one pass—alphabetical		
Rough and fine sort in one pass by account signature	3.46	1040
Check rack rough sort—table top fine sort—numerical		
Rough sort into check rack by account number	2.20	1634
Fine sort on table top by account number	3.98	904
Total for two pass check rack to table top sort	6.18	582
Check rack rough sort—table top fine sort—alphabetical		
Rough sort into check rack by account signature	2.28	1585
Fine sort on table top by account signature	4.25	846
Total for two pass check rack sort to table top fine sort	6.53	552

Table 8

Check Sorting Standards Summary

	Time in Seconds	Units per Hour
Check rack rough sort—fan items and fine sort—numerical		
Rough sort into check rack by account number	2.20	1634
Fine sort—fan items held in hand, intersort with items on table by account number	6.65	542
Total for two pass, check rack sort to fan and intersort fine sort	8.85	407
Check rack rough sort—fan items and fine sort—alphabetical		
Rough sort into check rack sort by account signature	2.28	1585
Fine sort—fan items held in hand, intersort with items on table by account signature	6.96	517
Total for two pass, check rack sort to fan and intersort fine sort	9.24	390

Table 9

Instalment Loan Operations Standards Summary

Instalment loan prescheduled payment system	Time in Seconds	Units per Hour
Operation description		
1. Pick up and open envelopes using a letter-opening machine	1.58	2278
2. Pick up envelopes, remove coupons, and check and compare dollar amount	8.13	443
3. Adding machine list of coupons (full keyboard)	2.87	1256
4. Adding machine list of checks (full keyboard)	2.58	1399
5. Sort coupons by control number or due date—on table top	1.94	1865
6. Sort coupons into account number sequences—on table top	2.22	1622
7. Locate and remove ledger cards from manual file tray, intersort coupons	14.12	255
8. Preschedule posting. Post payments by hand using a date stamp	10.20	353
9. Replace ledger card in manual file tray	10.73	335
Miscellaneous operations		
Operation description		
10. Search ledger file tray for past-due payment accounts	2.66	1353
11. Preschedule ledger cards on Burroughs Class P-600 machine	25.43	142
12. Make up installment loan payment coupon book (12) equal payments	32.01	112
13. Teller payment—receive cash payment for exact amount	34.64	104
Variations to prescheduled payment system		
Operation description		
14. Pick up and manually open envelopes with letter opener	2.73	1319
15. Adding machine list coupons (ten key machine)	2.63	1369
16. Adding machine list checks (ten key machine)	2.35	1536
17. Sort coupons by control number of due date into sorting rack	- 2.88	1252
18. Locate ledger card and remove from Electrofile tray	7.85	459
19. Replace ledger card in Electrofile tray	.83	4348
20. Teller payment—receive check payment for exact amount	16.33	220
21. Teller payment—receive check payment with cash returned	26.35	137
22. Post payments on conventional machine	19.16	188
23. Post payments on conventional machine (zero proof)	22.96	157
24. Post payments on conventional machine (proof balance)	23.38	154
25. Post payments on electronic machine—Burroughs Sensitronic	12.69	284
26. Post payments on NCR Class 2000 machine	19.48	185
27. Make up instalment loan payment coupon book (11) equal (1) odd payment	41.29	87

Table 10

Bookkeeping Standards

Operation	Standard Time per Unit, sec.	Slowest[a] 20 Percentile Time per Unit, sec.	Fastest[b] 20 Percentile Time per Unit, sec.
Ledger posting[c]	8.3	10.2	6.5
Statement posting[c]	8.6	10.4	6.6
Check sorting, rough	1.94	3.25	1.20
Check sorting, fine	4.07	6.61	2.82
Check sorting, (one pass)[d]	3.77	7.37	2.43
Filing	3.12	4.73	1.97
Check examination	0.64	1.12	0.42
Statement rendering	33.9	49.8	18.1
Canceling	0.480	0.837	0.211
Listing	2.9	5.1	2.6
Transfer of balance	10.4	12.8	7.8
Trial balance	2.5	3.4	2.3
Microfilming	0.52	0.907	0.346

[a] Operators whose times exceed these are in the slowest 20% of all operators observed.
[b] Operators whose times are less than these are in the fastest 20% of all operators observed.
[c] Statement time per unit is based on an activity ratio of 2.0.
[d] Only a few observations of this technique were available.

APPENDIX D

PRACTICAL EXAMPLES
OF EFFECTIVE COSTING

The purpose of this appendix is to provide additional perspective concerning the costing process by

- First, discussing how a coster should approach a costing problem.
- Second, presenting three costing problems common to banks along with their solutions using the five costing steps.

HOW TO APPROACH A COSTING PROBLEM

Costing cannot be approached in a mechanical, step-by-step way. As the costing process proceeds, new insights are gained with the result that some areas already covered must be redone in slightly different contexts. The costing process was presented in Chapter 3 as consisting of five specific steps to be carried out, not with the implication that a mechanical approach is desirable, but rather to make the ingredients of a useful cost solution more apparent and understandable.

An effective way to approach a costing problem is to consciously develop a preliminary or "rough cut" answer. The rough cut has two benefits: (1) it uncovers some of the difficulties that will have to be dealt with (such as obtaining new data, making some basic resource capacity studies, etc.); (2) it enables the coster to determine the magnitude of error that can be tolerated in the solution without leading to an erroneous decision.

At this stage, the coster should direct his efforts towards calculating a cost that answers the purpose:

- With the least effort.
- Using available data as much as possible.
- Within the time allowed.

This means going through the costing procedures quickly, using data readily at hand and, if it is not immediately available, making best estimates to work out an approximate cost.

The first objective of the coster is to go through the costing procedures making decisions by using estimates and data already available. Taking time to gather additional data or to make surveys is not recommended. The coster in this way arrives at a tentative, albeit a crude cost approximation.

Anyone using the five costing steps as a guide can make this rough cut. A senior officer would use it to arrive at a "ball park" figure for his planning and perhaps again when he is reviewing detailed costs prepared for him by others. A department head would use the rough cut to prepare costs incidental to a presentation he is making to management. The bank controller already uses a rough cut as a matter of course to gain perspective. If a final calculation is found to be necessary, he now is in a good position to show management why he needs time and perhaps bank-wide participation to arrive at costs that can be relied upon for management's purpose.

Frequently, as one proceeds in this preliminary fashion, it can readily be seen that the information is not available and difficult to obtain, or that the reliability of the estimates used may be difficult to defend. Conversely, it may become apparent that the information will be easy to obtain and that its accuracy can be verified without difficulty.

The costing that results should then be tested in the context of the decision to be made. If the decision concerns taking action on the most profitable alternative, will the preliminary costs suffice? Or, is the decision of such importance that more precision is worth the cost to be incurred to provide that precision? Costs determined using the "rough cut" approach will not always make the coster's course of action obvious. Nevertheless, a decision will have to be made concerning the need for more precise or more detailed cost data. The rough cut provides a frame of reference for this decision.

THE FIVE COSTING STEPS—A SUMMARY

The five costing steps are:
- Define the purpose.
- Define the costing object.
- Specify the cost data.
- Specify the allocation process.
- Calculate the cost.

These steps were discussed in detail in Chapters 3 and 10. As a reminder to the reader, these steps are listed below with their substeps.

Define the purpose.
    State the range of alternative decisions.
    State the criteria.
Define the costing object.
    Identify component resources (a diagram of the flow of benefits is a simple way to do this)
Specify the cost data.
    Identify all related data.
    Identify sources of cost data.
    Screen out nonrelevant data.
    Determine capacity and utilization.
    Determine degree of precision required.
Specify the allocation process.
    Determine the allocation basis.
    Determine the transfer unit.
    Determine the allocation method.
    Specify the close-out sequence.
Calculate the cost.
    Collect nonmonetary data.
    Collect monetary data.
    Allocate cost.

THREE COSTING PROBLEMS

This book stresses that cost has meaning only in the context of the use to which it is to be put. The purposes for cost calculation fall into two general categories: resource use and resource profitability.

The first cost problem illustrates the use of costs in determining profitability—customer profitability. The second problem is a problem of resource use—incremental cost. The third problem is a variation of profitability—pricing.

The data that appears in these problems has been used throughout the text. The reader will recognize the monetary data that appeared in Figures B.8 and B.9 (Appendix B) and Figure 10.5 (Chapter 10). This data is shown in various forms in all three problems. The data required for allocation in all three problems is summarized in Figure D.1. It is used as needed in the three problems.

Presenting this data neatly in one place may give the reader the false impression that the data gathering phase of costing is being glossed over, either as being unimportant or not being particularly difficult. This is not so.

Benefit-Providing Unit and Transfer Units

| I
Benefit-Receiving Unit | Occupancy Square Foot
II | Communication | | Total Telephone Expense (Monthly)
V | Administration Man-Hour (Monthly)
VI | Data Center Time-Weighted Item (Annual)
VII |
		Instrument Charge (Monthly) III	Toll Charge (Monthly) IV			
Communication	220					
Administration	8,340	$ 400	$1,077	$1,477		
General overhead[1]						
Data center	1,890	30	397	427	43	
Tellers	10,400	330	6	336	15	
Proof and transit	1,720	80	27	107	15	590,000
Bookkeeping	1,420	80	2	82		298,000
Credit files	2,450	200	210	410	25	
Credit analysis	1,720	280	294	574	77	
Commercial loans	1,670	150	63	213	309	110,000
Real estate loans	1,230	170	76	246	185	68,000
Instalment loans	1,470	80	84	164	236	68,000
Credit card	490	80	166	246	12	137,000
Investment		20	29	49	31	34,000
Subtotal	33,020	1,900	2,431	4,331	948	1,305,000
Demand deposits—						
Regular checking:						
Promotion—goodwill					159	
Checks cashed						
Checks deposited						
Deposit tickets						362,000
Checks drawn						1,600,000
Special services						
Statements						300,000
Total demand deposits— regular checking					159	2,262,000
Demand deposits—						
Special and other					3	833,000
Savings deposits and C.D.'s					32	435,000
Cost of capital					25	
General overhead					123	14,000
Trust	3,780	300	169	469	250	151,000
Total transfer units	36,800	$2,200	$2,600	$4,800	1,540	5,000,000
Total demand deposits, regular checking and other[1]						
Promotion—goodwill					162	
Checks cashed						
Checks deposits						
Deposit tickets						403,600
Checks drawn						2,016,500
Special services						
Statements						674,900
Payroll checks drawn						
Nonpayroll checks drawn						
					162	3,095,000

[1] For use in Problem 3 only.

Tellers Man-Hour (4-Weeks) VIII	Proof and Transit Document (Annual) IX	Bookkeeping Time-Weighted Item (Annual) X	Checks Cashed Document (Annual) XI	Statements Prepared Document (Annual) XII	Credit Files Time-Weighted Inquiry (Annual) XIII	Credit Analysis Man-Hour (Annual) XIV	1 General Overhead Noninterest Expense (Annual) XV
							$ 136,800
							131,600
							63,600
							125,000
							147,000
72	154,000				98,000	4,730	105,600
107	193,000				33,800	860	50,000
115	154,000				84,400	1,550	110,000
					33,800	860	38,400
							34,000
294	501,000				250,000	8,000	942,000
70			46,400				32,400
298	898,000						
	3,142,000						
555	771,000	510,000					
		2,840,000	411,100				
97							
		1,690,000		40,000			
1,020	4,811,000	5,040,000	457,500	40,000			32,400
90	690,000	1,960,000	52,500	25,000			10,000
265	578,000						30,000
							72,000
1,669	6,580,000	7,000,000	510,000	65,000	250,000	8,000	$1,086,400

Checks Drawn

Tellers Man-Hour (4-Weeks) VIII	Proof and Transit Document (Annual) IX	Bookkeeping Time-Weighted Item (Annual) X	Checks Cashed Document (Annual) XI	Statements Prepared Document (Annual) XII	Credit Files Time-Weighted Inquiry (Annual) XIII	Credit Analysis Man-Hour (Annual) XIV	1 General Overhead Noninterest Expense (Annual) XV
70			46,400				$ 42,400
329	1,013,000						
	3,487,000						
614	1,001,000	599,000					
		3,731,000					
97							
		2,670,000		65,000			
			280,000		800,000		
			183,600		3,460,000		
1,110	5,501,000	7,000,000	510,000	65,000	4,260,000		$ 42,400

Figure D.1—Summary of All Data Used in Allocation

In fact, it is in data gathering that the coster usually has the most trouble. The task is made easier if the bank has already established a budgeting or work measurement program. In the absence of these sources, the coster must use methods such as those illustrated in Problem 1, Step 5. The amount of effort that he expends is largely a matter of his own judgment. The preliminary "rough cut" will be very helpful in determining the amount of effort to expend on data gathering.

Problem 1. The Customer—A Profit Center (Customer Profitability)

References: Chapters 12 and 13.

A bank is experiencing a downward profit trend. In an effort to correct this condition management has decided to introduce the profit center concept of management. As a first step customers will be divided into groups and full responsibility for each commercial customer group will be assigned to an officer. Consequently, in the future an officer's performance will be evaluated, in part, on the profitability to the bank of his customers, individually and as a group. Trust department activities are excluded at this time.

The coster has been asked to develop a simple system for calculating customer profitability. The coster does this by using the five costing steps.

Step 1. Define the Purpose

The purpose is systematic determination of the profitability to the bank of customers individually and in groups. Such profitability is defined by the following formula:

Annual Profit Contribution of Customer (or Customer Group)

Revenue from loans to the customer	$XXXX
A credit for the earnings on customers deposit balance that exceeds his loan requirements over the 12-month period	XXXX
Service charges for services rendered	XXXX
Total revenue derived from the customer	XXXX
Less:	
A cost of funds charge for the loan requirements exceeding deposit balances over the 12-month period (cost of investable funds)	XXXX
Cost of lending and investing	XXXX
Cost of handling the customer's account	XXXX
Loan loss provision	XXXX
Total Cost	XXXX
Profit Contribution	$XXXX

The results of this calculation may prompt the following actions:

- Encouragement of larger deposit balances.
- Promotion of larger loans to the customer.
- Revision of service charge fee schedules.
- Campaigning to acquire more profitable customers.

On a higher level, the profit contribution of an officer's assigned customer group could influence his promotion, salary adjustment, or reassignment.

Step 2. Define the Costing Object

The costing object is the aggregate of the resources that provide service to a customer. For convenience, however, the costing object will be referred to as "the customer." Based on the foregoing profit formula, the resources that provide banking services to the customers are grouped into the following major benefit-providing units, which are diagrammed in Figure D.2 and related detail figures:

- Handling regular demand deposit checking accounts (Figure D.3).
- Lending and investing (Figure D.4).
- Investable funds (Figure D.5).
- Loan loss provision.

The loan loss provision is considered a cost center that replaces funds lost by default of loans. Since the provision is made from current bank profits, it is in effect an allocation of capital.

The deposits of commercial customers are contained among the regular demand checking accounts and the loans to commercial customers are included among the commercial loans. Thus the costing object is confined to the activities of regular demand checking accounts and commercial loans.

Step 3. Specify the Cost Data

Because the purpose is relative profit contribution, general overhead is omitted. The allocation of general overhead would either reduce each customer's profit contribution in an equal proportion or be subject to question as to fairness. Further, the inclusion or exclusion of general overhead should not change the ranking of relative profitability.

The demand deposit service fees and lending fees are netted against their related costs. This conforms to the decision to use the net method of calculating customer profitability (Chapter 12). Also, because the level of activity is stable, the cost data for the previous year can be used without any adjustment.

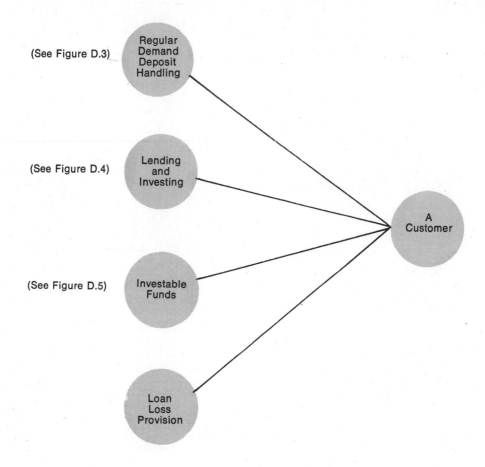

Figure D.2 (Problem 1)—Diagram Summary of Benefit-Providing Units Related to a Customer

The sources of the data are the general accounting system and a scale of rates developed by the credit department for loan loss provision. This scale of rates is based on the customers' credit ratings.

Although the time spent on credit investigation and lending officers' time in granting loans varies from customer to customer, it was decided not to include this cost in the profit formula shown in Step 1 because the manner in which the officer uses his time is felt to be only his concern. His overall effectiveness will be mainly judged on the profitability of his assigned customer group. This matter is left open for further study at a later date.

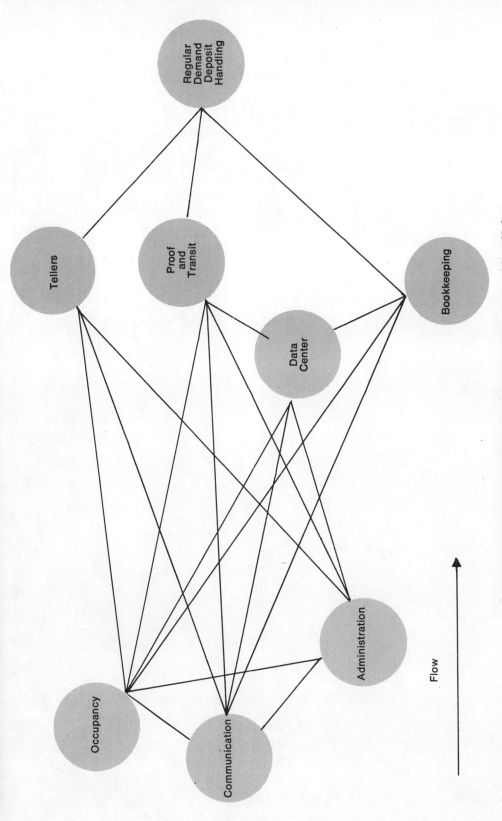

Flow

Figure D.3 (Problem 1)—Diagram Relating Benefit-Providing Units
to Handling of Regular Demand Deposit Checking Accounts

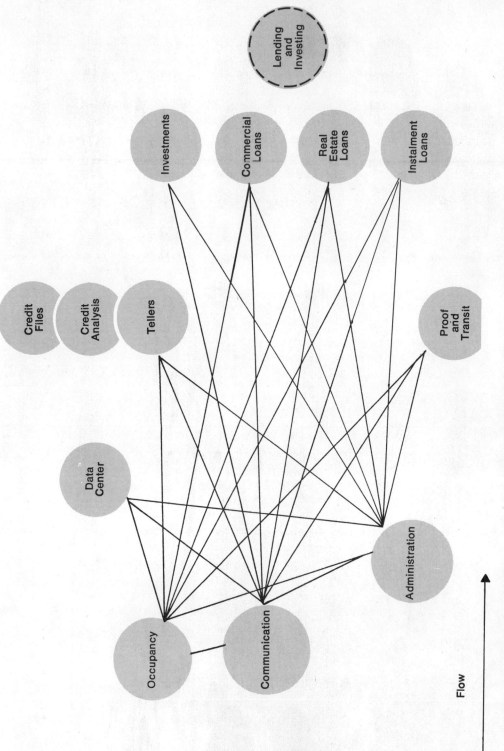

Flow

Figure D.4 (Problem 1)—Diagram Relating Benefit-Providing Units to Lending and Investing (Segmented for Clarity)

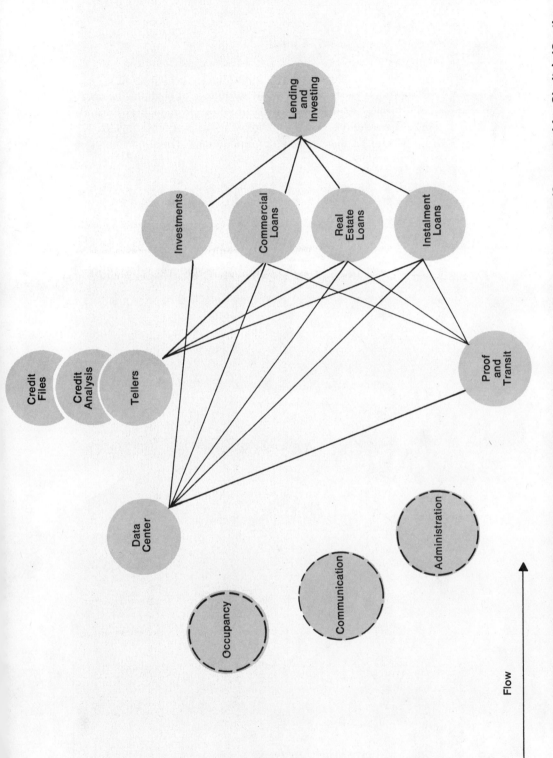

Flow

Figure D.4 (Problem 1)—Diagram Relating Benefit-Providing Units to Lending and Investing (Segmented for Clarity) (Continued)

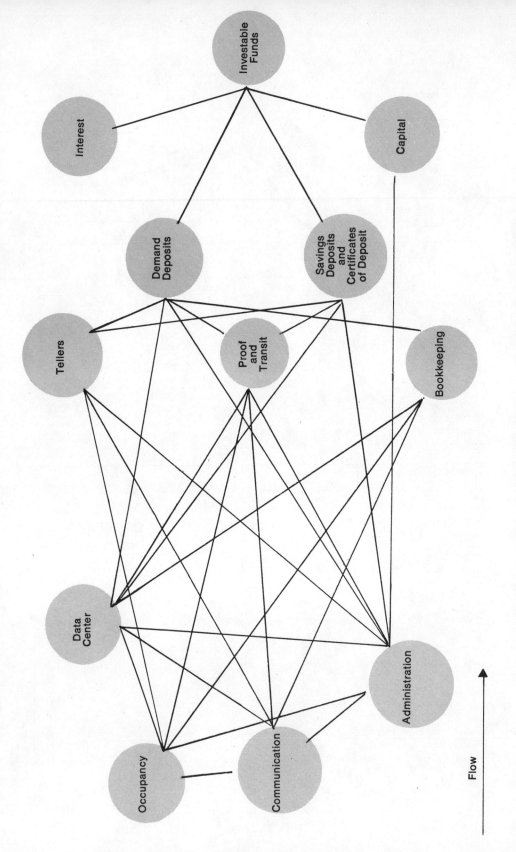

Figure D.5 (Problem 1)—Diagram Relating Benefit-Providing Units to Investable Funds

Flow

Step 4. Specify the Allocation Process

The connection between the various benefit-providing and benefit-receiving units shown in Figures D.3, D.4, and D.5 is reviewed by the coster so that the allocation bases can be determined and translated into transfer units. Because there are several levels of allocation, the step method (Chapter 10) is appropriate.

The cost center, handling regular demand deposit checking accounts (Figure D.5), is supported by the four benefit-providing units: tellers, proof and transit, data center, and bookkeeping. Analysis of the manner in which these units conduct their activities for the benefit of the customers and customer groups results in the addition of six intervening cost centers: checks deposited, checks cashed, checks drawn, statements, deposit tickets, and special services (Figure D.6). These additions permit equitable allocation of costs to the customers since each uses the services of tellers, proof and transit, data center, and bookkeeping in different proportions. The relationship of the added cost centers to the costing object is shown in Figure D.6. This addition is a retreat to Step 2 of the costing process to redefine the costing object and its components. The coster also must reexamine Step 3 to determine how the cost data for these new centers can be obtained.

In this instance, it was recognized that checks cashed would require additional consideration. In making the "rough cut" calculation it became apparent that cashing of checks involved services provided by the tellers and the proof and transit departments. Also a significant portion of the checks cashed were payroll checks, which could be identified with specific customers and which could affect their relative profitability. It was decided to defer the decision on how to reflect the cost of cashing checks in the customer profit formula until Step 5. At that time more information would be available, including the amount of cost allocated to the cashing of checks. Thus in Figure D.6 "checks cashed" is shown as a cost center but with only a tentative dotted line to the costing object, "handling regular demand deposit checking accounts."

Step 5. Calculate the Cost

The data for which allocations are to be made is collected in the following manner and is summarized in Figure D.1. In this Figure the data for allocation is arranged by benefit-providing units across the top in Columns II through XV and the benefit-receiving units are

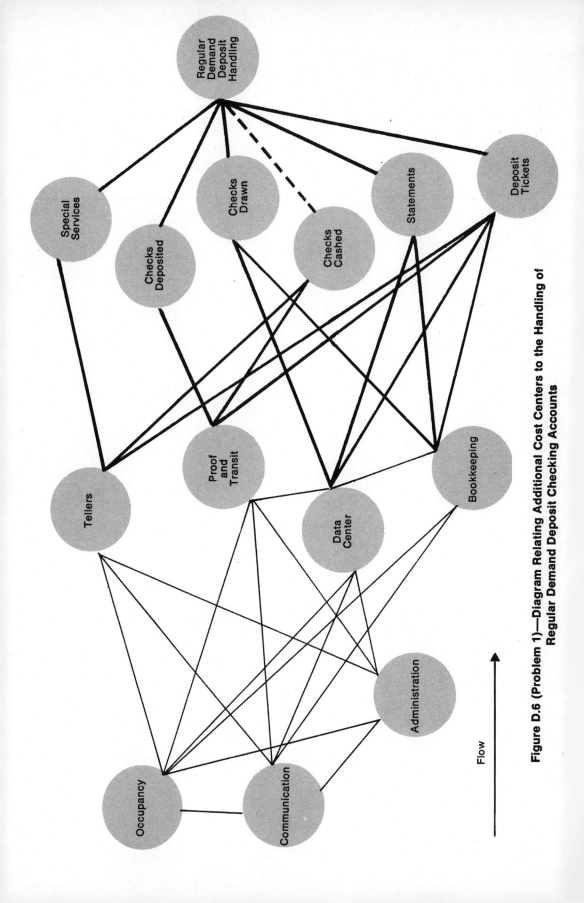

Figure D.6 (Problem 1)—Diagram Relating Additional Cost Centers to the Handling of Regular Demand Deposit Checking Accounts

Regular Demand Deposit Handling

Special Services

Checks Deposited

Checks Drawn

Checks Cashed

Statements

Deposit Tickets

Tellers

Proof and Transit

Data Center

Bookkeeping

Administration

Occupancy

Communication

Flow

listed in Column I. Problem I requires the data shown in Columns II through XI.

- The number of square feet occupied by each benefit-receiving unit is based on an analysis of existing use of floor space—Column II.
- The communication expense is analyzed and distributed by the number of instruments in use and the toll charges incurred. The resulting distribution of the one month's sample is reviewed by the heads of the various departments to ensure that it is reasonable—Columns III, IV, and V.
- Officers are asked to estimate their expenditure of time and an estimated distribution of administration time is made. It is reviewed by the senior executive officers to ensure that the distribution is reasonable—Column VI.
- The data center maintains statistics on inputs and outputs and has computed weighting equivalents. This is possible because the data center operates under a single program system—Column VII (see Chapter 16).
- A tally count is made of the tellers' activities for a representative four-week period—Column VIII (see Chapter 4). These counts are weighted as described in Chapter 10 and are shown in Figure 10.3. The 1,110 man-hours applicable to demand deposits in the Figure are further broken down between regular checking and special checking as follows:

Distribution of Tellers' Man-hours

| | Accommodation | Regular Checking Accounts | | | Special Checking Accounts | Total |
		Checks Cashed	Deposit Tickets	Special Services		
Demand deposits received						
Checks only			103		10	113
Cash only			108		13	121
Checks and cash			142		11	153
Cash returned			202		25	227
Checks cashed		298			31	329
Certified checks	35					35
Utility payments				44		44
Travelers' checks	35					35
Supermarket deposit				33		33
Change orders				20		20
Totals	70	298	555	97	90	1,110

.. The separation of time spent on special checking account transactions was obtained by sampling the transactions.

.. The statistics maintained by the proof and transit department (Column IX, Figure D.1) and the bookkeeping department (Columns X and XII) provide the basis for the distribution of costs for the documents processed by those units.

It was mentioned earlier that checks cashed would call for further investigation. By sampling it was found that the checks cashed fall into five categories:

	Percentage of Checks Cashed	Estimated Annual Volume
• Payroll checks drawn by customers and cashed by their employees	54.9%	280,000
• Other checks drawn on regular checking accounts	25.7	131,000
• Total checks drawn on regular checking accounts	80.6	411,100
• Checks drawn on special checking accounts	10.3	52,500
• Checks cashed drawn on other banks, principally social security checks as an accommodation	9.1	46,400
	100.0%	510,000

The estimated volumes are also included in Figure D.1, Column XI.

The large percentage of payroll checks cashed points to the possibility that, when identified with specific customers, varying volumes of checks cashed could affect the profitability of such customers. Further, the proportion of checks cashed to checks drawn was much higher for payroll checks:

	Payroll Accounts	Other Regular Checking Accounts	Total Regular Checking Accounts
"On us" checks cashed	280,000	131,100	411,100
Total checks drawn	800,000	2,587,000	3,387,000
Percentage of "on us" checks cashed to checks drawn	35%	5%	12%

The nonpayroll checks cashed do not present a problem. Their cost can be added to the cost of nonpayroll checks drawn without risking inequities. This is not so for payroll checks. There are three ways in which the coster can treat this matter:

1. Apply a separate cost for payroll checks cashed.

2. Apply a separate cost for payroll checks drawn. The cost of payroll checks drawn would be a new cost center to which a portion of the cost of checks drawn would be allocated.

3. Ignore the high proportion of payroll checks and simply include the cost of checks cashed with the cost of checks drawn.

The first two ways would involve an additional factor in the profit formula. This should be avoided for the sake of simplicity. Therefore, it was decided to defer a decision until the total cost allocated to cashed checks was known.

To proceed with the cost calculation, the costing object was defined in Step 2 as a "customer" and is summarized in Figure D.2. The major benefit-providing units are: handling regular demand deposit checking accounts, lending and investing, and cost of funds. The step method of allocating costs to these units is described in detail in Chapter 10 and is illustrated in Figure 10.5. The present cost calculations are carried out in Figures D.7 and D.8. Both these worksheets rework the figures introduced in Figure 10.5 (the total annual cost of $3,960,000 in Figure 10.5 is reduced by lending and investing fee revenue of $80,000).

The total costs of each benefit-providing unit are allocated to the benefit-receiving unit on the basis of the data accumulated in Figure D.1. For example, there are 36,800 square feet of floor space over which occupancy cost is allocated. The transfer unit is one square foot and thus the average unit transfer cost is $\dfrac{\$150,000}{36,800}$ or $4.08 per square foot. The officers occupy 8,340 square feet; therefore, the occupancy cost allocated to administration is 8,340 $\times$ $4.08 or $34,000 per year. Similarly, the proof and transit department handles 6,580,000 documents a year at a total cost of $170,700, or an average unit transfer cost of $\dfrac{\$170,700}{6,580,000}$ or $.02594 per document. There are 3,142,000 checks deposited annually. Therefore, the proof and transit cost allocated to checks deposited is 3,142,000 $\times$ $.02594 or $81,500. All the allocation calculations in Figures D.7 and D.8 are carried out in similar fashion.

As will be seen from Figure D.7, the cost allocated to checks cashed is $57,000, of which $45,900 is applicable to regular checking accounts as follows:

	Annual Costs	Occupancy	Communications	Administration
Benefit-Providing Units				
Occupancy	$ 150,000	$(150,000)		
Communications	57,600	900	$(58,500)	
Administration	447,200	34,000	18,000	$(499,200)
Data Center	192,400	7,700	5,200	13,900
Tellers	136,800	42,400	4,100	5,000
Proof and Transit	131,600	7,000	1,300	5,000
Bookkeeping	63,600	5,800	1,000	
Total Benefit-Providing Unit Cost	1,179,200			
Regular Demand Deposit Handling				
Checks Cashed				
Checks Deposited				
Deposit Tickets Processed				
Checks Drawn				
Statements				
Special Services				
Total Regular Demand Deposit Handling Costs				
Lending and Investing Costs				
Credit Files	125,000	10,000	5,000	8,000
Credit Analysis	147,000	7,000	7,000	25,000
Commercial Loans	105,600	6,800	2,600	100,000
Real Estate Loans	50,000	5,000	3,000	60,000
Instalment Loans	110,000	6,000	2,000	76,600
Investments	34,000		600	10,000
Fee Revenue	(80,000)			
Total Lending Costs	491,600			
Other Costs				
Credit Card	38,400	2,000	3,000	3,900
Trust	72,000	15,400	5,700	80,900
Promotion Demand Deposit	32,400			51,400
Special Checking and Other Deposits	10,000			1,000
Savings Deposits and C.D.s	30,000			10,500
Cost of Capital				8,000
General Overhead	116,000			40,000
Interest	2,012,400			
Demand Deposit Service Charge Revenues	(102,000)			
Total Costs not included	2,209,200			
TOTAL	$3,880,000	—0—	—0—	—0—

| | Allocation | | | | | | Total Costs of Cost Centers that Provide Benefits Directly to Customers |
Data Center	Tellers	Proof and Transit	Bookkeeping	Checks Cashed	Credit Files	Credit Analysis	
$(219,200)							
	$(188,300)						
25,800		$(170,700)					
13,000			$(83,400)				
	33,700	23,300		$(57,000)			
		81,500					$ 81,500
16,000	62,700	20,000	6,000				104,700
70,000			34,000	45,900			149,900
13,000			20,000				33,000
	11,000						11,000
							380,100
					$(148,000)		
						$(186,000)	
4,800	8,000	4,000			58,000	110,000	399,800
3,000	12,000	5,000			20,000	20,000	178,000
3,000	13,000	4,000			50,000	36,000	300,600
1,500							46,100
							(80,000)
							844,500
6,000					20,000	20,000	93,300
6,600							180,600
		7,900		5,200			96,900
36,700	10,000	17,900	23,400	5,900			104,900
19.200	30,000	15,000					104,700
							8,000
600							156,600
							2,012,400
							(102,000)
							2,655,400
—0—	—0—	—0—	—0—	—0—	—0—	—0—	$3,880,000

Figure D.7—Problem 1—Cost Calculation—Regular Demand Deposit Handling Cost and Lending and Investing Costs

Benefit-Providing Units	Annual Costs	ALLOCATION						Total Cost of Benefit-Receiving Units
		Occupancy	Communications	Administration	Data Center	Tellers	Proof and Transit	
Occupancy	$ 150,000	$(150,000)						
Communications	57,600	900	$(58,500)					
Administration	447,200	34,000	18,000	$(499,200)				
Data center	192,400	7,700	5,200	13,900	$(219,200)			
Tellers	136,800	42,400	4,100	5,000	25,800	$(188,300)		
Proof and transit	131,600	7,000	1,300	5,000			$(170,700)	
Total benefit-providing units cost	1,115,600							
Cost of Providing Funds								
Interest expense	2,012,400							$2,012,400
Demand deposits	42,400			52,400	135,700	125,300	142,700	498,500
Savings deposits and C.D.'s	30,000			10,500	19,200	30,000	15,000	104,700
Bookkeeping	63,600	5,800	1,000		13,000			83,400
Cost of capital				8,000				8,000
Service charges—revenue	(102,000)							(102,000)
Total cost of providing funds	2,046,400							2,605,000
Other Bank Costs								
Credit files	125,000							
Credit analysis	147,000							
Commercial loans	105,600							
Real estate loans	50,000							
Instalment loans	110,000							
Fee revenue of lending departments	(80,000)	52,200	28,900	404,400	25,500	33,000	13,000	1,275,000
Credit card	38,400							
Investments	34,000							
Trust	72,000							
General overhead	116,000							
Total expenses not included	718,000							1,275,000
Total	$3,880,000	-0-	-0-	-0-	-0-	-0-	-0-	$3,880,000

Figure D.8 (Problem 1)—Cost Calculation—Cost of Providing Funds

	Annual Number of Checks	Cost Allocated On Number of Checks	Percentage of Total Demand Deposit Handling Cost of $380,100
Payroll	280,000	$31,300	8.2%
Nonpayroll	131,100	14,600	3.8
Total	411,100	$45,900	12.0%

After due consideration management and the coster decided that, for the present, the cost of cashing payroll checks should be included with the cost of all checks drawn. They were anxious to get a system of evaluating customer profitability started and wanted to keep the formula as simple as possible. They agreed that a refinement could be made later if the circumstances warranted.

These computations result in the cost of handling regular demand deposits ($380,100), the cost of lending and investing ($844,500), and the cost of providing funds ($2,605,000). These costs are then expressed as average unit transfer costs in the following manner:

Benefit-Providing Unit	Annual Cost	Transfer Unit	Annual Number of Transfer Units	Unit Transfer Cost
(From Figure D.7):				
Checks deposited to regular demand deposit accounts	$ 81,500	Check	3,142,000	$ .026
Deposits made to regular demand deposit accounts	104,700	Deposit Ticket	771,000	.136
Checks drawn on regular demand deposit accounts	149,900	Check	3,387,000	.044
Statement	33,000	Statement	40,000	.825
Special services	11,000	Man-hour	1,261	8.723
Lending and investing	844,500	Dollar of average investable funds	87,540,000[1]	.00965
(From Figure D.8):				
Cost of funds	2,605,000	Dollar of average investable funds	87,540,000[1]	.0298

[1]See Figure 11.4.

343

The controller noted that the estimated cost of $11,000 a year for the special services performed by the tellers is not considered to be a material cost item to either the bank or the customer. Therefore, he dropped it from the basic profit formula stated in Step 1.

With calculation of the unit transfer costs, the costing portion of the system for calculating customer profitability is complete. The controller has the remaining tasks of designing the necessary forms, writing instructions, and establishing procedures for an annual review of the cost data and basic costing assumptions.

The smoothly operating system for calculating customer profitability centers around a worksheet form (Figure D.9). The example worked out in this Figure uses the above unit transfer costs.

Credit for excess of deposits is calculated as follows:

Historical or projected or target interest rate for the bank as a whole expressed as a percentage of investable funds— hypothetical rate	6.000%
Less cost of lending and investing	.965
Credit for excess funds	5.035%

The factor for converting deposit balances to investable funds is the percentage that the investable funds derived from regular demand deposits bears to average daily deposit balances. For this problem the amounts, with respect to regular demand deposits, have been taken from Figure 11.4 as follows:

$$\frac{\text{Investable funds}}{\text{Average deposit balance}} = \frac{\$25,952,000}{\$33,826,000} = 76.7\%$$

In summary, in this example the cost factors finally adopted by management consist of the following factors as used in Figure D.9. These costs are:

- Cost of funds.

- Cost of lending and investing.

- Costs of handling regular demand deposit checking accounts.

These costs are valid and happen to be satisfactory to management in these particular circumstances. However, they do not constitute the only set of valid costs.

	Loans Outstanding	Average Daily Deposits Balance	Revenue Interest	Service Charges and Fees	Checks Deposited	Deposits Made	Checks Drawn	Statements
Jan.	$ 270,000	$ 50,000	$1,350	$ 35	800	25	1,020	5
Feb.	200,000	40,000	1,000	38	840	27	995	6
Mar.	100,000	50,000	500	44	900	30	1,100	5
Apr.	—	75,000		47	800	22	1,005	5
May	—	75,000		40	400	24	940	6
June	—	75,000		42	500	21	600	5
July	—	80,000		36	450	22	575	5
Aug.	—	68,000		32	400	20	625	5
Sept.		70,000		37	375	21	750	5
Oct.	100,000	50,000	500	40	400	20	800	6
Nov.	250,000	60,000	1,250	48	425	19	900	5
Dec.	400,000	75,000	2,000	50	300	22	1,000	6
Total ÷ 12	1,320,000	768,000	$6,600	$489	6,590	273	10,310	64
Monthly Av.	÷ 12 110,000	÷ 12 64,000		Unit transfer costs	$.026	$.136	$.044	$.825
Conversion factor		76.7%			$171.34	$37.13	$453.64	$52.80

Average investable funds   49,088

Excess Loans $ 60,912

Charge for excess loan at 2.98% $ 1,815

Credit for excess funds at 5.035% $

Earnings

Interest revenue	$6,600
Fees and other revenue	489
Credit for excess funds at 5.035%	
Total earnings	$7,089
Less costs	2,585
Profit	$4,504

Costs

Charge for excess loans	$1,815
Checks deposited	171
Deposits made	37
Checks drawn	454
Statement	53
Loan loss provision at .005% of average loan	55
Total costs	2,585
Less earnings	
Loss	$

Figure D.9 (Problem 1)—Customer Profitability Worksheet

Equally dependable costs could have reflected credit analysis cost, payroll check cost, and the costs of special services. For the various reasons noted management decided against including these costs in the formula. A different management with a different outlook operating under different circumstances and experiencing a different set of numerical values might have included any of these refinements. This discussion illustrates the discretionary nature of costing, which is, after all, an art.

Problem 2. Cost of Increased Activity (Incremental Costs)

References: Chapter 6 and 7.

Because a major industry has moved into the community, the bank expects a significant increase in business. The controller has been asked to calculate the cost of additional resources that will be required to provide needed capacity to handle the anticipated increase in volume of banking activity and customer transactions. Management expects that this increased activity will take place in the following areas: commercial loans, 5%; real estate loans, 20%; instalment loans, 20%; regular checking, 15%; special checking, 50%; savings accounts, 10%. The costs that are to be calculated are to be compared to various revenue estimates for use in future planning.

Using the five costing steps, the controller computes the cost of this expansion.

Step 1. Define the Purpose

The purpose of the cost calculation is to determine the cost of providing additional resource capacity to meet the projected expansion of activities. The range of decisions is whether to encourage or discourage this expansion. The criterion for the ultimate decision is incremental cost in relation to the incremental revenue resulting from increased banking activity.

Step 2. Define the Costing Object

The costing object is the aggregate of several fund-using and fund-providing bank functions. They consist of commercial loans, real estate loans, instalment loans, regular checking demand deposits, special checking demand deposits, and savings deposits.

The component resources are new funds deposited, new funds loaned and invested, new personnel employed, newly acquired facilities and equipment, and the additional supporting services required of the bank's other benefit-providing units (Figure D.10). Because the

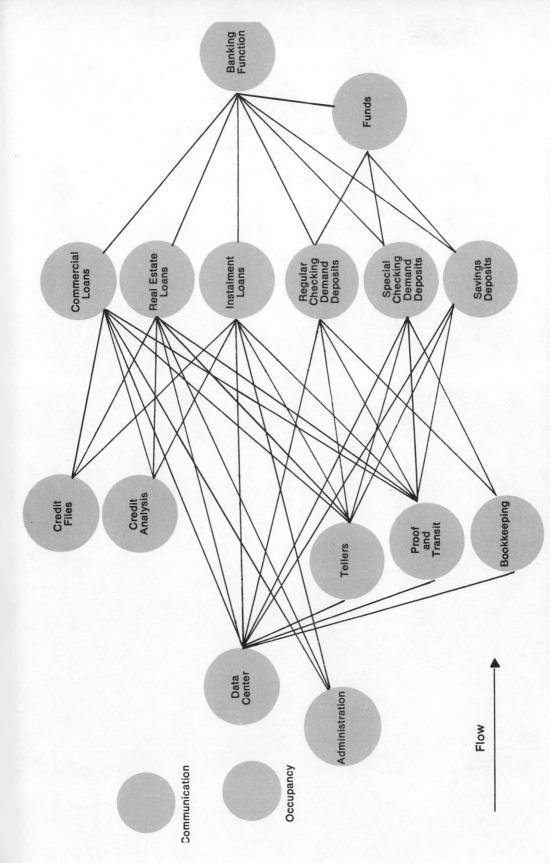

Figure D.10 (Problem 2)—Principal Benefit-Providing Units Related to the Banking Function

Flow

purpose of the cost calculation involves possible additions to resources, the emphasis in the diagram is on those resources most likely to be affected and accordingly, not all related cost centers have been shown.

Step 3. Specify the Cost Data

To specify the required cost data the coster must identify the benefit-providing units that require additional resources. This is accomplished by estimating the present capacity of each benefit-providing unit and comparing this capacity with projected utilization. It is assumed that the transaction mix within each unit will remain the same so that a valid projection can be made by applying the percentage changes expected to the present level of utilization.

The coster, by conferring with department heads, estimates the existing utilization and capacity of the various resources, using whatever methods described in Chapter 4 that may be applicable. As stated in the introduction to the problems, the basic current utilization data has been accumulated in Figure D.1.

This data is summarized in Figure D.11 for the clerical departments and is projected in accordance with the percentage increases specified by management. The capacity is estimated by experienced department heads and various subordinate supervisors.

It appears that the teller department is already exceeding estimated capacity and that two new full-time tellers and one additional part-time teller will be required. Six teller windows are currently in operation and they barely handle the traffic during peak periods. The projected increase of activity will aggravate this crowded condition. Therefore, the bank must add more windows and is considering expanding its physical facilities by installing a drive-in window.

The proof and transit department will be operating near capacity but it should not require additional help. However, two clerks will be required in the bookkeeping department.

The five percent increase in work for the commercial loan department can be absorbed by present personnel. The real estate loan department is currently staffed with three employees and requires the full-time attention of an officer. The 20% increase in activity will require one additional employee and an assistant vice president (an administrative expense). The instalment loan department now employs six persons and requires the attention of two officers. The increased activity will require one additional clerk.

Based on the estimated percentages of increase, the expected increase in deposits is expected to satisfy the increase in volume of loans (Figure D.12).

Additional required resources are summarized below. The costs of these resources constitute the specified cost data:

Benefit-Providing Unit	Resource Required
Real estate loans	1 clerk
Instalment loans	1 clerk
Credit files	1 clerk
Tellers	2 tellers (a drive-in window)
Bookkeeping	2 clerks
Administration	1 assistant vice president
Savings deposits	$3,752,000 investable savings deposit funds

The benefit-providing units that require additional resources are highlighted in Figure D.13. Only the costs of these cost centers will be involved in the calculation.

Step 4. Specify the Allocation

Each of the additional resources are wholly applicable to the additional activity, and these costs are transferred directly and in total to the costing object. Therefore, the allocation basis and the transfer unit are the increment of the resource directly applied to the costing object. This is summarized in the calculation shown in Step 5.

Step 5. Calculate the Cost

The cost calculation is the summation of the required resources as identified in Step 3.

Resource Required	Cost
Annual salaries and fringe benefits	
2 Loan clerks	$ 15,000
1 File clerk—credit files	6,500
2 Tellers	16,000
2 File clerks—bookkeeping	13,000
1 Assistant vice president	12,000
Total salaries and fringe benefits	$ 62,500
Annual increase in interest cost on $3,752,000 investable savings deposits at 4.62%[1]	$173,300
Fixed asset cost	
Estimated cost of drive-in window	$ 50,000

[1] Current rate of 4.5% adjusted for reserves.

Benefit-Receiving Units and Expected Increases

Clerical Benefit-Providing Unit and Transfer Units	Commercial Loans 5%	Real Estate Loans 20%	Instalment Loans 20%	Regular Demand Deposit 15%
Tellers, man-hours 4-week period				
Current utilization	72	107	115	1,020
Projected utilization	76	128	137	1,170
Proof and transit, annual documents processed				
Current utilization	154,000	193,000	154,000	4,811,000
Projected utilization	162,000	232,000	185,000	5,533,000
Bookkeeping				
Time-weighted items				
Current utilization				5,040,000
Projected utilization				5,796,000
Data center, annual time-weighted items				
Current utilization	110,000	68,000	68,000	2,262,000
Projected utilization	116,000	82,000	82,000	2,600,000
Credit files				
Time-weighted inquiries				
Current utilization	98,000	33,800	84,400	
Projected utilization	102,900	40,600	101,300	
Credit analysis				
Man-hours				
Current utilization	4,730	860	1,550	
Projected utilization	4,966	1,032	1,860	

Special Demand Deposit 50%	Savings Accounts 10%	Proof and Transit 10.8%	Bookkeeping 25%	Other	Total Current and Projected Utilization	Practical Capacity	Additional Resource Required
90	265				1,669		
135	292				1,938	16,000	2 tellers
					16% Increase		
690,000	578,000				6,580,000		
,035,000	636,000				7,783,000	7,800,000	None required
					18.3% Increase		
,960,000					7,000,000		
,940,000					8,736,000	7,250,000	
					25% Increase		2 clerks
833,000	435,000	590,000	298,000	336,000	5,000,000		
,250,000	480,000	653,000	372,000	336,000	5,971,000	8,000,000	None required
					19% Increase		
				33,800	250,000		
				33,800	278,600	250,000	1 clerk
					11% Increase		
				860	8,000		
				860	8,710	9,000	None required
					9% Increase		

Figure D.11 (Problem 2)—Projected Utilization and Practical Capacity of Clerical Benefit-Providing Units

	Present Average Balance of Investable Funds	Expected Increase	Projected Investable Funds
Projection of investable funds:			
Regular demand deposits	$25,952,000	15%	$29,845,000
Special demand deposits	2,968,000	50%	4,452,000
Other demand deposits	400,000		400,000
Regular savings	37,523,000	10%	41,275,000
Club savings	800,000		800,000
Certificates of deposit	6,897,000		6,897,000
Federal Reserve funds purchased	5,000,000		5,000,000
Capital	8,000,000		8,000,000
Total investable funds	$87,540,000		$96,669,000
Projection of loans and investments:			
Commercial loans	$35,935,000	5%	$37,732,000
Real estate loans	11,681,000	20%	14,017,000
Instalment loans	19,299,000	20%	23,159,000
Credit card	1,022,000		1,022,000
Other loans and investments	19,603,000		19,603,000
Total loans and investments	$87,540,000		$95,533,000

**Figure D.12 (Problem 2)—
Projected Funds Available and Fund Projected Requirements**

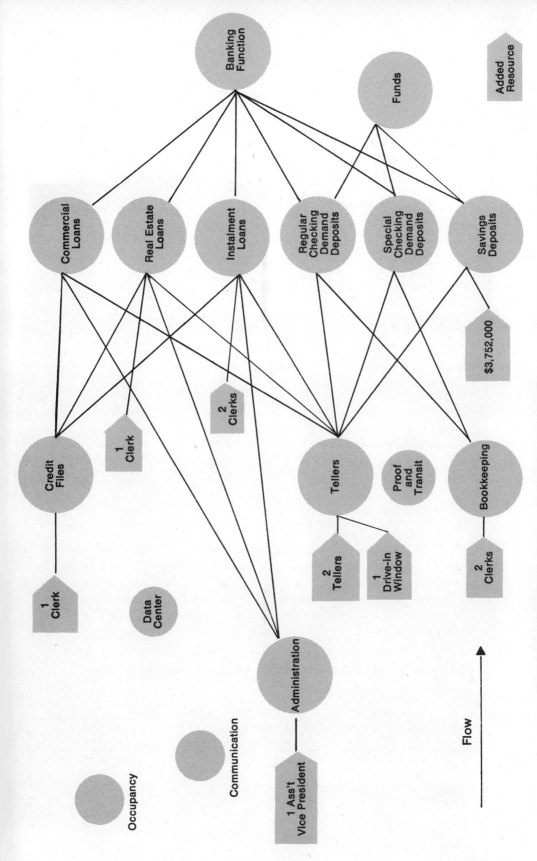

Figure D.13 (Problem 2)—Diagram of Resources Required to Accommodate Increased Activity

With the calculation of the foregoing costs the controller has completed his assignment. As a practical matter, however, if information is available to him, he should test the costs against the ultimate purpose of the calculation. Using the percentage of increase already given, together with current average yields, he calculates an estimated incremental profit as follows:

Annual Incremental Revenue:

Commercial loans, $1,797,000 at 5.15%[1]	$ 92,500
Real estate loans, $2,336,000 at 4.71%	90,000
Instalment loans, $3,860,000 at 5.44%	210,000
Incremental revenue	392,500

Annual Incremental Costs:

Funds

Added investable saving deposits	173,300

People

Salaries and fringe benefits	62,500

Facilities

Depreciation of drive-in window at composite rate of 10%[2]	5,000
Total annual incremental cost	240,800
Incremental profit	$151,700

[1] Rates obtained from Figure 12.4.
[2] Takes into consideration the varying useful life of the building as well as equipment.

The incremental profit of $151,700 markedly favors the encouragement of the additional business. Further refinement of the cost calculation by including stationery and other expenses and the incremental service charge revenue would not significantly affect the result; therefore, these items are rightly ignored as not being material.

Problem 3. Are We Charging Enough?
(Cost for Pricing Demand Deposit Services)

Reference: Chapter 14.

The bank management wants to review its schedule of charges for items handled for all demand deposit account customers and has asked that costs of handling these items be calculated and compared to the bank's current fee schedule.

Current fee schedule:

A check included in a deposit	$ .02
A deposit ticket handled	.10
A check drawn	.04

The coster proceeds with the calculation, applying the five costing steps.

Step 1. Define the Purpose

The purpose of the cost calculation is to provide management with the cost information necessary to enable them to review the demand deposit fee structure. This review could result in a change in the fee schedule. The criteria that will be used in making the decision include the profitability of the routine services provided the customer, the marketing impact of any fee changes, and other factors.

Step 2. Define the Costing Object

The costing object is the demand deposit checking account services provided to a customer. These activities employ the resources of people and bank facilities. The costs being sought are the costs of these resources allocated to the costing objects. They are grouped into the following benefit-providing units: tellers' department, proof and transit department, bookkeeping department. These departments in turn are supported by other benefit-providing units: occupancy, communication, administration, data center, and general overhead. In addition, as a result of a survey conducted through the use of a self-logging activity questionnaire (Figure 4.4), it was found that check cashing and statement processing also constitute significant demand deposit function activities, and are considered cost centers. The relationship of these cost centers to each other and to the handling of a demand deposit account is diagrammed in Figure D.14.

Step 3. Specify the Cost Data

All costs, including general overhead, are applicable to these costing objects because the costing purpose is price evaluation and these activities constitute a major bank service. The sources of the data are the general accounting system, the self-logging activity questionnaires, and tally counts.

Step 4. Specify the Allocation Process

Working from the benefits provided by the various units, the allocation bases and the transfer units are determined (Figure D.1). Step allocation is used because there are several allocation levels

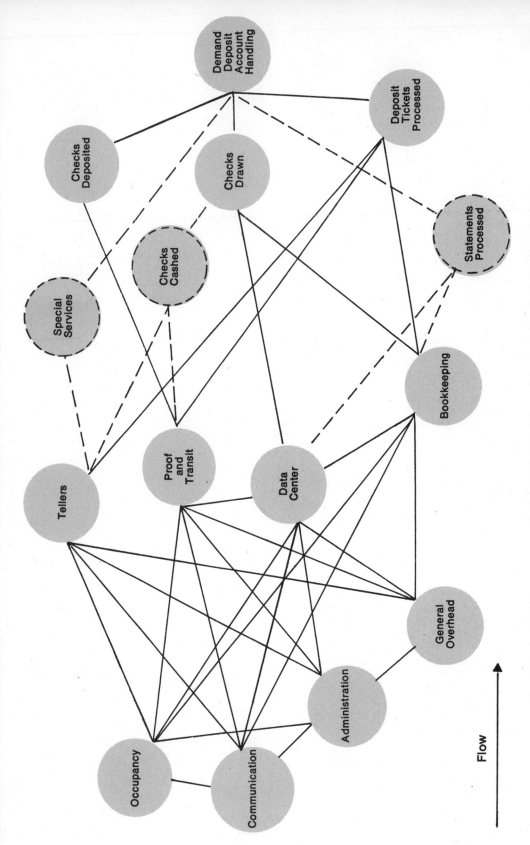

Figure D.14 (Problem 3)—Diagram Relating Benefit-Providing Units to a Single Customer

Flow

involved. The sequence of allocation indicated in Figure D.14 is shown in tabular form in Figure D.16.

Step 5. Calculate the Cost

The nonmonetary data is collected by a tally count and weighting of tellers' transactions (Chapter 4 and Figure. 4.2; Chapter 10 and Figure 10.3). The necessary data is summarized in the condensed summary of nonmonetary data (Figure D.1).

The four-week transaction count and weighting that is summarized in Figure 10.3 shows that a substantial amount of tellers' time is devoted to cashing checks:

	Man-hours (Per Figure 10.3)	Percentage
Receiving deposits	614	55%
Cashing checks	329	30
Special services: Supermarket deposits, change orders, utility payments	97	9
Certified and cashiers' checks	70	6
Total teller time spent on demand deposits	1110	100%

This requires, in effect, that the coster return to Step 2 to refine the definition of the costing object.

Further analysis established that checks cashed fall into four categories. These are shown below with percentages applied to estimated annual volume.

	Percentage	Estimated Annual Volume
Accommodation checks, "on others" checks cashed, principally social security checks	9.1%	46,400
"On us" payroll checks	54.9	280,000
"On us" nonpayroll checks cashed— regular checking accounts	25.7	131,100
"On us" nonpayroll checks cashed— special checking accounts	10.3	52,500
Total checks cashed	100.0%	510,000

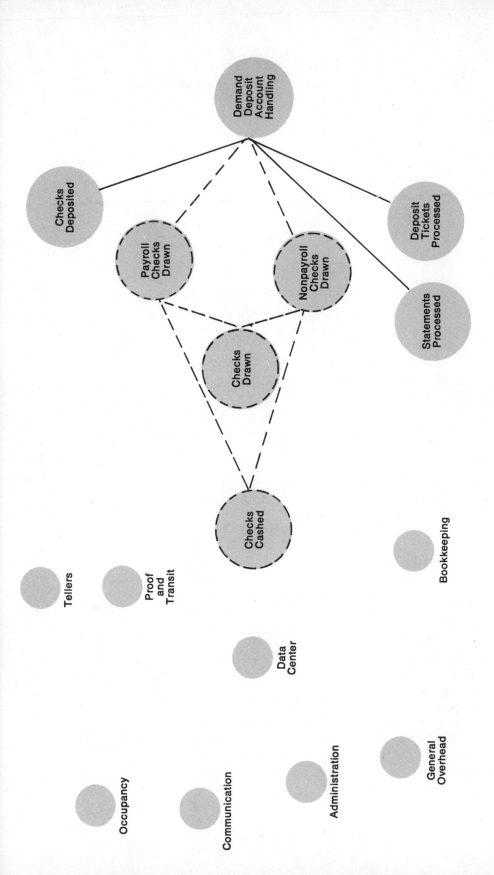

Figure D.15 (Problem 3)—Diagram Showing Additional Cost Centers

The accommodation checks are a goodwill measure; their cost is not applicable to demand deposit account customers. The payroll checks cashed warrant a separate charge to customers drawing them. Similarly, the cost of nonpayroll checks is allocable to the remaining demand deposit account customers. The cost of cashing nonpayroll checks can be added to the cost of nonpayroll checks drawn.

In order to accomplish the necessary cost allocation, it is necessary to create two new cost centers: "payroll checks drawn" and "non-payroll checks drawn."

The relationship of these cost centers to the cost centers already defined in Step 2 is shown in Figure D.15. The studies indicated that 800,000 of the 4,260,000 checks drawn annually are payroll checks.

The cost of processing customer statements also constitutes a significant portion of the cost of handling demand deposits. This cost does not vary entirely with the number of checks and deposit tickets. There is a fixed cost per statement regardless of activity. The activities that comprise the fixed and variable costs of statement processing were examined by the coster and found to be:

Benefit-Providing Unit	Costs That Are Relatively Fixed Per Statement	Costs That Vary with Activity
Data center	Printing of statement heading, opening balance, paper handling, master file data	File updating
Bookkeeping	Envelopes, preparation for mailing, handling	Filing, postage

By one of the various methods of work measurement (measurement of activity) described in Chapter 4 and existing statistics, the coster was able to obtain estimates of time-weighted items reflecting "fixed" activities carried on in the data center and bookkeeping department. These are shown on the line marked "Statements" in Figure D.1.

One item remains to be considered: special services. The study of the tellers' department showed that nine percent of the time was spent on services performed for customers, including change orders, coin counting and wrapping, supermarket deposits, etc. Although the bank does not charge for these services, the president and controller agreed that, at least tentatively, special services should be costed separately. This decision in effect goes back again to Step 2 and redefines the costing object by adding "special services" as a benefit-providing unit.

	Annual Costs		Cost Allocation		
		Occupancy	Communication	Administration	Data Center
Costs of Handling Demand Deposit Checking Accounts					
Occupancy	$ 150,000	$(150,000)			
Communication	57,600	900	$(58,500)		
Administration	447,200	34,000	18,000	$(499,200)	
Data Center	192,400	7,700	5,200	13,900	$(219,200)
General Overhead	116,000			40,000	600
Tellers	136,800	42,400	4,100	5,000	
Proof and Transit	131,600	7,000	1,300	5,000	25,800
Bookkeeping	63,600	5,800	1,000		13,000
Checks Cashed					
Checks Deposited					
Deposit Tickets					17,700
Checks Drawn					88,400
Statements					29,600
Special Services					
Payroll Checks					
Nonpayroll Checks Drawn					
Total Demand Deposit Checking Account					
Other Costs					
Credit Files	125,000				
Credit Analysis	147,000				
Demand Deposit:					
Promotion, Goodwill	42,400				
Service Usage Revenue	(102,000)				
Savings Deposits and C.D.'s	30,000				
Commercial Loans	105,600	52,200	28,900	435,300	44,100
Real Estate Loans	50,000				
Instalment Loans	110,000				
Credit Card	38,400				
Investments	34,000				
Trusts	72,000				
Capital					
Interest	2,012,400				
Total Other Costs					
Total Costs	$3,960,000	—0—	—0—	—0—	—0—

General Overhead	Tellers	Proof and Transit	Bookkeeping	Checks Cashed	Checks Drawn	Total Cost of Benefit-Receiving Units
			Cost Allocation (continued)			
$(156,600)						
19,700	$(208,000)					
19,000		$(189,700)				
9,200			$(92,600)			
	41,000	28,800		$(69,800)		
		100,700				$ 100,700
	76,500	28,900	7,900			131,000
			49,400		$(137,800)	
			35,300			64,900
	12,100					12,100
				38,300	25,900	64,200
				25,100	111,900	137,000
						509,900
108,700	78,400	31,300		6,400		3,450,100
						3,450,100
—0—	—0—	—0—	—0—	—0—	—0—	$3,960,000

Figure D.16 (Problem 3)—Cost Calculation

The cost calculation was completed as shown on the cost calculation worksheet (Figure D.16), and the corresponding unit transfer costs were calculated as follows:

Cost Center	Cost	Number of Transfer Units	Unit Transfer Cost
Checks deposited	$100,700	3,260,000 checks	$ .031
Deposit tickets	131,000	790,000 tickets	.165
Nonpayroll checks drawn	137,000	3,460,000 checks	.0396
Payroll checks drawn	64,200	800,000 checks	.0825
Statements	64,200	77,000 statements	.834
Special services	12,100	1,261 man-hours	9.58

With the completion of the calculation (Step 5), the cost process is complete. Nevertheless, the coster should apply the results of his efforts to the purpose of the calculation as a final check on the reasonableness of results. Accordingly, the unit transfer costs are compared with the pricing schedule:

Transfer Unit	Cost	Price
A check included in a deposit	$ .031	$.02
A deposit ticket handled	.165	.10
A nonpayroll check drawn	.0396	.04
A payroll check drawn	.0825	.04
A statement prepared	.834	no charge
One man-hour devoted to special services	9.58	no charge

These comparisons, except for the cost of special services, seem to the coster to be generally reasonable. The $9.58 a man-hour seems high; therefore, he breaks down the teller cost as follows:

	Annual Cost	Cost per Man-Hour
Salary and fringe benefits	$109,000	$5.02
Other direct costs	27,800	1.28
Total direct cost	136,800	6.30
Occupancy	42,400	1.95
Communication	4,100	.19
Administration	5,000	.23
General overhead	19,700	.91
Total teller cost	$208,000	$9.58

This information was included in the cost information submitted to management for their deliberations regarding pricing policy.

BIBLIOGRAPHY
AND INDEX

BIBLIOGRAPHY

The following abbreviated bibliography has been compiled for the purpose of providing the reader with a means for pursuing the subject matter of this book in greater depth. The bibliography has been kept to reasonable length and is not intended to include all material that may pertain to the subject.

BOOKS

American Bankers Association. *Cost Analysis Procedures for Smaller Banks.* Country Bank Operations Committee. New York, 1969.

American Bankers Association. *Recommended Cost & Accounting Procedure for Trust Departments.* Trust Division. New York, 1949.

American Bankers Association. *Role of Investment on Bank Asset Management: Study 4, Objectives and Principles (The).* Bank Management Committee. New York, 1966.

American Institute of Banking. *Principles of Bank Operation.* New York, 1966.

American Institute of Certified Public Accountants. *APB Accounting Principles: Vol. II, Original Pronouncements as of August 1, 1969.* New York, 1969.

Anton, Hector R., and Lirmin, Peter A. *Contemporary Issues in Cost Accounting.* Boston: Houghton Mifflin Co., 1956.

Bank Administration Institute. *Bank Administration Manual.* Park Ridge, Ill., 1970.

Bank Administration Institute. *Evaluating Instalment Loan Operations: Vol. I System and Performances Standards.* Research Division. Park Ridge, Ill., 1965.

Bank Administration Institute. *Performance Standards for Bank Operations.* Research Division. Park Ridge, Ill., 1967.

Bank Administration Institute. *Study of Dual Posting Fully-Deferred Demand Posting Accounting.* Park Ridge, Ill., 1959.

Bank Administration Institute. *Study for Improving Commercial Teller Operations.* Vols. I and II. Park Ridge, Ill., 1963.

Bank Administration Institute. *Study of Proof and Transit Operations (A),* Vol. I. Park Ridge, Ill., 1961.

Bank Administration Institute. *Study of Time Deposit Accounting Methods and Systems.* Park Ridge, Ill., 1960.

Bank Administration Institute. *Successful Profit Planning for Banks.* Park Ridge, Ill., 1970.

Baughn, William H., and Walker, Charls E. (eds.). *Bankers Handbook.* Homewood, Ill.: Dow Jones-Irwin, Inc., 1966.

Chase, Fred. *A Cost Accounting System For Banks of Medium Size.* Commercial National Bank of Peoria. Peoria, Ill., n.d.

Corns, Marshall C. *Practical Cost Accounting for Banks.* Boston: Bankers Publishing Co., 1959.

Corns, Marshall C. *The Practical Operations and Management of a Bank.* 2nd ed. Boston: Bankers Publishing Co., 1968.

Demski, Joel S., Feltham, Gerald A., Horngren, Charles T., Jaedricke, Robert K., and Sprouse, Robert T. *Cost Concepts and Implementation Criteria (An Interim Report).* American Institute of Certified Public Accountants, New York, 1970.

Dickey, Robert J. (ed.). *Accountants' Cost Handbook,* 2nd ed. New York: Ronald Press Co., 1967.

Federal Reserve System. 1966, 1967, 1968, and 1969. *Functional Cost Analysis for 11 Federal Districts.* Washington, D.C.

Gillespie, Cecil M. *Cost Accounting Control.* Englewood Cliffs, N.J.: Prentice-Hall, Inc., 1957.

Hengazy, Mohamad Abbas and Blakely, Edward J., Jr. *An Application of Budgetary Control to Commercial Banks with Reference to The Principles of Commercial Bank Management.* Madison: University of Wisconsin, 1965.

Horngren, Charles T. *Cost Accounting: A Managerial Emphasis.* 2nd ed. Englewood Cliffs, N.J.: Prentice-Hall, Inc., 1967.

Jessup, Paul F. (ed.). *Innovations in Bank Management: Selected Readings.* Chicago: Holt, Rinehart and Winston, 1969.

Kelly, Charles W. *The Construction and Use of Organizational Profit and Loss Statements in Commercial Banks.* First National City Bank, New York.

Kennedy, Walter. *Bank Management.* Boston: Bankers Publishing Co., 1969.

Kohler, Eric L. *A Dictionary for Accountants.* 4th ed. Englewood Cliffs, N.J.: Prentice-Hall, Inc., 1970.

Lasser, J. K. (ed.). *Handbook of Cost Accounting Methods.* New York: D. Van Nostrand Co., Inc., 1949.

Matz, Adolph, Curry, Othel J., and Frank, George W. *Cost Accounting*. 4th ed. Cincinnati: Southwestern Publishing Co., 1967.

National Association of Accountants. *The Analysis of Manufacturing Cost Variances*. Research Series, Number 22. New York, 1952.

National Association of Accountants. *Standards to Aid Control of Manufacturing Costs*. Research Series, Number 12. New York, 1948.

Newner, John J. W., and Frumer, Samual. *Cost Accounting: Principles & Practices*. Homewood, Ill.: Richard D. Irwin, Inc., 1967.

New York Clearing House Association, The. *Bank Cost Accounting Principles and Procedures*. Committee on Accounting Procedures. New York, 1961.

O'Brien, James A. *Impact of Computers on Banking*. Boston: Bankers Publishing Co., 1968.

Philadelphia National Bank, The. *Profitability Analysis of Commercial Customers*. Philadelphia, 1965.

Shillinglaw, Gordon. *Cost Accounting: Analysis & Control*. Homewood, Ill.: Richard D. Irwin, Inc., 1967.

Steiner, George A. *Top Management Planning*. Three Volumes. London: The MacMillan Company, 1969.

Thomas, William E., Jr. (ed.). *Readings in Cost Accounting, Budgeting and Control*. 3rd ed. Cincinnati: Southwestern Publishing Co., 1968.

Vaughn, James A. and Porat, Auner M. *Banking Computer Style (The Impact of Computers on Small and Medium-Sized Banks)*. Englewood Cliffs, N.J.: Prentice-Hall, Inc., 1969.

Walker, John R. *Bank Costs for Decision Making: Costing Procedures for Pricing Bank Services*. Boston: Bankers Publishing Co., 1970.

THESES

Benedict, George W., III. "Accounting for Bank Computer Costs." Rutgers University, June, 1964.

Bierer, William E. "Profit Planning for a Branch Organization." Rutgers University, June, 1965.

Blanchette, Ernest E. "How Small Banks Can Use a Functional Analysis of Income and Expense." Rutgers University, June, 1965.

Kemper, Robert L. "Methods of Computing Earnings Credit Allowances for Branch Banks." Rutgers University, April, 1963.

Olson, Ronald L. "Profit Planning in Commercial Banks." Indiana University, 1964.

PERIODICALS

American Accounting Association. "Report of the Committee on Concepts and Standards," *Accounting Review,* Vol. 27, 1952.

American Accounting Association. "Tentative Statement of Cost Concepts Underlying Reports for Management Purposes," *Accounting Review,* Vol. 31, 1956.

American Accounting Association. "Report of the Committee on Concepts and Standards—General," *Accounting Review,* Vol. 39, 1964.

Boras, Theodore E. "Cost Analysis for Smaller Banks—Now," *Banking,* Vol. 62, Oct. 1969, pp. 49-53.

Buek, Charles W. "Cost Accounting—Benefits for Trust Department," *Trust and Estates,* Vol. 10F, June 1969, pp. 551-552.

Crouse, Morris L. "Cost Accounting and Bank Pricing," *Auditgram,* Vol. 37, Oct. 1964, pp. 10-15.

Falkenberg, John F. "Profitability Analysis: A Marketing Tool Part I," *Robert Morris Associates,* February 1970, pp. 2-16.

Falkenberg, John F. "Profitability Analysis: A Marketing Tool Part II," *Robert Morris Associates,* March 1970, pp. 2-23.

Ferrara, William L. "Responsibility Accounting and the Contribution Approach," *National Accounting Association Bulletin,* Vol. 45, Dec. 1963, pp. 11-20.

Ferrara, William L. "Responsibility Reporting vs. Direct Costing—Is There a Conflict?", *Management Accounting* (National Accounting Association), Vol. 48, June 1967, pp. 43-54.

Larkin, Eugene L., Jr. "Financial Reporting by Banks," *American Banker,* Oct. 6, 1965.

Mason, Paul. "EDP Systems For Functional Cost Analysis," *The Magazine of Bank Administration,* Vol. 44, July 1968, p. 28.

Murphy, Neil B. "The Cost of Operations in Trust Departments," *The Magazine of Bank Administration,* Vol. 44, Nov. 1968, pp. 18-39.

Radius, David A. "Work Measurement + Cost Analysis = Improved Costing/ Pricing Decisions," *Auditgram,* Vol. 44, June 1968, pp. 20-23.

Shipley, Edward T. "Bank Accounting Principles," *Banking,* Vol. 42, Oct. 1969, pp. 41+.

SPEECHES

Ellis, Charles C. *Pricing Bank Services.* A speech given before the Bank Public Relations and Advertising Association, Miami, Florida, Nov. 3, 1969.

Larkin, Eugene L., Jr. *Pricing Banking Services.* A speech given before the Junior Bankers Conference of the Georgia Bankers Association, Sept. 1967.

INDEX